GAZA: VOLUME ONE

GAZA
VOLUME ONE
7th OCTOBER
to
18th DECEMBER
2023

Alan Dent

When a real and final catastrophe should befall us in Palestine the first responsible for it would be the British and the second the Terrorist organizations built up from our own ranks.
I am not willing to see anybody associated with these misled and criminal people.

Einstein.

First published November 2024

© Alan Dent

The author asserts his moral right to be identified as the author of the work.

All rights reserved. No part of this publication may be reproduced, stored in a retrieval system or transmitted in any form or by any means, electronic, mechanical, photocopying, recording or otherwise, without the prior permission of the publishers

ISBN 978-1-913144-64-7

PENNILESS PRESS PUBLICATIONS
Website : www.pennilesspress.co.uk/books

7th OCTOBER 2023

What happened on 7th October was one episode in a long and tragic history. It can be traced back a very long way, but to remain recent, 2006 gives sufficient context. Hamas won general elections in both Gaza and the West Bank; not only a surprise but an affront to those claiming to uphold democracy. The response was Israeli violence and a siege, followed by waves of attacks cutely termed "mowing the lawn". The aggression originated with the Israelis who have wilfully blocked every peace effort. Whatever criticism can be levelled at Hamas, it didn't originate what followed. Israel was the originator of oppression, occupation and violence, but in the eschatology of the "West", Israel is an angelic nation, a beacon of "progress", the "only democracy in the Middle East", the society which "made the desert bloom" and it is from that Pollyanna view the terrible massacre flowed.

The security fences breached by Hamas were formidable barriers, built at significant expense and trusted by Israelis, particularly it may be assumed, those who lived close by. Some of those were offered incentives to live near the Gaza border: reductions in income tax for example. There was always the risk of rocket attacks, but the Iron Dome system was well-tested and highly effective. There were watchtowers, remotely-controlled machine guns, patrols. The incursion should have been impossible, or at least so difficult its attempt would alert the ubiquitous IDF. According to Michael McCaul chair of the US House foreign affairs committee, Israel was warned three days prior by Egypt about the possibility of "something big". 70% of Israel's armed forces were busy in the West Bank, but that left something like 60,000 regular soldiers. This was a monumental intelligence failure, on behalf of both the US and Israel. Some estimates suggest planning might have taken a year. Bulldozers were, it seems, parked on the Gaza side for a day or more before the assault. The IDF later admitted the failure, an unusual occurrence. Perhaps it was nothing more than arrogance, the belief that such a thing was simply unthinkable. On the other hand, perhaps someone didn't care enough. In the closing days of October a row erupted between Netanyahu and Lapid after the PM posted a message blaming the Israeli security forces; an astonishing attribution given his position and responsibility. The leader withdrew his statement. This leaves begging the question, who was responsible. Netanyahu did not accept blame. Jeremy Bowen, the BBC's veteran man-in-the-Middle-East, pertinently pointed out that prior to 7th October Netanyahu was in serious trouble, facing not only the end of his political career, but a possible jail sentence. The war saved him, though it was clear within a fortnight that a substantial number of Israelis blamed him and wanted a ground invasion delayed until the hostages were safely home. Just how the failure happened may never be known, but one thing is clear: it wasn't the fault of Hamas. They exploited Israeli laxness and the assault raises serious questions about the nature of resistance, but a State such as Israel, which had illegally occupied the West Bank for fifty-six years, imposed an equally illegal siege of Gaza for a decade and a half and relied on supreme vigilance to keep its citizens safe, could not afford the negligence which permitted hundreds of Hamas fighters to invade its border settlement.

This is not to argue against Hamas agency, to suggest that they lacked the will or the means to do what they did without Israeli negligence. The attack was well-planned and executed and may well have been hard to repel had Israel been fully prepared. The point is not to denigrate Hamas capacity and by implication Palestinians in general, but to raise proper concerns about Israel's stance, and in particular the high claims of Netanyahu that he had made Israel impregnable.

Comparisons have been made between 7th October and slave revolts: Haiti in 1791 or Nat Turner's rebellion of 1831. When people are denied their humanity, even for short periods, they will resist. Sooner or later something ugly will happen. This is no intellectual theory, it's as obvious as knowing if you go out in the rain you'll get wet. Nor is there any great difficulty in defining "humanity" in this context: colonisers and exploiters are perfectly aware of what it means. They have to propose a dehumanised version of their victims to justify their behaviour. Not being subject to someone else's will, having the space to choose your own actions, these are fundamental facets of being human. By definition, the powerful expect to be able to act as they choose, and in the same way, to deny that right to those they make use of. Abuse people and they'll hit back, the question is: does their abused position absolve them of moral or legal responsibility? Have any populations been more abused in modern times than the Jews, Romanies, Polish Catholics, homosexuals and so on during the Nazi genocide? Would it be legitimate to argue: the Jews were systematically dehumanised and slaughtered, so they have fought back? Yes, they may exaggerate, but what do you expect? Do we excuse the terrorism of Lehi, the Hagana and the Irgun? Do we conflate Zionism with Jewish freedom? Don't we, on the contrary, condemn Jewish terrorism and expect Israel to obey international law? Can we, then, justify the killing and taking hostage of civilians on the grounds the people who did it were cruelly oppressed? Had Hamas fought the IDF and the Israeli police there would be no argument; they were the agents of oppression and occupied peoples have both a moral and legal right to resist. Nat Turner's slogan is said to have been "kill all the white people." An injunction he didn't himself obey. Was he right? William Lloyd Garrison was white but on Turner's side. What is understandable is not necessarily justifiable.

Yasmin Porat, a 44 year-old mother of three was grazed on the left thigh by a bullet during the attack. She and her partner, Tal Katz, were at the rave, escaped to the Be'eri Kibbutz where they were kindly sheltered in the home of Adi and Hadas Dagan. Her first call to the police went unanswered. The time of that call is uncertain. Discovered by the fighters, they were taken to another house where there were eight captives and one dead victim. Ms Porat said she and her partner were treated "humanely", though at one point she was used as a human shield by a Hamas commander who wanted to give himself up, stripped naked and held her in front of him as he approached the police who were on the house's lawn. She called to the police not to shoot. The fighter released her a few metres from the police. According to her account her captors said, "…we're not going to kill you. We want to take you to Gaza. So be calm, you're not going to die." They were waiting for the police to arrive, seemingly because they imagined they could conduct the matter of taking the hostages to Gaza under their supervision.

It was eight hours after the attack before the police appeared. Half an hour prior, Ms Porat had succeeded in contacting them by phone. An immediate gun fight broke out. In the crossfire, Ms Porat said, some Israelis were killed. Interviewed by Aryeh Golan on Israeli State Radio on 15th October at 5.49 a.m., Ms Porat claimed that "undoubtedly" Israelis were killed by their own side. Given the Israeli claims about the bloodthirsty nature of the attack and their initial tally of 1,400 dead, establishing how many were killed by the Israeli police is a crucial matter. Ms Porat's testimony was quickly and easily available online, but the mainstream British media ignored it virtually entirely. She commented "For ten hours the kibbutz was abandoned." She also recounted that two tanks shells were fired into a house occupied by Israeli residents. Hamas has no tanks.

Tuval Escapa, security co-ordinator at Kibbutz Be'eri commented, "Israeli commanders made difficult decisions, including shelling homes on their occupants in order to eliminate the terrorists along with the hostages." Danielle Rachiel was nearly killed by Israeli fire as she fled the Nova festival. The images of the Kibbutzim presented by Israel showed utter destruction. The Hamas fighters were armed with machine guns and grenades. Charred bodies dumped in a skip were Hamas fighters. Concrete structures had been destroyed. Maybe some of this was by grenades, but the extent of the destruction was consistent with shell fire. Israeli Apache helicopter pilots were hard pressed to distinguish Hamas fighters from Israeli civilians and at least some fleeing Israelis were taken for Hamas men. .

The immediate Israeli response to the attack was horror, dismay, the invocation of The Holocaust and avowal to hunt down and destroy Hamas, who were portrayed as monsters motivated by "pure evil" and an unmediated desire to exterminate Jews. Crucial to the story was the extreme violence of the attack and its sickening results. Of course, to admit that even one Israeli death was the result of Israeli fire would have been catastrophic. It had to be true that all fourteen hundred dead, who turned out to be twelve hundred, had been wickedly slaughtered by the morally bereft Hamas fighters. Yet if what is recounted above is even marginally true, it may be that dozens or even hundreds of Israelis were slain by their own side.

Netanyahu made no apology for the security failure, if such it was. Political leaders in the "West" were quick to offer unconditional support to Israel reiterating at every opportunity the principle that Israel had the right to defend itself. No one in leadership questioned this principle, yet it holds only if the dehistoricization of the Hamas attack is assumed. It was some days before Antonio Guterres argued the event didn't take place in a vacuum, a comment which caused Israel's leaders to call for his resignation. Guterres was right and his point undermines the obvious principle: aggressors can't cite resistance to their aggression as a justification for defence against that resistance, otherwise no aggression could ever be criticised. Who is the aggressor in Israel/Palestine? Going back only a far as 1967, it's Israel. Casting back to the Jewish terrorism of Lehi, the Irgun and Hagana, and the ethnic cleansing of 1948, inculpates the violent Zionists (Zionism had a liberal wing which never envisioned a purely Jewish State) and the Israelis even more definitively. This is not to excuse the Hamas attack, but it does permit it to be understood. How could the violence of the ANC be understood without the context of South African apartheid, or the violence of the IRA without that of partition and the gerrymandering of Ulster? To understand is not to condone, but to refuse to understand is the worst of all mistakes.

The response of the "Western" leadership was a wilful refusal of understanding. Everyone lamented the loss of Jewish lives, rightly of course, but no one argued the loss could have been avoided had the Palestinians been granted equal rights. On the contrary, Israeli leaders were permitted to call Palestinians "animals" without demur from leaders in the US, Europe and elsewhere. On 10th October Joe Biden gave a response which Marwan Bishara, Al Jazeera's chief political analyst, typified as a demonisation of the entire Palestinian people and a rehashing of Netanyahu's customary rhetoric. The following day, Keir Starmer, interviewed on Radio 4, refused to say Israel must stay within the law, asserting rather it must do what was necessary. This remarkable valorisation of fascism (power not law) went uncommented in the mainstream media. On 19th October Biden made his opinion (and it was mere opinion rather than argument) clear: Israel must win for US security and world leadership. What Biden meant by "win" is anyone's guess, but the frank cynicism of this remark illustrates the gross hypocrisy of US, and therefore European, foreign policy.

The initial responses were crucial. If the US was going to determine the course and outcome of the violence, which is what Biden meant, it needed to be ahead of the curve. Instead, by permitting its position to be defined by Israel, it found itself lagging and losing the capacity to direct. The USS Ford was sent to the Mediterranean on 10th October to be joined by the Eisenhower a few days later with the intention of deterring Iran and Hezbollah. Biden visited Israel on 18th during which he made a stunning speech. Beginning by saying to Israel "You are not alone", he went on to speak of "rape, beheading, bodies burned alive" on 7th October. He did so because these were Israel's claims, none verified by objective third parties. That this was irresponsible hardly embraces its recklessness. For the world to hear from its most powerful politician that beheadings had happened when no one had been able to confirm them was to valorise a response which dispassionate evidence might find hard to justify. Adding to his wayward claims, he said the "atrocities..recall the worst ravages of ISIS." To assimilate Hamas to ISIS is much more than exaggeration: Hamas has no international reach. It is a nationalist organisation whose aim is limited: equal rights for the Palestinians. Further, it is a political body which won the elections in the West Bank and Gaza in 2006, after which it made an offer to George W Bush: recognition of Israel and renunciation of violence in return for significant steps towards a two-States agreement. Bush's response was typical of the US: silence. The EU withdrew its funding after the Hamas win, Blair said they shouldn't have been allowed to stand. Thus, the world's democracies rebelled against democracy when it produced the wrong result.

Biden continued, "brutality..cuts deeper here in Israel." This shocking attribution of greater worth to Israeli than other lives, was another concession to Israel's dubious contentions. It tallies with Biden's evocation of "a millennia (sic) of antisemitism and the genocide of the Jewish people". Did he mean the genocide has been going on for a thousand years? That the Jews have suffered prejudice, exclusion, hatred and the appalling madness of the Nazi genocide is beyond question, but there have been periods when Jewish culture has flourished. Maristella Botticini and Zvi Eckstein argue that Jewish success in some economic and cultural areas was not because they were excluded from others, but because their independent learning and education after A.D. 70, gave them a comparative advantage. This is not to play down the suffering, but to recognise it hasn't been uniform across the last two thousand years. Today, Jews are flourishing in Biden's US. Some 60% have college degrees and about 28% post-graduate qualifications. Both religious and secular Jews have much higher educational attainment than average. 70% of Jews are married to non-Jews. Marrying outside the group is always a good indicator of success. According to the Pew Research Group at least 50% of Jews have an income of at least $100,000, much higher than the percentage of all US households at that level. There are nine Jewish senators and 26 in the House of Representatives, not bad given that about 2.4% of the total population is Jewish.

"The State of Israel," he added, "was born to be a safe place for the Jewish people of the world." The idea of a Jewish

State was born for no such reason. Nor was the Balfour Declaration inspired by concern for Jewish safety. On the contrary, Balfour was a self-confessed Jew-hater who wanted them out of the UK as he felt they'd done enough damage. "If Israel didn't exist," Biden waxed, "it would be necessary to invent it." Whether he's read Voltaire is an open question, but that anyone today would dream of creating the State of Israel if it didn't exist is about as sensible as suggesting if Ulster didn't exist it would be a good idea to partition Ireland. "For decades," he boasted, we've ensured Israel's qualitative military edge", apparently with no inkling this might be a substantial part of the problem. He confidently asserted the attack on the Al-Ahli hospital of 18th October was by "an errant rocket fired by a terrorist group". Hananya Naftali, an IDF spokesman, posted this message shortly after the attack (6.59 p.m.): "Israeli Air Force struck a Hamas terrorist base inside a hospital in Gaza".It was quickly deleted, perhaps because Mr Naftali was brought into the loop of the Israeli party line. Biden's willingness to accept Israel's account without third party confirmation is shocking. The concessions Biden made to the Palestinians were that Hamas and the people were not coterminous and that Israel had agreed to allow aid to move in from Egypt. There was , predictably, no mention of the occupation, ethnic cleansing or Israeli non-compliance with UN resolutions. Biden's moral idiocy reached its peak when he claimed that like the US, Israel lives by the rule of law, as if invading Vietnam and Iraq and the occupation of the West Bank were legal actions. Biden was in full Angelic Nation mode, that delusion which permits the self-appointed global angels to colonise, exploit, murder and oppress at will because they are superior by nature. "Israel is a miracle," he declared. Just what is miraculous about the terrorism of Lehi, the Irgun and Hagana, or the ethnic cleansing of 750,000 Palestinians he didn't bother to explain. Israel, he proposed, is a "nation of conscience" like the US. The genocide of the native Americans, slavery, the Jim Crow laws, the mass incarceration of coloured people and the extreme violence and cynicism of American foreign policy for decades are apparently matters of conscience. "You inspire hope and light for so many around the world." Biden appeared to have no inkling of the attitude of the global south. Across the world for decades support for the Palestinian cause has been growing and with it, of course, severe criticism of the State of Israel. Somehow this has failed to register on Biden's consciousness. The sheer cruelty of typifying as a beacon of hope and light a State which has dehumanised an entire population for nearly a century suggests a radical dissociation. Finally, he told his fond, homely story of meeting Golda Meir as a young senator and recycled her remark about the Jews having nowhere else to go. The Jews are welcome in most countries and flourish almost everywhere they settle. They are not today a persecuted minority. It's the Palestinians who have nowhere else to go. Biden might have mentioned Meir's comment that Israel is not a line on a map; wherever there are Jews, that is Israel.

In March 2019 Netanyahu said: "Whoever opposes a Palestinian State must support delivery of funds to Gaza because maintaining separation between the Palestinian Authority in the West Bank and Hamas in Gaza will prevent the establishment of a Palestinian State." In 2019 Ehud Barak said of Netanyahu: "His strategy is to keep Hamas alive and kicking..even at the price of abandoning the citizens…in order to weaken the Palestinian Authority in Ramallah." Netanyahu declared war on Gaza on 8th October, hours after the assault. This was not an "operation" he said, not a "round" but war. At that point, he showed scant regard for the Israeli hostages, the very young and the very old among them. An all-for-all prisoner swap might have secured their release. It was at least worth a try. Qatar would almost certainly have been willing to broker negotiations. Further, a pause would have permitted reflection on the best way to proceed. If the aim was to remove Hamas as a military force, the crucial matter was to cut off its funding, but for years Netanyahu had been doing the opposite. He had ensured the money which paid for the weapons which killed Israeli citizens because their safety was less important to him than scuppering a two-State agreement. His rush to war was ludicrously eager.

On 8th October, Efraim Halevy, former Mossad chief said: "Israel had no inkling what was going on…We didn't know they had that quantity of missiles." Blinken, asked about the shocking intelligence failure said, "There will be plenty of time to see what anyone missed." . Daniel Hagari commented "First we fight, then we investigate", displaying his profound respect for due process. Hamas had a dress rehearsal for the attack, a video of which was posted on social media on 12th September. During the previous year the group had posted more than a hundred videos of its preparations, all scrutinised by APnews. Bradley Bowman, an ex-US army officer was reported as saying: "There clearly were warnings and indications that should have been picked up…Or maybe they were picked up but they didn't spark the necessary preparations.". Bowman's "maybe" is worth thinking about. If it was simple arrogant negligence, it was criminal. The world seems not yet to have considered the possibility it may have been worse.

According to the Israeli response to the Hamas attack, history began on 7th October, a position absorbed, at least in the first days, by Israel's allies. If we take for granted, as in a way is wise, that all countries lie to protect their interests, that diplomacy is essentially high quality lying, and as Lord Salisbury would have contested, the morality which governs our life as individuals can't apply to international relations, we can understand why Israel was blind to its responsibility. Yet this requires the assumption that our moral sentiments extend no further than our national borders, an essentially primitive view. It's also naïve in its contention that our domestic morality is any better than our international. Israel was unable to reflect that its occupation of the West Bank and siege of Gaza might have played any part in the dreadful events of 7th October 2023 because it's an Angelic Nation. Whatever it does is right because it's serving "progress". In his speech at the opening of the second session of the twenty-fifth Knesset on 16th October, Netanyahu said:

"This is a struggle between the children of light and the children of darkness, between humanity and the law of the jungle…They want to return the Middle East to the abyss of the barbaric fanaticism of the Middle Ages, whereas we want to take the Middle East forward to the height of progress of the 21st century."

Such a Manichean view is bound to be wrong, because nothing ever divides so simply. What is shocking is the absolute assumption of virtue. It's the mentality of James Hogg's "justified sinner". Once you are convinced of your perfection, no barbarity is beyond you. We don't expect political rhetoric to be truthful- power and truth are sworn enemies- but the "barbaric fanaticism" Netanyahu evokes ignores that without Muslim learning and culture during the period, we might never have heard of Aristotle, Galen, Hippocrates or Euclid. It requires the most profound ignorance to pretend the Muslim culture of the Middle Ages didn't make enormous contributions to literature, chemistry, maths, astronomy, architecture and more. Netanyahu's claim is pure supremacism, which was hardly nugatory as he was the man guiding the military response.

ALL-OUT ASSAULT

On the 12th October Reuters reported Israel had imposed a total blockade of Gaza. Article 3 of the first chapter of the Geneva Convention reads:

In the case of armed conflict not of an international character occurring on the territory of one of the High Contracting Parties, each Party to the conflict shall be bound to apply, as a minimum, the following provisions:

1) Persons taking no active part in the hostilities, including members of the armed forces who have laid down their arms and those placed hors de combat by sickness, wounds, detention or any other cause, shall in all circumstances be treated humanely, without any adverse distinction founded on race, colour, religion, faith, sex, birth or wealth or any similar criteria.

Clearly, the civilian population of Gaza was not taking an active part in the hostilities. The adjective is vital. Civilians can't be targets because they hope their armed forces will prevail. Even providing support for active soldiers, food, shelter, hiding, would be moot. According to a Reuters report of 16th October, Hamas has some 40,000 fighters. To date, more than 11,000 civilians have been killed in Gaza. Had they all been Hamas fighters, its capacity would be severely damaged. Israel claims some 1,500 Hamas fighters were killed on 7th October, the number killed since is impossible to ascertain. There are no reports, Israel is not issuing figures. The media are full of images of devastation and death for civilians, the very people protected by the Geneva convention. Nothing about Hamas casualties.

The Israeli claim is that the fighters hide behind the population, but the topography of Gaza makes it impossible for them to distance themselves. The truth is, Israel has created, by its cruelty and intransigence, a nationalist force embedded in the "open air prison" in which it holds 2.3 million Palestinians. Its military operations have proven impotent to put an end to Hamas. It has had to secure itself behind a panoply of defences which no civilised, democratic culture could wish to have. Defeating Hamas, a nationalist idea and effort, through war is impossible. Hence, Israel's unrestrained offensive against Gazan civilians.

On 22nd October there were reports of increased attacks on the Israeli-Lebanon border with Hezbollah attacking the Shebaa Farms (an area on the Lebanon-Syria border in the Golan Heights which were seized by Israel in 1981). 24 Hezbollah fighters died. On the same day, there were pro-Palestinian demonstration in Kuala Lumpur, Lagos, where a call was made for a boycott of products produced by Israel and those supporting its campaign, Canada, where 30 MPs called for a ceasefire, Washington and other places in the US. Two days earlier the release of two hostages, Judith and Natalie Raanan was announced, but Hamas claimed on 22nd that Israel was blocking further releases. Netanyahu's rationale was both the destruction of Hamas and the release of the hostages, but his position was barely rational: if Hamas was destroyed, who would Israel negotiate with for the release? If the hostages were released, that implied sufficient restraint to prevent them dying through Israeli violence. If, as Netanyahu claimed, the release of the hostages was the first priority, the sensible strategy was to refrain from violence until they were home. Israel was not under threat of renewed attack. Its own logic was the 7th October was a colossal intelligence and strategy blunder. The possibility of another breaching of the fence and incursion was impossibly small. The goal of wiping out Hamas was undertaken with no thought for how it could be accomplished militarily or for what would follow the fighting. From the outset the hard-line Israelis were obviously intending to ethnically cleanse the entire Palestinian population.

On 9th October, Yoav Gallant, looking pale, gaunt, tense and displaying an absence of thought, declared Gaza would have no water, no food, no fuel. By 22nd the second convoy of trucks was admitted, seventeen in total. Martin Griffiths, UN Under Secretary for Humanitarian Affairs, insisted more be permitted. While the essential supplies were reduced to a dribble, the Pentagon supplied more missiles. Two Palestinians were killed in an air strike in Jenin while in Tel Aviv people demonstrated for the release of the hostages. Rafah City was hit, Jabalia refugee camp was attacked, thirteen were killed, mostly children and twenty-seven injured. The Israelis hit an Egyptian position in what they claimed was an accidental strike. There were pro-Palestinian protests in Sarajevo. Meanwhile *The Guardian* sacked its long-time cartoonist, Steve Bell. Bell had produced a cartoon, inspired by David Levine's 1966 image of Lyndon Johnson raising his shirt to reveal the Vietnam-shaped scar from his gall bladder removal; it showed a supine Netanyahu wearing boxing gloves, a scalpel in his right hand carving the shape of Gaza on his midriff. The newspaper's asinine response was that it evoked Shylock and the pound of flesh, but as Bell retorted, there was nothing in the cartoon about *The Merchant of Venice* or Shakespeare. The clear meaning of the image is that a clumsy man is damaging himself.

Netanyahu was slicing open his own abdomen by attacking Gaza. Behind the cartoon is the obvious knowledge that prior to 7th October, Netanyahu was in deep trouble, facing the end of his political career and a possible jail sentence. It is unreservedly anti-Netanyahu but not in the least Jew-hating. That it could be interpreted as such is a measure of the febrile, paranoid atmosphere generated by the long-standing malicious campaign to conflate all criticism of the State of Israel, however mild, with Jew-hating.

The Guardian's illiterate view of Shakespeare is also interesting. The play is thought of as Jew-hating only by those who haven't read it properly or have an axe to grind, like Harold Bloom, who dismisses Shakespeare's defence of Shylock's humanity as superficial. According to Bloom, it might have been a revelation in the 1590s that Jews shared their humanity with rest of us, but in the modern world only skinheads and psychopaths question it. On the contrary, Shakespeare's evocation of a common humanity is not recognised by most of the world's leaders. The USA engages in mass incarceration of coloured people because its mentality is supremacist. Change places and handy-dandy and the failure to recognise the Jews as human is exactly the fate of the Palestinians today. Members of the Israeli government have called them "animals". "If you prick us do we not bleed" is Shakespeare telling us we have a given, shared human nature. That isn't superficial and the ruling global doctrines, though they might pay lip service, don't accept it.

That Bell could be sacked as a Jew-hater for a cartoon which evinced not a glimmer of Jew-hating echoes the madness which seized the Labour Party amidst the welter of unfounded claims of "institutional anti-

Semitism" and led to thousands of people being expelled and denied any right to defend themselves, merely for being accused. Small wonder that in such an atmosphere the slaughter of innocent Palestinians got under way quickly and with the full support of "the West".

On 21st October Israel dropped leaflets over Gaza telling residents to move south and warning that anyone remaining in the north would be considered an ally of terrorists. On 22nd and 23rd, southern Gaza came under attack and people began to flee north.

Alog Cohen MK interviewed on Radio 4 claimed Israel would invade Gaza to destroy Hamas, cited the beheadings of 7th October as a cause and suggested annexing the West Bank. During the Israeli occupation of Gaza, he argued, there were no rockets fired at Israel. He likened Hamas to Isis, asked why Gazans were not going south as advised, and claimed there were no air strikes on the road south. Hamas, he asserted had started the conflict on 7th October.

Mazen Sinokrot, the Palestinian capitalist, argued that the twenty trucks so far admitted were nowhere near enough. He accused the US of a shameful failure of diplomacy, said fuel was needed as much as medicines and argued Egypt was right to refuse to accept the expulsion of Gazans to the Sinai. The solution, he said, was not the removal of the Gazans. They won't leave their homeland.

In advance of the London demonstration on 21st, the Home Secretary, Braverman, met Sir Mark Rowley, Head of the Metropolitan Police. On the 30th she would call the protests "hate marches". Ken McDonald, former Director of Public Prosecutions (fined a small amount when a student for sending cannabis in the post), interviewed on Radio 4 called for a balance between security and free speech. "Jihad" he pointed out had multiple meanings. The word "insult" he suggested might be removed from Section 5 of the Public Order Act. The police had to be operationally independent. It wasn't right for the Home Secretary to make operational decisions.

Braverman was clearly playing politics. A typical sharp-elbowed greasy-pole climber, she was perfectly aware of the absurdity of her claims. What is most to note about her interventions, however, is how quick the right was to seize the opportunity to close down on protest. In France and Germany people were banned from the streets, though they still turned up in their thousands. Prohibitions of what people want to do out of principle or for their own satisfaction never work. It's a measure of how the Israel lobby, through the misuse of the Nazi genocide, has engendered widespread paranoia that people chanting "from the river to the sea" were said to be dangerous because they want to wipe out Israel, while Israel remained secure and the Palestinians were being wiped out. Israel has become an iconic matter because it represents the right of rich, "progressive" States and movements to wipe out the "backward" the "barbarians". This is the principle on which the world order rests. Everything else is flummery.

Two weeks into the assault, the Jabalia, Beit Lahia and Jalazone refugee camps were targeted. 95 were reported dead in the latter. Yoav Gallant predicted a three-month campaign, an indication of how difficult expected the urban fight to be. On 20th Judith and Natalie Raanan were released and on 23rd Yocheved Lifshitz, 85 and Nurit Cooper, 79, Qatar and Egypt being the mediators. Israel offered nothing in return. Hamas called those held "guests" and claimed they would be well-treated. In

Karachi there was a protest calling for an end to diplomacy with Israel and in South Africa people took to the streets in support of the Palestinians. Meanwhile, Israel struck 320 targets overnight including in southern Gaza where people had been warned to move. Hundreds were killed. Bombs fell in the vicinity of the Al Quds hospital. Mark Rutte, Prime Minister of the Netherlands, said it was impossible to tell if Israel was observing international law, tantamount to saying it wasn't. UNICEF warned that without fuel incubators for premature babies would cease to function. James Cleverly, Foreign Secretary, observed that it wasn't simply up to Israel to ensure supplies got through. On the other hand, Finnuala Ni Aolain, UN Special Rapporteur for Human Rights, said Israel was guilty of "profound violations of international law". Her view seems to have been that the application of such law was ineffective and the terrorism of Israel's attacks worse than the Hamas outrage of 7th October.

Marwan Bishara, Al Jazeera's chief political analyst, who proved to be one of the most astute commentators ,argued there should be a ceasefire to permit the release of the hostages. Biden insisted the hostages should be released first. This, however, was not an offer to impose a ceasefire if Hamas complied. The taking of civilian hostages was, of course, a morally despicable act and also outside of what the Gazans were permitted to engage in legally to lift the siege; but given the hostages were in their hands and Gaza was being pounded by Israel, what incentive was there for them to release, unless a serious reward was available.

A row broke out between Netanyahu and Gallant. The Prime Minister blamed the security forces for the debacle. Gallant, previously sacked by Netanyahu and reported to loathe him, fought back. This was the first sign of a crack in the Israeli war cabinet. Reports suggested Gallant saw Netanyahu as a lying populist concerned only for himself while the IDF had a concern for the well-being of the military.

An Israeli spokesman interviewed on Radio 4 and asked about the blockade responded: "Water, electricity, are you kidding me?" indicative of Israeli's sense of entitlement. The 7th October had rocked its delusion that the Palestinians could be permanently contained and also sparked the customary view of itself as under threat from bloodthirsty enemies, making any criticism or resistance an existential threat and also, crucially, reinforcing the view of Israel as an Angelic Nation.

On 24th October Jordan's Foreign Minister, Ayman Safadi, condemned the 7th October attack and called for peace, pointing out that the "elephant in the room" was the occupation, the widening of the war was possible and a ceasefire was the way to avoid it. His warning was accompanied by Hezbollah's attacks on southern Israel engaging some 100,000 IDF troops. The Saudi Foreign Minister, Faisal bin Farhan Al-Saud, said a ceasefire was an "absolute necessity" as was the lifting of the siege. The UAE's representative to the UN also called for a ceasefire, dialogue, a just and lasting, comprehensive solution, the implementation of a 2-States agreement and the fulfilment of the legitimate aspirations of the Palestinian people. All relatively predictable but nevertheless a sign of Israel's isolation in the region. Whatever the moral and legal objections to the Hamas assault, one thing was clear, it had shattered the Abraham Accords and scuppered Israel's attempt to portray itself as Arab-friendly as a way of implying the problem in its relations with the Palestinians had nothing to do with its supremacism, but was the result of their intractable wickedness.

Sergey Lavrov put the Russian point of view: the US was sabotaging a solution and offering palliative measures only; the long encroachment of Israeli settlers in the West bank was sure to lead to something like 7th October; either a two-States agreement must be accepted or a solution was impossible; the 1967 borders should be accepted; East Jerusalem to be the capital of a Palestinian State; a widening of the conflict had to be avoided; Russia could not accept a resolution which fell short of a complete ceasefire; Russia would advance such a resolution and seek co-sponsorship.

All this sounds very reasonable and high-minded, but it's somewhat hard to swallow from a State waging war on a neighbour, however provoked Russia may have been. It could be argued there was symmetry between the Russian invasion of Ukraine in February 2022 and Israel's unrestrained assault on Gaza after 7th October. In both cases, a heavily armed, powerful State, believed violence was its best method. Neither stood back to contemplate a more sober response. There's no doubt the Hamas attack, by killing and abducting civilians was legally and morally inadmissable, nor that NATO's willingness to place weapons in Ukraine was a wayward provocation, but both Russia and Israel had many more possibilities than simply unleashing Armageddon. Such is the logic of massively over-armed States: don't stop to think, just drop the bombs.

The Chinese also advanced rational arguments: a humanitarian catastrophe must be avoided; if the war were to spread it could consume the entire region; the aid getting through was a trickle; Israel must lift the siege and open the Rafah crossing; there must be no forced resettlement; the context mattered; two-States was the only way out. All perfectly sane, until you think about the Uighurs.

Japan called for a two-States agreement. Two Palestinian prisoners were killed in prison in the West Bank. The death toll in Gaza was reported to be 5,800. 1,300 Palestinians had been arrested in the West Bank.

Marwan Bishara agreed with Antonio Guterres that 7th October did not happen in a vacuum. 56 years of occupation were hardly nugatory. A ceasefire and sufficient humanitarian aid were essential. Israel had lost its mind. The killing was on an industrial scale, three times that of the 2021 war. It was simply murder. The UN was bickering while 2,400 children had lost their lives. This was the behaviour of psychopaths. Blinken was lying about the refusal of Arab States to condemn 7th October, the Cairo meeting of Arab leaders had done so explicitly. The US refused to condemn the murder in Gaza. It was sheltering Israel in every way and complicit in the debacle. Macron was engaging in the typical double-speak of the US and EU. To compare Hamas to ISIS was racist, farcical, Islamophobic nonsense.

This was available to UK viewers on Al Jazeera, but most people got there news elsewhere and those who relied on social media witnessed systematic dehumanisation of the Palestinians.

BLUNDER

On 25th October it was announced that Keir Starmer and Angela Rayner had to meet Labour's Muslim MPs after the leader made an appalling gaffe during an interview with LBC's Nick Ferrari on 11th causing significant dismay among Labour's Muslim supporters. Subsequent to asserting the usual principle that Israel had a right to defend itself ("herself" in Starmer's words) he was asked whether a siege was appropriate, "cutting off power, cutting off water". His response was worthy of a sixth-form debating society and revealed starkly just how out of his intellectual and moral depth he was. "I think Israel does have that right" he said. It was a blunder of enormous proportions followed immediately by the feeble declaration that Israel must act with the limits of international law. Here was a trained lawyer who had once headed the CPS granting to Israel a right which any barely legally literate undergraduate could have confirmed as a breach. In those few seconds, Starmer lost the Muslim vote. It wasn't long before tens of Muslim Labour councillors had resigned. Leaving aside matters of principle and looking at the matter from the point of view of cynical expediency, exactly the position taken consistently by the so-called centrists (John McTernan being a seasoned exponent) Starmer alienated two million Muslim voters, 80% of whom were loyal to Labour. On the other hand, he had bent double backwards to placate the UK's 300,000 Jews, 70% of whom vote Tory. There is a principle at work here: we back the rich and powerful in every situation, because that's what unflinching support for the State of Israel is about. It has been the US strategic asset since at least 1967 and Europe falls into line. Apply a little principle, however, say the principle upheld by international law, that States have no right to move their populations onto land seized in war, and Israel needs to be condemned out of hand.

Starmer had made apparent opposition to supremacism the heart of his bid for the Labour leadership. He would eliminate anti-Semitism. This was to drape himself in the flag of anti-supremacism, to lay claim to the high ground of equality, to have no truck with prejudice based on skin colour, religion or ethnic characteristics. At the first hurdle, he fell flat. The Israeli siege of Gaza, the denial of water, food and fuel was a war crime, but it was also clearly supremacist: there was no need to treat these people according to the rules because they were "animals", the word used by an Israeli spokesperson. Starmer, the self-appointed noble enemy of prejudice and irrational hatred, embraced what he claimed to reject. Effectively, he declared his support for starving people to death as a valid weapon of war. That he displayed his moral idiocy while maintaining a statesmanlike demeanour, shone a bright light on his superficiality.

Nineteen Labour councillors resigned. One hundred and fifteen signed a letter of protest. Labour lost its majority on Oxford council. Thirty-seven Labour MPs supported a ceasefire.

Meanwhile, Sir Stephen O'Brien, ex-Tory MP and Under Secretary for Humanitarian Affairs at the UN, interviewed on Radio 4, said Antonio Gutteres' remark about 7th October not having taken place in a vacuum was "ill-judged". Hardly a surprise for a representative of a party which has made itself the USA's lapdog. Israel refused a visa to the current Under Secretary, Martin Griffiths, who had the temerity to question whether slaughtering children was a sensible way to disable Hamas.

Benzi Sanders, a 2014 IDF War veteran, interviewed on *Sky News* on 26th October dispelled the lie that being Jewish and supporting the State of Israeli in all its actions are coterminous. "Axiomatic change" in Israel's behaviour towards the Palestinians was necessary. In simple language, Sanders put the simple argument: if Hamas were to be defeated physically, the resistance to Israel's occupation and siege would remain. Indeed, the present assault on Gaza was a recruiting sergeant for Hamas. The only way to defeat the ideology of resistance was to make resistance unnecessary: the Palestinians had to be granted autonomy and the rights which Israel's cherished for themselves. These are not highly abstract arguments. They don't require great learning or remarkable intellectual powers. They are easily accessible to all. Why then were they anathema to a majority of Israelis, the entire US Republican Party, and supposedly informed and civilised opinion in Europe, all of whom took the view on the day of Sanders's interview, that there was no alternative to a brutal attack on Gaza? The answer is simple: the propaganda system teaches people to fear and hate. Hamas is not a resistance movement which will wither and die if the Palestinians gain freedom, but a manifestation of "pure evil". Its demands can't be met because they are those of "the devil". Hamas operatives aren't human beings but animals. They don't want independence, but the annihilation of Israel, and indeed of all democracies (in spite of the fact that since the early 1970s Hamas has been willing to recognise Israel). They are like ISIS. All this is deliberate distortion and exaggeration. The people who peddle it know they are lying. Netanyahu knows Hamas will give up violence if the Palestinians gain independence; but this dishonesty, the dissemination of paranoia, are the means to hold onto power and wealth. That's where the threads always lead back to.

Once it has been hammered into people's heads that Hamas is a sub-human bunch of murderous psychopaths, it's easy to get them to accept what they object to. It's vile, but it has to be done. Of course, as we do it we regret it (shoot and cry). We are highly moral as we slaughter children because we do it to save them from "pure evil". Millions, of course, saw through this. Sanders expressed the opinion of people across the globe who can see the wood for the trees. The crucial constituency, however, US politicians, was marinated in the propaganda.

It's worth observing that what's going on here is the old ploy of accusing your enemy of what you're guilty of. Hamas which had nowhere near the capacity to wipe Israel off the map was accused of intending to while Israel, one of the most powerful militaries in the world, was wiping Gaza off the map.

Qatar and Tunisia pushed for a political settlement. The former is a hereditary dictatorship which gained independence from the British only in 1971. Interesting that a State effectively under the rule of one man can show greater concern for peace than the so-called liberal, progressive democracies. Erdogan of Turkey declared Hamas not to be a terrorist organisation and called for an international conference. The Turkish Foreign Minister, Fidan, said it was necessary to act fast or there would be "dark days" ahead. Oxfam declared food was being used as a weapon of war, clearly a crime. Their estimate was that supplies were meeting about 2% of Gaza's needs. Water was restricted to about three litres per person per day, well below the recommended UN minimum. Antonio Gutteres defended himself against the accusation he was justifying the Hamas attack by his remark that it didn't occur in a vacuum. Clearly, he was explaining not justifying. That he was accused of the latter is a measure of the low intellectual level of debate and the maliciousness of the propaganda system.

Interviewed on Radio 4 on 25th October, retired British Army officer Rupert Jones pointed out that during urban warfare everything is accentuated. It took a hundred thousand troops nine months to clear Mosul. Daesh was prepared to fight to the death. Trying to clear every building meant getting nowhere fast. In Gaza there was the added difficulty of the tunnels. Fighting underground would be very tough and hostages might be held there. Though he reiterated the empty mantra that Israel had a right to defend itself, he argued the operation might take longer than the plans suggested.

Interesting that a military veteran could pour a fair dash of cold water on the IDF's confident assertions. That he parroted the line about Israel's self-defence is not surprising. It was a feeble argument because no one questioned what was meant by "Israel". Were the proponents of this nostrum intending "Israel" as the illegal occupier of the West Bank or besieger of Gaza? If so, what right of defence existed? No State which illegally occupies territory has a right, legal or moral, to defend itself against resistance to that occupation. No aggressor has a right of defence against resistance to their aggression. Zionists were visiting terrorism on both the Palestinians and the British before any retail terrorism on the Palestinian side was thought of.

Hamas and Islamic Jihad met with Hezbollah in Lebanon. The Qualandiya refugee camp in the West Bank was attacked by 30 IDF troops. One resident was arrested. A more or less typical raid this was indicative of Israel's dishonesty: there were no Hamas fighters in Qualandiya. Eliajah Magnier, a veteran war reporter and analyst, speaking on Radio 4, argued that three out of nine Israeli divisions were engaged with Hezbollah on the border. What he wondered might be Hezbollah's red lines? He gave expression to the anxiety of a widening of the war and questioned whether Israel could avoid a ground invasion.

On 25th October there was a strike very near the Al-Wafa hospital, a regular target when Israel assaults Gaza. The UN Security Council voted against the Russian and US resolutions, the latter receiving ten votes out of fifteen, with Russia, China and the UAE voting against and Brazil and Mozambique abstaining. The resolution would have permitted humanitarian pauses but was otherwise a justification of Israel's action. The right to veto of the five principal members showed itself, once more, to be outdated and a barrier to good decisions. Why should these five retain their special status after seventy-eight years, just because they were founders? As if the world hasn't changed. In order to avoid these kinds of logjams the UN needs to move to consensual decision-making. Not a winner takes all system, but a requirement to work out a position acceptable to all in which, in all probability, no one gets all they want but no one gets nothing.

A world body in which one State has supremacy is a form of lunacy, and pre-eminence for five States is just as bad. The UN should be what it calls itself. All States should meet on an equal footing. Of course, the rich and powerful baulk at such an idea, however much they crow about their commitment to democracy.

Biden announced there could be no return to the status quo ante. There had to be a vision for the future and that must involve two-States. Settler violence was unacceptable. However, the timing of the ground invasion would be left to Israel. The problem with Biden from the outset was he seemed to be talking into a void. He said one thing, Netanyahu said and did the opposite and Biden lacked the resolve to tell Israel to comply. It was pitiful to watch the world's self-appointed super-power following Netanyahu like a timid poodle. The Prime Minister declared "we have killed thousands of terrorists and this is only the start." There was a nuance of difference in his rhetoric, however: releasing the hostage had become more crucial, no doubt a response to domestic and US pressure. His claim to have bagged a brace of terrorists wasn't confirmed by any verifiable evidence. On the other hand, the evidence of civilian deaths was all too obvious.

Dan Gillerman, ex-Israeli Ambassador to the UN in an interview on Sky News on 26th October said, "I am very puzzled by the constant concern which the world is showing for the Palestinian people, and is actually showing for these horrible inhuman animals who have done the worst atrocities this century has seen, and the worst atrocities the Jews have suffered since the Holocaust." He went on to establish equivalence between the Twin Towers attack and 7th October, to point out that Britain joined the US in the war on Iraq, that no one shed any tears for dead Iraqis and added that no one was worried about dead Russian soldiers in the Ukraine conflict. He was wrong on most points. That the Hamas fighters were not "inhuman animals" goes without saying. When the Irish resisted British occupation they were portrayed as less than human in the British media. This is the cliched stock-in-trade of oppressors and colonialists. The 7th October attack was nothing like the shock and awe visited on the Iraqis. According to the Watson Institute at Brown University at least 250,000 civilians died as result of the US-UK assault. The 7th October toll was 1,200 and some of those were almost certainly killed by Israeli fire. Further, pending an independent investigation, no one has unequivocal evidence of what happened on 7th October. Claims of beheading haven't been confirmed. As whatever crimes were committed took place on Israeli territory, it is their responsibility to ensure they are investigated properly, which means by objective agencies. People across the world responded to the deaths in Iraq and there has been plenty of criticism of Putin's willingness to treat his soldiers as fodder. As for the worst atrocity since the Nazi genocide, some two and half thousand IDF soldiers died in the Yom Kippur War. The evocation of Nazism is standard Zionist fare: Israel is always facing a bloodthirsty enemy which is about to wipe out all Jews, never resistance to its illegal occupation.

By the 25th October, thirty-five UNRWA staff had been killed. Jasmine El-Gamal, an ex-Pentagon adviser on the Middle East, interviewed on Al-Jazeera said Gazans were unable to move, aid needed to get through, Israel had complete control of the borders. Frances Leach of Action Aid raised concerns about over-crowded hospitals, babies in incubators whose energy supply might soon run dry and called for aid to be brought in through the Rafah crossing. Yasmin Querish, MP for Bolton East, called Israel's action collective punishment and called for a ceasefire. Khalid Mahmood, MP for

Birmingham Perry Bar, spoke for the twelve Muslim Labour MPs, saying they were united, not intimidated and were meeting on 26th. Clive Betts, MP for Sheffield South East declared Israel's blockade of Gaza wrong in principle and called for a ceasefire. Shaista Aziz, Oxford City Councillor who resigned from Labour, interviewed on *Newsnight* linked the 7th October killings to Palestine's colonial legacy, blamed the occupation and called for a ceasefire. On the other hand, that ubiquitous talking head, John McTernan, still dining out on having been Blair's right-hand man, on the same programme argued both sides would have to stop fighting for a ceasefire to work, claimed Hamas would never agree and therefore those asking for a cessation of hostilities were effectively demanding Israel's surrender. Hamas had started the conflict and, in any case, only the US had any influence over Israel. The UK is a tiny country with no influence. We are powerless and must simply fall in line with Israeli-US policy. The latter point was at least honest. The UK is the US's lapdog. We do what the US wants in pursuit of its global dominance. The relationship is one-sided. The US has little if any concern for Europe, except in so far as it assists its aims. McTernan's view, however, was cowardly and morally bankrupt, as you would expect from someone able to stomach a high-priest of expediency like Blair. The UK has significant influence by being a member of the UN Security Council. Voting for a ceasefire there would be more than symbolic, Further, the UK has a moral responsibility because of its historic role in Palestine. For the country which produced the Balfour Declaration to refuse support for Israel's genocidal attack would hardly go unnoticed. McTernan declared Hamas a terrorist organisation, claimed that Corbyn had "poisoned" the Labour well and concluded Labour must support Israel.

McTernan expressed not only in his language, but in his tone and demeanour, the dismal vision of the UK's political elite. That small countries can't stand for what they consider morally right, but must prostrate themselves before the world's super-power, is a very peculiar notion for anyone who has any faith in democracy. Perhaps the comment about Corbyn was the most telling. In the light of the devastation of Gaza, the concerted campaign to brand Corbyn a supremacist and therefore unfit to be Prime Minister, takes on a tragic hue. Were he leading the country now, can anyone doubt he would be calling for a ceasefire? For the US, that would be sacrilege. The UK's role is to obey. McTernan's talk of poison turned reality on its head: Corbyn expelled the poison of submission to wealth and power from the Labour Party, which is why so many rallied to him and the Establishment had to destroy him.

IRRESOLUTE RESOLUTION

Interviewed on Radio 4's Today on 26th October, Andrew Fisher, former adviser to Corbyn, argued the reason Starmer hadn't sacked Yasmin Qureshi for voting with the SNP call for a ceasefire was fear of a revolt. He pointed to the polling: 76% of the UK population in favour, rising to 89% among Labour voters. Justin Webb's response was illustrative: that's just because people want peace; they don't understand the complexities. Fisher defended the public against the accusation of ignorance. Webb's position is stunning: there's something wrong with wanting peace. It's a sign of mental simplicity, of not being sophisticated enough to understand the world. Perhaps unsurprising for a seasoned BBC journalist. Having to tack permanently to the Establishment view must result in a tendency to take it for the truth. The public's desire for peace is sane. It's the willingness of the rich and powerful to plunge the world into extreme violence time and again which is out-of-kilter. Fisher cited the councillors, Labour members and Shadow Cabinet members who wanted movement and were insistent war crimes were being committed by Israel.. Starmer was weak on this. As Antonio Guterres had said, there needed to be proportion. There was much more at stake then merely Starmer's skin in the next General Election: it was a life and death matter. Some principle needed to be shown. In any case, the Tories' condition was terminal. There was no need to be cowed by electoral considerations.

Was the BBC showing its impartiality by permitting Fisher a chance to speak? Webb's response hardly suggests so. This was a rarity. Debate ran between very narrow lines. Virtually no one was permitted to question the essential rightness of Israel's response. No one argued the sensible response might have been to apologise to the Gazans for a decade and half of siege, invite the Palestinians to immediate negotiations about the creation of an independent society, commit to withdrawing the settlements from the West Bank and agree to abide by UN resolutions. Without exception, spokespeople supported Israel's assault. Such is the reality of the world order. A people oppressed for seventy-five years fights back through violence and the official view is the oppression is not to be discussed.

Chris Gunnes, former spokesperson for UNRWA, said the Global South saw the struggle between Israel and Palestine as an anti-colonial struggle. Richard Falk, a professor at Princeton and Chair of the Board of Trustees of the Euro-Mediterranean Human Rights Monitor, called for a ceasefire and negotiations. The Jordanian Foreign Minister argued Israel appeared to be above the law. Lula da Silva bemoaned the weakness of the United Nations. Hamas asked the Arab States to cut ties with Israel. Meanwhile, Israel claimed two hundred and fifty strikes against Gaza in twelve hours. How many did anything to weaken Hamas? Demonstrators in Tel Aviv called for negotiations for the release of the hostages to continue. Biden declared he had no confidence in the Palestinian death count. Settler violence against Palestinians in the West Bank was increasing.

Professor Abdehamid Siyan of Rutgers claimed the UN was paralysed. The Arab world was united but if their resolution passed in the General Assembly, it would have no legal power, in spite of its moral weight. Israel was behaving with its usual arrogance. The root causes needed to addressed. "Normalisation" was no solution. Popular pressure was driving in the right direction.

In Brussels there was hope of a humanitarian pause but the EU was divided. Germany, partly through its historical guilt, was uncritically with Israel. Pedro Sanchez of Spain, on the other hand, called for a ceasefire. In a UN Emergency Special Session, Jordan called for an immediate cessation, a somewhat futile effort given the veto. Riyad Al Maliki, Palestine's Foreign Minister called for war crimes trials in The Hague. The ICC agreed to investigate violations by both Hamas and Israel. Riyad Mansour, Palestine's Ambassador to the UN pleaded for the bombs to stop and lives to be saved. "Is this the war some of you are defending?" he asked. "These are crimes. This is barbarism." Hospitals were being turned into morgues. Gaza had been devastated by five wars. Vengeance is a dead end. The only way forward was justice.

Unfortunately, it was the kind of barbarism the civilised "West" likes. It was clear from the start Israel was not engaging in a campaign to root out and kill or seize Hamas fighters but was using 7th October as an excuse to slaughter Palestinian civilians, mostly women and children. What was to follow was fully approved by the US and most of the rest of the so-called advanced States, in spite of the views of their populations. Had democracy prevailed, including in the US, the war would have been stopped in days. The 66% percent of Americans who wanted a ceasefire weren't supporters of Hamas, they were simply able to see the chopped logic: wholesale slaughter of civilians and physical devastation weren't the way to deal with attacks like 7th October. The propaganda system might have convinced people Israel's right to defend itself was beyond question, but it cracked over the extremity of the attack on Gaza. As time passed, as we shall see, the gap between the elite leadership and the people grew wider and the US became ever more isolated.

Gilad Erdan, Israel's Ambassador to the UN claimed the organisation was burying its head in the sand regarding Hamas. 7th October had nothing to do with relations between Israel and Palestine. Israel was at war with a genocidal Hamas who are modern-day Nazis. Their one aim was to murder every Jew on the face of the earth, as expressed in their charter. The denial of history in this is remarkable, but was repeated over and over in the media and by spokespeople. The Hamas charter was written in 1988 and is the work of a handful of people. It was long ago repudiated by the Hamas leadership. After its election victory in 2006, Hamas approached G.W. Bush. They offered to recognise Israel, something the Palestinians had been putting forward since the early 1970s, and renounce violence in return for real moves towards a two-States agreement. Bush's response was silence. The EUs response to Hamas's democratic win was to withdraw funding from Palestine. Blair said they shouldn't have been permitted to stand. Think also about Likud's charter. Likud grew from Herut which in turn emerged from the Irgun. Its position has always been that the land of Israel belongs exclusively to the Jews. It explicitly rejects 2-States. Israel has spent the last twenty years fighting unity between Gaza and the West Bank. There was a unity agreement between Fatah and Hamas in April 2014. That was a real problem for Israel. First of all, because Israel's long-standing excuse for not negotiating is it has no one to talk to, the Palestinians being divided, but also because unity between Gaza and the West Bank is the first step towards an autonomous Palestinian society. Gaza faces Europe across the

Mediterranean. A unified Palestinian society with Gaza as the gateway to the outside world would be a disaster for Israel. Keeping Gaza and the West Bank separate is the way to imprison the latter. Erdan was also insinuating that anyone who didn't support Israel was by definition a Hamas supporter. This distorted thinking was ubiquitous. Hamas is Hamas's problem. The millions protesting on the streets across the world weren't defending Hamas, they were opposing their governments in their vicious, murderous actions. Hamas is not the responsibility of people marching in London, Manchester, Paris, Washington, Colombo, Karachi, but the actions of their governments is. Erdan's rank dishonesty and phoney logic were the essence of Israel's position.

Nine hundred more US troops were sent to the region. Since 7th October, there had been one hundred and thirty-eight attacks by settlers in the West Bank. Prior to the Hamas attack, there was an average of three firearms incidents daily, now it was seven. The EU said its greatest concern was for the deteriorating humanitarian situation. There was a call for an international peace conference. Hamas announced fifty hostages had been killed by Israeli bombing. Twenty-four journalists had been killed by Israel. Twelve trucks of aid had passed the Rafah crossing. The Israeli war cabinet discussed pre-emptive strikes against Hezbollah. Marwan Bishara commented that Lebanon was, more or less, a failed State. The EU was a mess, bickering over semantics: a window or a pause. It was simply following its US master. Martin Griffiths, UN Under-Secretary for Humanitarian Affairs said aid was barely trickling in.

Overnight from 26th to 27th October, the US attacked military targets in Syria. There were, apparently, two hundred UK citizens trapped in Gaza. Putin welcomed Hamas representatives to Moscow. According to Reuters, almost fifty per cent of Israelis wanted to hold off a ground invasion of Gaza, out of concern for the hostages. Important to recall Israel's declared war aims: to eliminate Hamas (though whether that meant its leadership, all its fighters and supporters and its ideology was never stated); to release all the hostages; and to ensure another attack from Gaza could never happen. It was clear all three were impossible through military means. In this regard, it was interesting that on Radio 4 on 27th October, Jeremy Bowen argued that Netanyahu was trying to save his skin. Though the fact that without the war his political career would have ended and his time in prison probably be drawing nearer were alluded to now and again, no one in the media was joining the dots. No one knew how informed Netanyahu was about the warnings of an attack, but there was enough information to permit speculation and more, importantly, serious questions. Israeli spokespeople were given a relatively easy ride. No one asked how many Israelis were killed by Israel on 7th October. No one asked exactly who had seen the Jericho Wall document. No one asked how it could be that investors in the Tal Aviv stock market seemed to be forewarned but Netanyahu wasn't. These were too near the knuckle. The story had to be that all the people killed on 7th October were slaughtered by Hamas and Israel was justified in its response.

Interviewed on Radio 4's Today programme, Rosena Allin-Khan, Labour MP for Tooting and a doctor, called for a ceasefire. She agreed with Israel that the Hamas attack was a crime against humanity, but condemned the Israeli bombing as collective punishment of civilians. She cited her work as a doctor in Gaza for a period of thirteen years. There was no slack in the system for Palestinians. Justin Webb excelled himself once more, by claiming Hamas ruled Gaza and was therefore to blame for all its woes. This parroting of the Israeli line was typical of the British media. The idea that during the decade and half siege, Hamas made all the decisions is laughable. With the exception of the Rafah crossing, tightly monitored by Egypt, all entry to and exit from Gaza was controlled by Israel, for people and everything else. The Palestinians had no right to leave the Strip as they wished, to trade beyond it, and even trade within was limited by what Israel would permit. Most Palestinians were refugees. Half of them were children, giving the lie to the notion the Gazan people had chosen Hamas. None of this is hard to discover, yet the BBC lets a veteran broadcaster promulgate the lie that Hamas was in control of Gaza.

Mediated by Qatar, negotiations regarding a ceasefire and prisoner release were under way. The case of Gilad Shalit was cited. For his return, Israel released a thousand Palestinian prisoners. To get the hostages home safely, something similar might be necessary. There were some six thousand Palestinians in Israeli prisons, many under "administrative detention", a euphemism for denial of all legal rights. No one in the British mainstream media commented that such practices might have contributed to the radicalisation of Hamas fighters, and help explain, though not justify 7th October. It was as if Palestinians simply had to live with such things. Such is the implicit racism of the British media.

Hamas's position was, no release of hostages without peace, though it didn't specify if that meant a truce or a permanent ceasefire. Marwan Bishara's view was that Israel might be ready to pay a big price in release of prisoners to get the hostages home, but he felt the US was concerned over such a release triggering a land invasion. Israeli public opinion was 69% in favour of a land invasion, a shift from the previous position. There were multiple fires on the Lebanon border. Israel targeted residential areas in Khan Younis. Muslims were prevented from attending Friday prayers by blockades in the West Bank.

Jeremy Bowen interviewed an Israeli, Roy, at Ashkelon police station: "The other side aren't human. They are monsters. Gaza belongs to us."

How did Roy arrive at his conclusions? Presumably, 7th October proved Hamas are less than human while the terrorist outrages of Lehi, the Irgun and Hagana are proof QED of the sweet gentleness and commitment to international law and human rights of the followers of Herzl. No doubt Gaza belongs to Israel because Israel decided to take it by force, proving the Israelis are marvellous, generous, folk dripping with the milk of human kindness. Lady Macbeth accuses her husband of too much of that. She understands that power requires all-round dehumanisation; but the powerful, of course, cover their tracks by invoking a phoney humanity. Power is morally vacuous which is why it has to consistently promote hysterical moralism.

Andy Burnham, Sadiq Khan and the leader of Scottish Labour called for a ceasefire. That's no small matter. The Mayors of a major European capital and an important UK city and the leader of Starmer's party north of the border, were opposed to unconditional support for Israel. Yet the media made little of it. It was mentioned and passed over.

Marwan Bishara commented that Israeli fanatics wanted to retake Gaza and impose a military occupation. Israel felt invincible because of US and EU support and complicity. The invincibility Bishara invoked was a product of America's protection racket. Israel looks after the US's interests in the region and if there's trouble, in come the thugs to sort it out. Of course, the thugs don't need to turn up in person, which is part of the beauty of the arrangement; they send the weapons, supply the training and advice and convey the message: "Do what you like. We can take on anybody." Israel is the little psychopath defended by the muscular bully. Trace back the threads and what do you find: the Monroe Doctrine and its interpretations which turned an ostensible defence against European colonialism into a pretext for the US version; George Washington's enlightened belief that the native Americans should accept the ways of the founding fathers or be "extirpated" as recalcitrant savages and the entire history of American supremacism, slavery, the Jim Crow Laws and the current mass incarceration of coloured people. What lies behind this is the pursuit of lucre. Making the accumulation of material wealth the central aim of life robs it of its moral character. Hence the high-sounding rhetoric of freedom, independence, democracy and human rights side by side with oppression, tyranny, exploitation and genocide.

UNRWA predicted the breakdown of civil society in Gaza, no doubt delighting Netanyahu and the fascists in his cabinet. Lazzarini, its Commissioner General, asked why there was no global will to stop the war. Amongst the common folk, there was but the world isn't ruled by them. The corporates control and slaughtering Arabs is all right with them. Marwan Jilani of the Palestinian Red Crescent said no aid was getting to the north. Conveys were going to be hit. There were no safe places. The situation was impossible. The international community should stop the fighting at once. The technical aspects of the war were shocking. Who was speaking for the Palestinians? All communications in Gaza had been cut.

Meanwhile, at the UN, Linda Thomas-Greenfield whimpered that the resolution calling for a ceasefire didn't mention Hamas or the hostages, who were innocent civilians. The only surprise is that she didn't complain about it not mentioning Yasser Arafat's birthday. On 27th October the General Assembly rejected proposal A/ES-10/L.26, eighty-eight votes for, fifty-five against and twenty-three abstentions and passed A/ES-10/L.25, one hundred and twenty for, forty-four against and forty-five abstentions. The former condemned the Hamas attacks, the latter called for humanitarian ceasefire and greater aid. Gilad Erdan, Israel's Ambassador to the UN responded by claiming the UN no longer had a shred of credibility. Something of an astonishing comment given the body's historic record of vetoes of any resolution calling for restraint by Israel. Of course, this was the General Assembly. It's the Security Council which matters and there America gets its own way. The UK is an obedient poodle, France makes no more than mild objections; if Russia and China see eye to eye the US still has a permanent guaranteed majority.

The UN Charter is clear: no State shall engage in aggression without the permission of the Security Council: more in the breach than the observance. The US has engaged in aggression in pursuit of its perceived interests over and over in blank defiance of the UN. As it operates, the UN is impotent to ensure the rule of international law. It needs radical reform. The only sensible outcome would be one State one vote and consensus decision-making. Winner takes all is always a bad idea. It's the logic of the casino, not of serious diplomacy.

The appeal to the international community was, of course, baying at the moon. There is no such community. There is a global system run in the interests of the rich and appealing to that is like asking Harold Shipman to treat your sick grandma.

The World Food Programme reported only forty trucks had entered Gaza in the recent period. Only two bakeries were operating. Food was running short in the West Bank. Much more upscaling was needed. Joe Biden, however, saw fit at this juncture to question the figures for deaths provided by the Gazan Ministry. This deliberate insult to the Palestinians, based on no evidence, was typical of the President's pusillanimity and crass partiality. That the US backed Israel was taken for granted, but that Biden should descend to gratuitous sneering was an indication of the low moral tone of his administration. Omar Shakir of Human Rights Watch said the organisation had been monitoring Gaza for three decades and the Gazan Health Ministry numbers were always reliable. In this case, they were in line with the intensity of the attack and the bodies were mounting up quickly. Exactly what Netanyahu wanted and Biden was willing to endorse.

FRIEND OF HAMAS

Overnight from 27th to 28th October, four Palestinians were killed in Jenin in the West Bank. From the beginning, Netanyahu was intent on fighting on at least two fronts. There was no pretext for increased raids in the West Bank. Yet the pleas from Biden and the UK and elsewhere made no difference. Stephane Dujarric, spokesperson for Guterres said "the world will judge us." Unfortunately, the world's judgement meant nothing to either the Israeli War Cabinet or Biden and his colleagues. What did Dujarric mean by "the world"? Presumably some fairly democratic entity in which people's revulsion at wholesale slaughter, notwithstanding the Hamas attack, could sway policy. Hundreds of millions protested. There could be little doubt most of the world's population would have been glad of a ceasefire, but power doesn't lie with the people.

On 27th October the UN General Assembly passed resolution A/ES/10/L.25. by 121 votes. The amendment (L.26) condemning the Hamas attack the taking of hostages and calling for their immediate and unconditional release failed to attain the required two-thirds majority. The main problem with the amendment was its demand for an unconditional release of the hostages. That was to grant safety to the Israeli victims of 7th October with no reciprocal guarantee for the Palestinians. An all for all swop might have had more chance. Best of all would have been a ceasefire in return for the safe release of the hostages. To expect Hamas to give up its advantage, however questionably it might have been attained, and for the vicious assault on Gaza to continue unabated was unrealistic. That the US backed the amendment gave it the hue of a pro-Israeli move. Further, the condemnation of the Hamas attack was too crude. Occupied peoples have a legal right to armed resistance. A more subtle wording, granting Hamas the right of resistance but condemning those of its actions which fell outside the law might have been more sensible; but the US was intent on supporting Israel in spite of its blatant transgressions of law, the pattern for many decades. Israel's war on Gaza was Biden's war, the Democratic Party's war, every death was on Biden's conscience. Whatever he thinks of himself, to posterity he will be a mass murderer.

Brigadier General Pat Ryder presented the Pentagon's view on Radio 4: the US would respond to Israel's defence needs; it would work with "partners in the region"; it had the capability to protect its forces. The laws of war would be adhered to. Protecting civilians was essential. The US was not involved in Israel's operation. The US had a long-term relationship with Israel, which was viciously attacked. Hamas was using the ISIS playbook.

What would you expect from a career militarist but apologetics for the US's ally? However, Ryder's comments go beyond that: assimilating Hamas to ISIS was pure propaganda. It picked up on Netanyahu's line, a deliberate attempt to widen the conflict, to draw the US into the action. This was the Pentagon behaving as a political actor. The principle in democracies, of course, is supposed to be that politicians make the policy having been empowered to do so by the people, the armed forces carry it out. It isn't for the military to intervene politically. They may have to make difficult decisions in the heat of battle, but they remain, always, servants of the elected politicians. Who empowered Ryder to claim

Hamas was behaving like ISIS? A minimal familiarity with the two outfits reveals serious differences. Hamas isn't an international body. It's a resistance movement with a nationalist aim. It hasn't engaged in terrorism outside Palestine. It's also a *bona fide* political organisation which won elections in the West Bank and Gaza in 2006, much to the consternation of the lovers of democracy in the US and Europe. Its offer to recognise Israel and renounce violence, made to George W Bush after that victory was met by silence, as mentioned above. Democracy has to bring the "right" result. If people vote for Hamas or Jeremy Corbyn, democracy must be subverted. Ryder's intervention ought to bring outrage among the people. They ought to push back; but this, in the current arrangements, is utopian. The Pentagon has power, the people can shut up.

Marwan Bishara commented that the US, Canada and Israel were operating in the theatre of the absurd. The US was engaged in thoroughgoing deception. Its presence in the region was a threat of wider war. Canada refused to condemn genocide. Do you think there is no hierarchy of death? Yes, there is. Palestinians are children of a lesser god. The UN resolution was symbolic but had no muscle. Israel's position was that the world can say what it likes, we do what we want. If Israel does not accept UN resolutions it resorts to insulting the organisation. Should Israel be reprimanded, expelled? The question was purely rhetorical. Israel will simply defy.

In the wake of the resolution, Israel expanded its ground operation. In Nablus, thousands rallied in protest. Drones dropped tear-gas on Hebron. There was an average of three settler attacks per day in the West Bank.

The UN had voted, but the US and Europe had granted Israel a green light for massacre.

Mustafa Barghouti, one of the founders of the Palestinian National Initiative and probably the wisest voice for Palestinian autonomy, accused the Israelis of refusing to listen. Barghouti is disliked by the US, Canada and the EU. When he stood for the leadership of the P.A., they worked diligently against him. He is a dangerous figure because he rejects violence and fundamentalism, both very useful for the Israelis and their backers. His logic is impeccable: violence and fundamentalism play into the hands of those who claim Israel is defending itself against irrational, unreasonable enemies. Commitment to non-violence and rejection of fundamentalism raise the Palestinian cause to a moral level which disturbs Israel. Barghouti's family suffered under British rule, his grandfather and great-uncle having been imprisoned during the Mandate. He has been subject to physical attacks by the Israelis and his visa for a lecture tour to Canada was conveniently processed too late. He illustrates beautifully how the US requires hot-heads and gun-toters to justify its own addiction to aggression. Barghouti's principled, disciplined stance is far and away the best strategy the Palestinians have. He spoke of a huge massacre. The aim of the ground operation was total destruction. Everything was being razed. Everyone killed. The bomb power so far unleashed was close to that visited on Hiroshima. As for Hamas, it was being used as pretext. The Israelis were going after the entire population. Ethnic cleansing was under way. Biden was lying about the casualties.

On 28th October a communications blackout was imposed on Gaza. Four hundred thousand civilians were still in the north. Women and children were among the many casualties. According to Medical Aid for Palestine more than three thousand children had died. Gilad Erdan, Israel's Ambassador to the UN in his response to the previous day's resolution claimed it had nothing to do with peace. Nor did 7th October have anything to do with the Palestinians or Israel-Palestine. Israel was at war with a genocidal Hamas who were modern day Nazis with one goal: to murder every Jew, as laid out in their charter. Even if you grant that Erdan is lying, this is hysterical. Hamas didn't have the capacity to kill all the Jews in Tel Aviv let alone in the world. Israel is a big military power. Twenty percent of its arms funding comes from the US. It has nuclear weapons, and of course, it has the greatest, most grotesque military force the world has known on its side. That it could wipe out Israel is laughable. It managed to kill, with the assistance of the Israelis, slightly more that eleven hundred on 7th October. A tick bite on a herd of cattle in terms of scale, though, of course, devastating for the victims and their families. Israel responded with outlandish violence, not because there was any real fear of destruction or takeover, but because it had been itching for decades to find an excuse to obliterate the Palestinians.

Nine hundred more US troops were sent to the region on 26th, a clear sign of a desire to avoid escalation. Had Iran moved nine troops towards Israel, doubtless it would have been seen in Washington, London, Brussels and Tel Aviv as a shocking act of provocation. There is, of course, a principle at work here: power knows no limits. Its reach can never be broad and deep enough. It can never have sufficient control. The slightest deviance from its impositions is an existential threat. Power can't be reasoned or negotiated with; that can be done only with those who accept others have interests and a case. The essence of power is that it alone is justified.

Settler attacks in the West Bank reached one hundred and thirty-eight, one third involving firearms. On Radio 4's Today programme on 28th October, Mishal Hussein pointed out that Israel claimed it had precise intelligence, sufficiently accurate for it to know where Hamas's tunnels were and what they were used for. In that case, she asked, how come its intelligence was so dismal on 7th October? She was interviewing Justin Cromp who styles himself a security and intelligence expert. He spent twenty years in the British military and has written about corporate security. In other words, his expertise is in defending the rich and powerful. He doesn't appear to have written about how trade unions, pressure groups or anarchists can look after themselves. Hussein asked him if Israel's key aims made sense. He responded that such aims weren't rational in the fight against ISIS. Terrorism, he averred, can't be beaten by violence. This might appear balanced, in fact it's the usual propaganda tactic: what Israel is doing is justified, it's just going about it the wrong way. There was no question of putting Israel's essential position in question. Such interventions provide a useful appearance of democratic debate: should Israel decimate the Palestinians this way or that way; but that they shouldn't is off the agenda. Meanwhile, Daniel Hagari, the IDF's ghoulish spokesperson, argued medical facilities were fair game, a claim greeted with resounding silence by the "West". Geoffrey Nice, the veteran KC and judge explained that theoretically medical facilities can lose their protected status but a warning must be given; the aim of the attack must be justified and proportionate and must be to prevent risk to other lives. Brought before a court, the precise reasoning leading to the attack would be required. The ICC has jurisdiction in such matters. It was doubtful Israel could fulfil the requirements. The law employs the caveat of acts "harmful to the enemy" but doesn't offer precise definition. Clearly, the Israeli claim from the start was that hospitals were being used as military bases, though no convincing evidence was adduced. Leaving aside the legal issue, however, from a moral point of view Israel's assaults on medical facilities were despicable. They weren't indiscriminate: they were intended to remove medical care for the wounded and sick; part of the Israeli effort to wipe out the Gazans.

Jeremy Hopkins of UNICEF said a million children were in need of supplies. There were no communications. An immediate ceasefire was the best way to bring aid.

Jeremy Bowen reported on radio 4 that the IDF were hitting the north, though they weren't saying much about their operations. The bombardments were very large. It was hard to get information. The UN was in contact with the south by satphone, otherwise communication was down. The IDF was trying to clear Hamas's tunnels. They seemed to be trying to take Gaza slice by slice.

Mark Regev, the robotic purveyor of the Israeli State's mendacity, interviewed on Radio 4, said the pressure to destroy Hamas would increase. As for the four hundred thousand civilians still in the north, everything was being done to spare them (this with a straight face). The figure of three thousand dead children couldn't be trusted because it came from Hamas. As for Israel, it was unable to provide numbers. Pressed on how he could know the figures provided by Hamas were wrong given he could provide none of his own, he replied the military was not the right body to provide such statistics. Odd that the IDF was rather less reticent about assertions concerning precisely how Hamas was using hospitals. The problem of getting the hostages out alive, he claimed, was there was no good will from Hamas; as if the Israelis had always bent double to secure peace and understanding. Hamas was lying, he asserted about the hostages killed in Israeli attacks. Once again, curious that one minute the Israelis know nothing and the next they have secure data. Regev made a strange admission: Israel had failed. Its mistake was believing it could live with Hamas.

Regev's capacity to lie is pathological. Netanyahu is on record as arguing in 2019 that anyone who wanted to isolate the Palestine Authority must support Hamas: "Whoever opposes a Palestinian State must support the delivery of funds to Gaza because maintaining separation between the Palestinian Authority in the West Bank and Hamas in Gaza will prevent the establishment of a Palestinian State." Hamas had no better friend in the world than Netanyahu. Funds to Gaza were funds to Hamas. In May 2019 Mubarak remarked: "Netanyahu isn't interested in a two-State solution. Rather, he wants to separate Gaza from the West bank, as he told me at the end of 2010." In the same year, Ehud Barak remarked: "His strategy is to keep Hamas alive and kicking.. even at the price of abandoning the citizens..in order to weaken the Palestine Authority in Ramallah." Netanyahu ensured funds kept flowing from Qatar and Iran to Hamas.

None of this is arcane. Yet Regev argues that Israel tried to "live with Hamas." It was doing no such thing: it was consciously and deliberately supporting them. Living with them implies putting up with them in spite of being opposed. Netanyahu wasn't opposed, he was enthusiastic: Hamas was his guarantee of a block on a

Palestinian State. He wasn't putting up with them, he was manipulating them. Regev's comment leaves this out entirely. It implies Israel did nothing to help Hamas but tried merely to find a *modus vivendi*. That is thoroughly dishonest. Netanyahu was boosting an organisation which he defined as terrorist. He scuppered the 2017 peace plan between Fatah and Hamas, brokered by Egypt: it might facilitate two-States. In January 2022 Gadi Eisenkot, a senior IDF military figure, revealed that Netanyahu consistently overruled the National Security Council in its efforts to engage with the PA and establish two States. His strategy was to ostracise the PA and strengthen Hamas.

Angela Davis, the veteran US civil rights activist, argued on Al Jazeera that Palestinian and coloured liberation were intertwined. Palestine was a moral litmus test. The movement against racism was expanding. There was no abstract answer, things had to play out in practicality. The Israeli police and the IDF were all of a piece. There was a comparison with the US where Atlanta, for example was a "cop city". The police were pushing for greater power. There were great corporate profits to be had from oppression. It was necessary to talk about capitalism. Though it might be hard to see a way through, it was crucial not to give up. Hope is the condition of all struggles.

Davis was perhaps the sole, at least one of the very few, who raised the question of the US as a business-controlled society. In the mainstream, of course, the connection was never made. The cause was simply a mad attack by Hamas . That the US used Israel as a strategic asset, that Israel, like its master, was a business society marked by serious inequality, that the people to suffer in Israel were the poor, that the assault on Gaza was necessary for US domination and that was driven by the corporates and their divine right to profit, was completely suppressed. As ever, whatever the US did was justified. The US was always on the side of freedom and justice, even when it invaded South Vietnam or brought down Allende. The underlying assumption of indefeasible virtue which has turned the US into the biggest threat not only to peace but to the survival of humanity, was simply taken for granted. Davies's remarks were relatively banal, yet the banality of the obvious had to be hidden from view. There was only one narrative: the US and Israel were defenders of peace, justice, humanity, the rule of law. Franz Kafka couldn't have made it up.

IMPECCABLE VIRTUE

Biden, Sunak , Starmer, Macron, Schultz all the accomplices in mass murder were willing to nod along. What was forbidden was to point out the obvious. Interviewed on Al Jazeera, Ilan Pappé argued that 7th October had been de-historicised by the acceptance of the Israeli narrative. This was an anaesthetising frame: to support Palestine was terrorism. There was nothing new about this. 7th October had brought about no fundamental change. The debate was taking place through soundbites, which was utterly inadequate. Space to air the issues was required. We should insist on conversation on our terms. We shouldn't apologise. It was necessary to be patient. The truth is on our side. To be accused of racism for criticising Israel was to be a victim of racism. Dima Khalidi of Palestine Legal warned of a descent into fascism. There was a crackdown on dissent. Conversations about the issues were being closed down. It was dangerous and hypocritical. Gilad Erdan was anti-UN. Israel was trying to deny all interests which uphold international law. The US, EU and UK were following Israel's line. The UN had been established post World War 2 to avoid genocide. Palestinian history was being erased. There had been an exponential increase in the need for legal help. Students were being harassed by their universities for taking part in activism. Israel is an ethno-nationalist State. There is no room for criticism, no nuance.

All this is true, but what lies behind it is American power. Everything Israel does is sanctioned and funded by the US. Israel is a client State. Noam Chomsky has argued that it isn't fair to dub Israel the fifty-first State because it receives more from the Federal government than any US state. Israel is the guarantor of US power in the region and has been so since 1967, when aid increased vastly thanks to the victory against Nasser. The US needs Israel in the region because of its desire to control world affairs and it needs to do that to protect the profits of US big business. That's the reason innocents were being slaughtered in Gaza. The US wasn't complicit, it was responsible. Biden could have ended the war at his choosing. He could have used the US vote in the UN to scupper Netanyahu. He could have pulled funding. Biden believed slaughtering Gazan civilians was right . They were hiding Hamas fighters. They were suspect. Simply, however much he might deny it, Biden was an anti-Arab racist. The people being killed didn't have blonde hair and blue eyes.

Harlan Ullman of the Atlantic Council, a think tank incapable of thinking, claimed on Radio 4 that Israel had no choice. Hamas's tactics were disastrous. Things were only going to get worse. There was no way out. There might be some kind of diplomatic initiative, but the Gazans had nowhere to go. Think of Stalingrad or Fallujah. Netanyahu's life was on the line. It was the war from hell and there were no good options.

Notice how this is cast to sound superficially rational and informed. That Israel had no choice is risible. It had multiple choices, but the best and obvious was to lift the occupation and the siege and to promise an autonomous Palestinian society. A pipedream of course as that would involve Israel thinking. Israel's leaders are involved in the systematic destruction of the capacity to think which accompanies all desire for power. The State of Israel wasn't brought into existence to guarantee the well-being of Jews. Had it been, why would there have been any reason to expel the Palestinians? It was brought into existence to be a supremacist State, as adumbrated in Herzl's famous book. Only its supremacist ideology explains the expulsion of nearly a million Palestinians and the appalling history of its oppression of Arabs since 1948. Yet supposed world leaders peddle the twaddle that Israel's "security" is that of Jewry. Jews in America live perfectly safely and thrive, as they do in the UK, France, Sweden, Australia. What guarantees the security of the Jews is universal equal rights. What Israel stands for is the exact opposite.

Erdogan called the Israelis war criminals and criticised the West. Israeli terror groups were not a country. Over the past few years there had been a softening of opinion about Israel in the Arab countries. That had all been lost. Governments had to take the Arab street into account. Protesters were demanding a Muslim peace-keeping force.

There was a significant demonstration in London, estimated by the police to be 100,000 strong. It was compared to the 15th February 2003 protest against the coming invasion of Iraq. A show of popular desire for peace dutifully ignored by the political elite, doing the bidding of big business. People expressed disbelief at the UK's abstention in the UN. There was a disconnect between policy and popular opinion. Sunak and Starmer were conjoined.

Anger was growing among Labour voters, but of course, the purge and imposition of authoritarianism had happened. Grassroot members were forbidden to discuss the issue, just as they were gagged from mentioning Corbyn. A quarter of Labour MPs were in favour of a ceasefire. Naturally, Starmer ignored them. That's democracy.

Antonio Gutteres, in Doha, called for de-escalation. Gaza was at the top of his agenda. He was "encouraged by what seems to be a call for a humanitarian pause," while at the same time "surprised by unprecedented escalation." He shouldn't have been. The US was granting Israel *carte blanche*, Netanyahu was fighting to stay out of jail. For both Biden and the Israeli P.M., sacrificing the Gazans was a perfectly reasonable price for their success. At the time of the Vietnam War, Stokley Carmichael, the American civil rights activist, said that as far as America was concerned, the Vietnamese were "just slant-eyed niggers." The same was true in Gaza. The Palestinians were just Arab niggers. The IDF wasn't going after Hamas fighters, it was treating every Palestinian as a legitimate target. Its tactics and morality were medieval.

Yair Lapid observed that if the media were objective, they were serving Hamas. If they showed both sides, they served Hamas. It's doubtful whether Lapid, in spite of his books, dramas, songs, television and journalistic career, understands what "objective" means. It simply means impersonal. Quite an assertion that to report from an impersonal perspective is biased, but perfectly in keeping with the dishonesty of power.

While Netanyahu made the usual claim that the IDF is the "most moral army in the world", a typical oppressor's expression of extreme virtue, Lapid, on 28th October, called on the PM to apologise for criticising the armed forces. Netanyahu, the man who staked his reputation on providing security for the Israelis, had to find someone to blame. His attribution of responsibility to the IDF, however, was at the level of adolescent clumsiness. It beggars belief he imagined he could get away with it, but desperate people try desperate measures. Gallant claimed the more Israel hit Gaza the more likely Hamas would be to negotiate. Quite what he based this logic on is hard to ascertain, but as Hamas had secured leverage by taking hostages (which it termed "guests" and promised to treat well) it was unlikely to renounce it except in exchange for at least a temporary ceasefire. Gantz asserted that Israel controlled the operational clock. Marwan Bishara pointed out that the three men hated one another. They had different aims. Netanyahu was in cahoots with fascists and his belief he could kill Hamas as an idea was unrealistic. Netanyahu was forced to withdraw his critical tweet in the face of outrage.

Navi Pillay from the Commission of Inquiry on Palestine and the Occupied Territories, interviewed on Al Jazeera, termed Israel an "apartheid State". In that, she concurred with Human Rights Watch and B'tselem. She argued Israel didn't want to see the occupation end and the European States were essentially for the status quo, but to what end? Interestingly, she was given an award for "outstanding achievement" by the International Law Association. On 5th October Hillel Neuer of UN Watch, wrote to the body calling for the recognition to be rescinded because recipients have to be impartial and Ms Pillay had previously made comments in support of Palestine and critical of Israel. Neuer is a lawyer who has made a name for himself as a human rights advocate. He has defended human rights in Darfur, Pakistan, Zimbabwe and elsewhere, but curiously enough, never Palestine. In 2009 he was involved in a row over his criticism of Naomi Klein (a Jew) for her support of the boycott of the Toronto Film Festival in protest at the showing of films from Tel Aviv. It's a cute tactic: defend human rights everywhere except Palestine. Argue for equal rights everywhere, except

Palestine. Stand against the abuse of all people, except Palestinians. Neuer gets away with it for two reasons: most people don't have the time or inclination to research his background and activities, and he garners the support of leading figures naïve enough not to question his Palestinian exceptionalism. Klein made the terrible mistake of being willing to criticise Israel. Neuer, in keeping with the current mad, Perlmutter brand of anti-Semitism ie to suggest Israel is anything but angelic is to be a Nazi, leaps on anyone, Jew or otherwise, who refuses absolute obeisance to the Israeli State. UN Watch was founded in 1993. Its first chair was Morris B Abram. As US representative to the UN Commission on Human Rights in 1990, Abram supported America's lonely veto of the UN resolution calling for right to development for all countries, calling it an "empty vessel" and a "dangerous incitement". In other words, doing the bidding of US big business. One of the board members of UN Watch before his death was David Trimble, once a member of the Vanguard Unionist Progressive Party which called for the "extermination" of the Provisional IRA. As with Neuer, Trimble's human rights concerns didn't extend to the victims of the colonialism from which he had benefitted and which he supported.

Israel warned Gazans to move south, as if they were going to spare them if they did . Gaza City had turned into a battlefield. Israel refused the Starlink communication system to Gaza while at the same time claiming Hamas was in total control of the Strip. Israeli missiles struck within twenty metres of the Al Quds hospital. Israel's excuse for its deliberate and concerted attacks on medical facilities was that they were command centres or hiding places for Hamas, but such evidence as it produced was quickly shown to be dubious. In the wings was the bleating voice of the sheepish Blinken insisting civilians must be spared. What was clear to anyone with eyes was that Israel was going after the sick and injured and its intent was to demolish the entire Gazan medical infrastructure.

Riham Jafari, an Action Aid worker, called for huge political pressure to force Israel to abide by international law and pleaded for an immediate ceasefire. Her call was principled and correct, but hopeless in the face of State which prides itself on its defiance of international law. Its array of Prime Ministers who have engaged in terrorism is impressive: Levi Eshkol was high commander of the Haganah, Ygal Allon and Yitzhak Rabin Palmach commanders; Begin led the Irgun and fought against the British who called him "leader of the notorious terrorist organisation" (things have changed somewhat, the British, effectively chased out of Palestine by terrorists, now define the Israelis as angelic; no Israeli could be a terrorist, a definition reserved for Palestinians, Arabs, Muslims, the Irish etc); Shimon Peres belonged to the Haganah as did Sharon. None of this, naturally, prevents Netanyahu from endless public declarations of total condemnation of terrorism. In the rosy light of retrospection, the terrorists who murdered and bombed their way to statehood are high-minded freedom fighters to whom statues must be raised and praises sung.

Bushra Khalidi of Oxfam called for an end to the siege and a genuine, time-bound plan. She pointed to calls by some six hundred organisations for a complete ceasefire and said it was the responsibility of elected leader to bring it about. Unfortunately, the elected leaders, drunk on their own power, were luxuriating in the delightful capacity of being able to assist in the murder of Gazan children. Not only were they not willing, with a few noble exceptions, to call for a ceasefire, but viewed it as dangerous capitulation. After all, Hamas, entirely unprovoked, had slaughtered, with a little help from the Israelis, some eleven hundred on 7th October. The British who killed a mere eight hundred thousand during the Indian Mutiny of 1857, would have been outraged beyond measure had the lesser race dared to launch an assault on British soil, yet found it the most natural thing under the sun to support tens of thousands of Palestinians being murdered for an incursion by a small para-military group fighting back against nearly a century of oppression.

On 29th October, Israel claimed there were no food shortages in Gaza. Fergal Keane, reporting for the BBC said: "It seems as if the world is broken." Who lives or dies, he observed, was a matter of chance. Of course, the world was functioning exactly as it should, according to the US and its allies. Who lives and dies has been a matter of chance for a very long time. It's taken for granted in the current arrangements that the lives of the poor are worth less than the rest, just as it's beyond question that people with blonde hair and blue eyes shouldn't be slaughtered. Certainly, those who own and profit from big business should be protected at all costs. Palestinians were being murdered because, as Richard Nixon's defence secretary put it, Israel is the "cop on the beat". Things were working marvellously. Thousands were being killed and displaced. People were being deprived of the basic means of life. That's what should happen in a world organised in the interests of the rich. Keane's heartfelt plea was full of the milk of human kindness, but when Lady MacBeth rules the world, it won't get you anywhere. Expressions of this kind were obvious: the assault could be stopped immediately, the threat to Israel removed, by ending the occupation. When this was tamely suggested, the robust response was: it was to play into the hands of terrorists, it would embolden Hamas who had vowed to repeat 7th October over and over. It was siding with terrorists against the rule of law. The rule of law, that is, which permits Israel to occupy the West Bank in its stark defiance. The language was always Orwellian. What else can it be when you are defending the indefensible and accusing your enemies of your own crimes?

Fourteen thousand people were sheltering in Al Quds hospital. There were reports of the wounded having white phosphorous burns. Israel admitted the use of WP against military targets in the 2006 war with Lebanon, and used it in the 2008-9 war with Gaza. On 15th January 2009 the UNRWA facility in Gaza City was hit by WP. Israel's hatred of UNRWA is not new. A State which can exist in its current form only by breaching international law every day is not going to be sympathetic to an international organisation which is part of a body seeking to ensure the world runs according to agreed rules. WP isn't banned but is subject to strict regulation. You're not allowed to walk through the door of a nursery and blast the kids with it. Or into an old folks' home and set them all on fire. The legislation is mad. The only rational thing to do about such a vile weapon is to ban it and bring to justice any head of State who uses it; but then a bow and arrow is vile enough if the barb sticks in your eye. Which leads us to the idea of banning aggression altogether, an idea from Jupiter if you're rich and powerful, but pretty attractive if you're poor and watching your kids get bombed.

Reports claimed surgeons were using ketamine. Hamas reported it had damaged two IDF tanks and killed two soldiers. Something Israel denied. An Israeli flag was flown in Gaza for the first time since 2005. Netanyahu denied he had been informed of a potential attack at which Benny Gantz was up in arms. Western media were more or less refusing to report on the obvious evidence that Hamas planning for the assault had been known by the Israeli security forces for months. The narrative had to be a surprise attack and over a thousand murdered by Hamas. Will the number killed by Israel ever be known? Nuseirat refugee camp was hit once more with dozens killed. Mads Gilbert, a Norwegian physician with long experience in Gaza warned of a "disaster of a magnitude not seen in modern times" unless there was a ceasefire. Gilbert spoke with the authority of his professionalism and humanitarian commitment. He's also, however, a member of the Red Party, a more or less orthodox Marxist organisation which, though it renounces violent revolution and upholds democracy, is heavily Statist. Easy to justify in a way: in a world of marauding corporates, to use the State as a defence for the common folk is politically and morally sensible. The problem for the Red Party, however, is that it is too readily associated with the punitive and controlling State which, as Bakunin pointed out, was the logical outcome of Marx's "dictatorship of the proletariat".

Rami Khoury, the New York born Palestinians journalist argued Israel had gone mad. Biden should think carefully and go easy. The war was a consequence of the League of Nations mandate. The Israelis were intent on inflicting pain. They had no military aim. The vehemence of Biden's support for Israel was puzzling. He had an election to fight and needed to calculate.

Israel was very good at getting western leaders on its side. The result was genocidal war. The same pattern had been repeated four or five times. Since 1948 Israel had relied on a display of military power. 7th October had shattered the *status quo* in the Middle East. A ground war could involve Hezbollah and Iran. To an extent it was already happening.

Khoury was right about the absence of military aims, but there was nothing surprising about Biden's unconditional support. The US doctrine is that it has the right to employ extreme violence whenever its "interests" are challenged. By its interests, it means the right to dominate the globe economically and militarily. Of course, it does this in the most angelic fashion. It is always on the side of democracy, freedom, human rights, even when its defoliating Vietnam or installing Pinochet in Chile. The US is in the grip of a delusion of impeccable virtue. Biden simply took it for granted Americans would understand this. Mostly they do. That he might have trouble with the US-Arab votes in Dearborn, Michigan, was a side issue. Using Israel as a proxy to decimate a people who had the nerve to resist American hegemony was just one more proof of what a morally superior State the US is.

FROM THE RIVER TO THE SEA

On 29th October, angry people stormed Makhachkala airport in Dagestan, a Russian republic on the west side of the Caspian sea, looking for Israelis. People on buses were interrogated. Passengers were locked inside planes. Some of the crowd carried Palestinian flags. Were they anti-Semites or anti-Zionists? Almost certainly some of them were the former but information hasn't been very forthcoming. Russia blamed Ukraine, predictably. If some of these people were anti-Semites looking for victims, their actions were despicable. If they were pro-Palestinians, they besmirched their cause. What can be concluded from this episode is that the surest way to give succour to anti-Semites is to pursue the colonialist doctrine of Zionism by conflating it with being Jewish. It is the Zionists who do this. Anti-Zionists are always scrupulous in effecting a distinction between their political and philosophical position and the irrationality of Jew-hatred. Zionists, on the other hand, make ill-use of anti-Semitism by arguing an identity between its most extreme and vile forms and any criticism of the Israeli State. This was witnessed egregiously in the false claims of "institutional anti-Semitism" in the Labour Party and the much-repeated claim that Jeremy Corbyn was an anti-Semite or friend of anti-Semitism. As the attack on Gaza unfolded, so did the flimsy claim that to refuse to line up with Israel is anti-Semitic. The threadbare ideology of Zionism was torn to shreds in the streets of towns and cities across the globe. Probably billions now see through the Israel claim that every criticism is an existential threat, that anyone who doesn't concur with all the actions of its State conceals a desire to exterminate all Jews. Our leaders still wear blindfolds.

Mads Gilbert argued he had seen no evidence of the use of hospitals as political or command centres during his thirty years of work in Gaza. The responsibility was on Israel to produce the proof. Israel's attempts to do so were at the level of the dog ate my homework, except that the school boy or girl seeking to evade imposition may be acting rationally. On Radio 4's Today programme on 30th October Peter Ricketts, a career diplomat who now sits as a cross-bencher in the Lords, said there was no military solution to political problems. There needed to be an endgame. Referring to Lebanon in 1982 he pointed out that the PLO had been expelled but that hadn't prevented the Sabra and Shatila massacre. There had been no political solution. Ricketts is a typically conformist product of Oxbridge and the diplomatic corps. Little in the way of genuine insight can be expected from such people: they have spent their lives serving the British State. Yet it's interesting he should make his first remark. If there is no military solution to political problems, what is war for? Has there ever been a war which wasn't fought over political claims? Ricketts was, inadvertently, pointing up the insanity of our international order. Specifically in relation to Gaza, he was ditching the government's and Starmer's line. They were fully supportive of Israel's unflinching assault and supported Netanyahu's mad aim of extirpation of Hamas.

In contradistinction, Elon Levy the eyebrow raising (both senses) Israeli spokesperson, argued Hamas had declared war on Israel on 7th October. Levy was brought up in London where he was privately educated, moving on, predictably to Oxford. He served in the IDF in 2014. Early in the Gaza debacle he revealed his jejune nature when in response to a speech by Hasan Nasrallah he thought boring, he observed his speech-writer had probably been assassinated by Israel. Perhaps the frank admission of Israel's vicious anti-democratic tactics should be welcomed. He went on, however, to claim Nasrallah was a coward hiding in a bunker defending the "paedophile rapists of Hamas." Nothing unusual in this exposure of the demented thinking of supporters of the Israeli State and the wild exaggerations of its spokespeople. 7th October, he claimed, was a genocide. Under the UN definition, his position might be defended as it covers the killing of part of a national, ethical, racial or religious with the intention of its elimination. Yet if his assertion is correct, how much more so is the demand the assault on Gaza be characterised as genocide, something Levy would never concede. He argued the Geneva Convention permits bombing of hospitals. Once again, possibly correct in some circumstances, but not when the aggressor can produce no significant evidence of their military use. Jihadists were on Israel's borders. Israel didn't want to hurt civilians. Should there be more aid? There was sufficient food and fuel in Gaza. Israel was happy to see aid delivered but had to be sure it didn't fall into Hamas's hands. UNRWA had admitted its fuel had been stolen. All information from UNRWA had to be taken with a pinch of salt. UNRWA workers were involved with Hamas. Anything Levy said which contained a grain of truth was rendered false by his pushing to extremes. As always when people are defending an unjust or dishonest position, refusal to temper their arguments to the evidence gives them away. Finally, Levy was asked for his reaction to the London protests. He responded they were difficult to watch. They were effectively a call to intifada, suicide bombings, terrorism. They were a contribution to the globalisation of the intifada, an example being the Manchester Arena bombing. They assisted anti-Semitism and Jews were afraid of being in central London when they were taking place. In other words, Levy doesn't like the democratic right to protest. His assertion that "Jews" feel afraid was a signal instance of speaking for all Jews by someone who has no authority to do so. Odd too that on all the London demonstrations, Jews were in evidence and there had been no reports of them being uncomfortable. On the contrary, Jews were especially welcome on the protests, for obvious reasons. Levy is an educated intellectual who, like so many of his ilk in the modern world, provides his intelligence to an unjust cause. Voices such as his silence those of millions who disagree. Many Jews across the world wouldn't have concurred with his stance. Many Israelis would have put release of the hostages first and would have questioned his unflinching support of Netanyahu, whose popularity was declining temporarily. The media like to feature intellectuals and academics, who, the assumption is, will bring objectivity to a question; but intellectuals today, especially in the social and behavioural sciences, are more likely to be servants of business and the State than independent minds willing to reach conclusions troubling for the rich and powerful. That Levy, educated in London and Oxford can sneer at the democracy that gives people the right to peaceful protest, claiming it's a threat to Jews, contains a sinister hint: either stand by Israel or Israel will condemn you.

Jeremy Bowen reported that the road south through Gaza, Salah Al Din Street, had been damaged. Tanks had fired on and destroyed an approaching car. According to the Israelis, Palestinians had been told to move south for safety. There were two routes only. Israel's allies dutifully praised them for their kindness in granting the people from the north the chance to escape the bombing.

On our televisions were pictures of carts piled shakily with families' belongings and pulled by donkeys as desperate people sought refuge where the IDF told them they would find it. What else could they do? Bowen speculated the IDF was trying to lay siege to Gaza. The truth is, the Israelis were playing a sadistic game with the Palestinians, as they have for decades: driving them south and shooting at them like targets at a fun fair. There is no description for this but psychopathic. Nothing about it assisted the searching out of Hamas fighters. Netanyahu had his excuse and was determined to push his opportunity as far as possible.

On Radio 4's World at One on 30th October Mohammed Galayini, an air quality scientist from Manchester who had gone to Gaza on a three-month career break to visit his family, said Hamas was not preventing anyone from moving to safety as the Israelis claimed. It was the bombardment which was preventing them.

Hamas released a video of three female hostages wearing Palestinian clothes in a white tiled room, one of whom spoke in Hebrew. She expressed fury with Netanyahu saying they had been in custody for twenty-three days and referred to a press conference (probably held three days earlier). She appeared to believe there had been an agreement to let them all go. She was angry the IDF hadn't protected them on 7th October. They wanted to go back to their families. From a simple humanitarian stance, it would have been impossible not to feel sorry for these women and to wish them reunited with those they wanted to be with. They appeared healthy and not to have been abused. Perhaps they were convinced Zionists who supported the oppression of the Palestinians, but maybe not. It was impossible to see them as anything but victims of mad violence, yet the responsibility for that had to lie with the Israelis and their protector, the USA. These women were caught up in the power politics of the most heavily-armed State the world has seen, willing to employ exorbitant violence to get its own way. Of course, our media took the opportunity to expatiate on the inhumanity of Hamas, as usual diminishing or ignoring the historical and political background. The greatest significance of the video, however, was what it meant for Netanyahu. Mr Security had failed. His assault was supposed to be the way to get the hostage released. He was getting nowhere. The question it should have raised in everyone's mind was whether Netanyahu was at all serious about saving the hostages, or was saving his skin what came first?

Andy McDonald, Labour MP for Middlesborough was suspended for making a speech in which he said: "We will not rest until we have justice. Until all people, Israeli and Palestinians, between the river and the sea, can live in peaceful liberty." A Labour spokesperson said the comments were "deeply offensive particularly at a time of rising antisemitism which has left Jewish people fearful for their safety." Thus, the Labour Party thinks it "deeply offensive" that one of its members should believe in "peaceful liberty" for "all people". Of course, the excuse is that mentioning "from the river to the sea" implies a desire to eliminate Israel. McDonald made himself perfectly clear: he wants Israelis and Palestinian alike to live in peace and justice. Yet the Labour Party is so absorbed into the thinking of Likud and Mossad, that anything but the present arrangement ie Israeli oppression, settlements in the West Bank, a siege of Gaza and full citizenship of Israel for Jews alone is interpreted as a desire to exterminate the Jewish people. It's often asserted that Israel has a right to exist. No State enjoys an abstract right to exist. The international order recognises functioning States, North Korea for example. Israel is a functioning State and a such protected by international law; but it breaches that law daily by the occupation of the West Bank. What do we mean when we say "Israel"? In its present iteration, it has no right to exist. It has no right to occupy territory gained in the 1967 war; it has no right to build settlements in the West Bank; it has no right to control Gaza's borders. It has a right to exist within the pre-1967 borders, but as Golda Meir's remark, asserts, Israel refuses borders; where there are Jews, that is Israel. A terrifying idea.

On 3rd November, the executive of Unite the Union called for a ceasefire, after dithering since 7th October. On 30th December, however, Unite members published a letter on Skwawkbox criticising the feeble nature of the 3rd November declaration, its drawing of an equivalence between the Hamas attack and the Israeli response and its failure to detail the putative breaches of international and humanitarian law. It was claimed the Unite leadership was prohibiting the display of the union's banners on demonstrations and attempts to use Unite premises to show *The Big Lie*, the film about the vicious campaign against Corbyn and to prevent presentation or discussion of Asa Winstanley's *Weaponising Antisemitism*, were clearly taking place. Not all unions were as tentative and dilatory as Unite. NEU banners, for example, were in evidence on London demonstrations. The response of the British Trade Union movement, however, was in general shameful. The TUC was fully behind the arming of the Ukrainians. There was no suggestion Ukrainian flags should not be flown. Whence the timidity? Of course, fear of being deemed antisemitic. European guilt over the Nazi genocide played a decisive role in dampening condemnation of Israel. That the Israeli State made use of this goes without saying. As Norman Finklestein and others have amply displayed, it is the stock-in-trade of post 1948 Zionism to manipulate the Nazi horror for political advantage. It took a very confused and cowardly mind, however, to hold back from calling for a ceasefire when unarmed men, women and children who had nothing to do with Hamas were being slaughtered. It required no political stance or knowledge of the history of Israel/Palestine, simply humanity. It's estimated that during the Troubles, the IRA killed about 1,700, mostly British soldiers, but some 500-600 civilians. Would that have justified bombing Londonderry, invading hospitals, displacing the population to the border with Southern Ireland? The analogy is not precise, but Israel's claim it was going after Hamas fighters was preposterous. The way to do that, long established, would have been to recruit informers. What Israel needed was intelligence. What evidence is there the bombing killed Hamas operatives? A clever strategy would have been to drive a wedge between the civilian population and Hamas and the way to do that would have been to look after the civilians. If Hamas had their support it was because of Israel's vile treatment of the Palestinians. The entire Israeli justification for its actions, backed by the US, the UK, France, Germany and more, was phoney. Netanyahu was intent on killing Palestinians. For a simple reason, like many Israelis, he was an anti-Arab Israeli supremacist.

During an Al Jazeera discussion on 30th October, Menachem Klein of Bar-Ilan University argued the Israeli economy was effectively on hold, the Shekel was falling in relation to the dollar, and Israel was fully dependent on the US both financially and for security. There was no endgame. It was impossible to predict economic consequences because there was no plan.

Natasha Lindstaedt of Essex University called 7th October Israel's 9/11 (from their perspective) and pointed out the US spent two trillion dollars on its military response (a complete failure, naturally). There was no mention of the effects of the war on the Israeli working-class but it goes without saying they were the ones suffering the most. What is striking is the willingness to lavish huge spending on death and destruction for aims impossible to achieve. As with the US response to the Twin Towers attack, it looked much more like unhinged revenge than any rational policy.

Netanyahu declared there would be no ceasefire, claiming Israel had great "moral clarity". Interesting to pause over this Orwellian usage. *Moral* is said to have been coined by Cicero to render the Greek for *ethics*, which relates to character, rule-following, custom. By its very nature, *moral* relates to adherence to a norm or set of norms and is therefore a recognition of duty. In other words, the opposite of doing what you like. It evokes, of necessity, the rights and needs of others and the requirement to adhere to principles which extend beyond what may be expedient. *Clarity* is derived from the Latin for brightness or splendour. *War*, of course, comes from words meaning chaos and confusion. Netanyahu was committed to "war" ie herding sheep into tight spaces and dropping bombs on them. There was a thoroughgoing absence of morality in his position. He was inimical to any international body which stood in his way, like a spoilt, narcissistic child who can't accept any defiance of its wilfulness. The obvious high moral intent of UNRWA, which for decades had done excellent work in difficult situations, had to be portrayed as low conspiracy with terrorism because it prevented Bibi from having his own way (perhaps the infantile nature of the diminutive is worth noting). As for brightness or splendour. At every turn, Netanyahu's and Israel's technique was to muddy the waters, to throw in red herrings, to ensure rational thinking was subverted by unfounded claims, rejection of evidence, refusal of compromise, unwillingness to listen to any voice which wasn't in total agreement. In a ridiculous effort to justify his wayward over-reaction he likened 7th October to Pearl Harbour and the attack on the Twin Towers. Of course, ninety minutes prior to the attack on Pearl Harbour, the Japanese attacked Malaya, and it was no surprise: Lord Halifax had predicted the "balloon would go up" days before. Perhaps Netanyahu gave away more than he intended in making the comparison. As for the Twin Towers, in July 2000, Richard Clarke, a counter-terrorism official warned: "Something really spectacular is going to happen here, and it's going to happen soon." Netanyahu's attempt to claim the three assaults came out of the blue was typically cack-handed.

What he intended, of course, was to gather "western" sympathy. Israel was a victim, like the US, and therefore justified in its retaliation. The US was no victim. Pearl Harbour was a military base on a colony and Osama bin Laden had made multiple statements about his opposition to US domination, stressing that if the US looked after its own people and let the Middle East decide its own fate, he had no argument with America. Netanyahu was simply behaving like his bully protector.

The US warned there would be no ceasefire and engaged in self-congratulation over the delivery of aid. John Kirby, the National Security Council coordinator claimed a ceasefire would benefit Hamas. Israel's "operation" (interestingly, just what Putin called his aggression in Ukraine) was against the Hamas leadership. Of course, the Israeli assault on the

Palestinians was a superb recruiting sergeant for Hamas and the deaths were overwhelmingly civilian and mostly women and children.

420 A DAY

On 30th October Uri Magidish, an 18-year-old Israeli soldier, was rescued by the IDF in an operation along with Shin Bet. The return of a young woman to her family is to be celebrated, but she was a serving member of an army which holds the Palestinians in a condition of submission no fully human person could accept. Naturally, the Israeli media had nothing but praise for the rescuers. As usual, there was not a glimmer of recognition that perhaps the kidnaps were because the Palestinians were at the end of their tether. The absolute refusal of the Israeli State to accept any responsibility betrays a need to believe in its perfection. On the same day, Phillip Lazzarini, Commissioner-General of UNRWA, declared nowhere safe in Gaza. The killing of children was not collateral damage. "We will not be able to say we did not know," he observed, which raises an interesting question: did Netanyahu believe his power was so great he would be able to control posterity? It seems people drunk on power do. Somehow power has the capacity to turn off the perception that the history sees with different eyes and its judgements are harsh. Presumably, Napoleon, Stalin, Pol Pot, Ceausescu, any tyrant you choose, believed their power was so absolute no one would ever look back on them in disdain and horror. Why else would a person behave in a way which ensures their eternal contempt? While the Magidishes, along with most of their fellow countrymen and women, delighted in the safe return of their child, their government was wilfully massacring children because they were Arabs. How do people fail to make the connection? The answer, we know, lies in dehumanisation. In war, the enemy has to be conceived of as vile, animal, unworthy of dignity and respect. The propaganda tricks which do this are well-known, what we have no idea about is what goes on in our brains to make it possible.

Catherine Russell of UNICEF spoke of "rampant, grave violations". 70% of victims were children. 420 a day were being killed. Humanitarian bodies addressing the UN Security Council called for a ceasefire or pause, the application of international law, protested the inadequacy of aid and pleaded for help to do their work. It was stunning to witness the number of occasions well-motivated, humanistic voices made this kind of appeal, always in the face of ugly defiance by Netanyahu, his cabinet and a majority of Israelis. It's reminiscent of Joseph K's inability to comprehend or have any influence on the court which has accused and will kill him. There is a psychological blindness associated with power which should make us distrust it and cleave to the doctrine that no one is good enough to have power over anyone else.

Marwan Kabalan of the Arab Centre for Research and Policy Studies criticised the UN as a talking shop. It was shameful it couldn't protect civilians. There should be more pressure but the US was buying time for Israel. His hunch was pressure from the families and the US might bring movement from Israel some time. The IDF wouldn't be able to release the hostages, there would have to be some kind of deal. The IDF's aims were contradictory: only negotiations could bring back the hostages. If Hamas was destroyed, who was there to negotiate with? In the first instance, Netanyahu didn't prioritise the captives. Also, in spite of the US efforts to contain Iran, there was a danger of contagion. The irony of Israel's action was the more vigour they applied, the greater the resistance.

Meanwhile, Youman Elsayed, an Al-Jazeera journalist working in Gaza, was told to move south at the risk of she and her family losing their lives. She lived in a block with six other families comprising some hundred people, but only her family was threatened. Such is Israel's respect for democracy and free speech. The assault would see many more deliberate attempts to intimidate or murder journalists. The US, of course, turned a blind eye.

Michael C Ryan, former US Assistant Head of Defense Policy for NATO, argued Israel's two main aims, releasing the hostages and destroying Hamas, were hard to achieve. Urban combat is tough. Hamas's positions were not necessarily easy to get at. Israel had overwhelming force but Hamas fought with small units. It was a game of cat and mouse. There was a great weapon on Hamas's side, global public opinion. In that regard, Israel was losing. The IDF might well try to surround Gaza. They were intending to isolate Hamas in the north (this becomes interesting by the middle of February 2024 when Netanyahu was claiming Hamas was holed up in Rafah which, therefore, must be attacked). It was an open question when Israel would be able to claim Hamas was no longer a threat.

Far from it being merely the case that Israel would struggle to assert the threat defeated, day by day it was increasing the likelihood of greater resistance. In the grip of his supremacist delusion, and surrounded by acolytes who shared it, Netanyahu was committing the dictator's classic mistake. It was true Israel was a democracy, of a flawed kind, but Netanyahu was imposing war Zionism. Any deviation from his doctrine was support for Hamas and collusion with the 7th October attack.

On 31st October, Filippo Grandi, UN High Commissioner for Refugees, called for statehood and security for both Israelis and Palestinians. International law was being ignored. A ceasefire was required. Another high-minded but vain intervention, like politely requesting a rapist to desist. The world's leaders and leading agencies continued to speak and act as if Israel was a thoroughgoing democratic State and well-behaved member of the international order, intent on spreading peace, justice and brotherhood. The ingrained reluctance to accept that Netanyahu was a thug, Israel a State founded in and led by terrorists and its political doctrine violently supremacist, was alarming.

Hezbollah continued its strikes on northern Israel, mounting three attacks. 15 were killed in the Nuseirat refugee camp in central Gaza. The Jabaliya refugee camp was attacked. UNICEF reported children were drinking salty water. The water output in Gaza had fallen to 5% of normal. Gaza was becoming a graveyard for children. Meanwhile, Biden and Blinken seemed to be asleep. The latter shuffled here and there, but utterly ineffectually. The US was being systematically humiliated by Israel, like an indulgent parent reaping the whirlwind of a spoilt child.

31 journalists had been killed, 29 Palestinians. Their families too were targeted. Sherif Mansour of the Committee for the Protection of Journalists said the number of killings of journalists in Gaza had trebled since 7th October. It was hard to verify if Israel was targeting them. Of course, the difficulty of verification was simply an effect of the chaos. In the previous 20 months only three had been killed., Shireen Abu Akleh

for example. In 2012, 2014 and 2021 media outlets had been bombed. No one was held accountable. Israel, accountable?

In Washington there was a demonstration at the Capitol. People had painted their hands red. Blinken declared we all wanted to protect human life but had to stand up when democracies were threatened. He made no mention of the deaths in Gaza. It's hard not to laugh out loud when a US Secretary of State talks about defending democracy and human life. Is that what the US was doing South Vietnam, Eisenhower in Iran and Guatemala, Kennedy in Cuba, Johnson in the Dominican Republic, Kissinger in Chile, Ford in East Timor, Reagan in Nicaragua, Bush in Panama and Iraq? US foreign policy has nothing to do with the protection of human life and democracy and everything to do with fulfilling Manifest Destiny. Like Israel's psychopathic treatment of the Palestinians, it's an expression of supremacism. The question is, do Blinken and his kind believe what they say ie are they deluded, or do they deliberately lie? Or maybe a bit of both. In any case, the US committed another $14 billion to Israel just to make sure the IDF could go on butchering children in the name of humanity and democracy.

By 31st October, eight thousand six hundred and twenty-five Palestinians, three thousand five hundred and fifty-two of them children, had been killed. Presumably Biden went to bed each night saying his prayers for more kids to die so Hamas could be defeated. Just how many Hamas fighter had been killed wasn't revealed, and wouldn't be as the assault continued. The US State Department called for the Rafah crossing to be opened so US citizens could leave. John Kirby admitted that the 66 trucks allowed into Gaza was a minute amount. Yet the velvet gloves weren't removed. Netanyahu was humiliating the US and the world's super-power which liked to boast it was pushed about by no one was being bullied by a pipsqueak country ruled by neo-fascists.

Bolivia, on the other hand, broke off diplomatic ties with Israel. Medea Benjamin of Codepink, the US-based, feminist peace movement, pointed out that 66% of Americans wanted a ceasefire, despite the one-sided coverage of the US media. Who did the politicians represent? She observed also that the global community wanted a ceasefire. Opinion was shifting every day. Jews were changing their minds. People were more concerned about the economy and the cost of living than with providing military aid to Israel. Lots of Americans felt their government wasn't attending to their needs. They didn't want more war. Biden, she predicted, would suffer.

That Americans were hurt by the neglect of their government is touching. Since when has the purpose of government been to look after the interests of the people? If that prevailed, the world would look very different. Only recently, in historical terms, have the people been permitted to have a say in who governs, and their entry into the arena has been accompanied by an unceasing campaign by media in corporate control to convince them their needs must be subordinated to those of the rich. When the people were excluded, there wasn't a great urgency about controlling their minds. If you can throw people in dungeons, behead them, shoot them, burn them at the stake, make them disappear, what does it matter what they think? Once what they think can influence who has power, thought-control becomes the order of the day. More than 60 million Americans are people of colour. Five times as many spend time in prison than in the white population. Is that the government looking after its people? According to Bernie Sanders, the three richest people in the US have more wealth than the bottom 50%. Is that the government looking after the people? It takes an extraordinarily effective propaganda system to prevent people seeing these simple truths.

The Al Qassam Brigades announced they would release some hostages in the next few days. Elijah Magnier, the veteran war correspondent, argued Hamas was playing a waiting game. Israel was trying to split Gaza to make its advance easier while Hamas was relying on urban warfare which takes time. The rubble of demolished buildings made for good hiding places. The IDF was hesitant in this arena. Hamas's tunnels were 15-18 metres deep and it was likely Hamas was using them to get beyond the Strip. There would be many surprises to come.

On 1st November the Jenin refugee camp was hit. Three Palestinians had been killed in the previous 24 hours. A general strike took place in the West Bank in response to images from Jabaliya. The IDF raided multiple targets multiple times. 50 were arrested in the West Bank. There were 50,000 pregnant women in Gaza, 5,500 due to give birth in November. C-sections, it was reported were being performed without pain killers or light. Jordan recalled its ambassador from Israel and prohibited Israel's ambassador from returning to Amman. Jordan was one of the few Arab countries to have diplomatic relations with Israel. Chile and Colombia also withdrew their ambassadors.

Gil Hoffman, an Israeli journalist who has lectured worldwide on Israel and lays claim to objectivity claimed the mood in Israel was sombre. There was no real pressure yet, no deep mood change. Netanyahu would remain in power till the war was over then the would be forced out. So far, so balanced. Hoffman went on, however, to claim there were 50 terrorists in the Jabaliya camp. What evidence there was for this he didn't explain. The IDF he claimed had done more than any in history to avoid civilian casualties. At this point you appreciate what Hoffman means by objectivity. It's perfectly reasonable, of course, for journalists to have a *parti pris*, as it is for commentators, intellectuals, academics, artists. What matters, however, is that when arguments are advanced and analysis undertaken, the evidence has to take precedence. It's risible that the IDF in Gaza has been protecting civilian lives. Simply the toll of dead children shows that. There has been no war in the past century in which the same proportion of children has been killed. Hoffman observed that Hamas couldn't be believed, as if Israel is a fount of unbiased comment. He is a product of the immunity Israel has enjoyed since 1948. The immunity of the powerful. He is typical of that phoney face of balanced, reasoned perspectives behind which the Israeli State hides its vicious supremacism.

Ismail Haniyeh, recognised as the current leader of Hamas, argued that Netanyahu was saving his skin. And willing to obliterate Gaza to do so. The US must take a step back and stop providing funding for fascists. It was on the wrong side of history. Palestinian rights must be restored. Haniyeh may have been right or wrong, but at least he didn't claim he was objective. He was putting things from his point of view. All the same, many might have agreed with his assessment of Netanyahu's motives.

Siyan Abdehamid, professor of Political Science at Rutgers, said the position of the West was blind. They were behaving as if history began on 7th October. The majority of the global population condemned Israel. He hoped more countries would withdraw their ambassadors, Egypt for example. The Arab street was boiling. The regimes in the Arab dictatorships were not popular. Israel too had a problem with public opinion. It was inflicting maximum damage on Gaza, intending to cut off Gaza City, drive people south and exterminate the north. Ultimately, Israel would have to leave Gaza. It's aim of destroying Hamas was impossible. The Palestinians were an occupied people and they needed to be able to give expression to their desire for autonomy.

On 2nd November the Rafah crossing was opened to let two hundred UK citizens leave Gaza. The process was slow. People were kept waiting for long periods and could get out only if their names were on a list. Naturally, the UK media were somewhat scandalised by this inhuman treatment. Meanwhile, nine thousand Palestinians had died. On Radio 4's *The World At One*, Labour M.P. Jess Phillips said there wasn't much movement. She had constituents who were trapped and could only sit and wait. She was unable to get information about them. They were running out of water. She'd never known such a thing before. She had helped constituents escape from Afghanistan and Ukraine when there had been more communication and co-ordination. The government wasn't getting UK citizens into Egypt. There seemed little prospect of a ceasefire. Hamas had declared publicly it would repeat 7th October (which might mean, of course, the Israelis would know it was coming and possibly ignore the warnings). A military solution wasn't going to work. There had to be a political resolution. What was the rationale of Israel killing tens of thousands of civilians?

Ms Phillips got away with comments her leader would never have made because she was talking principally about her efforts to release her constituents. Starmer was resolute in his support of Israel's actions. His position was that of Biden and Blinken, as befits a lapdog: Hamas started it, Israel had a right to defend itself, no one wanted civilians to die. But, heigh-ho, civilians die in their thousands. Get over it. Ms Phillips, like all Labourites, was under orders from Commissar Evans to avoid demonstrations, to stay away from those supporting the Palestinian cause. You never knew who you might be consorting with. The cowardice which ran through the Labour movement at this moment when its minimal adherence to principle was tested was sickening to witness. There were noble exceptions, but mostly MPs, members and affiliated unions kept their heads down. No doubt Hodge, Ellman and their cronies were gleeful at the sight of the State of Israel proving its god-given right to exterminate Arabs. After all, anything else would be antisemitism.

THE MAN WHO SHOT LIBERTY VALANCE

On the same Radio 4 news programme, Mark Regev deemed Israel's attack proportionate. Israel could not accept living next door to an Isis type enclave, he asserted, failing to reflect that no State has done more to promote ISIS than the USA. Hamas had engaged in rape and beheading. The latter claim, entirely without evidence, went unchallenged. As for civilian casualties, the question was if Israel didn't take on Hamas, who would? He invoked article 13 of the Geneva Convention, which asserts the provisions of Part 2 shall apply to the entire population in question. Part 2 is about the protection of civilians, the creation of agreed safe zones, the need to ensure the sick and injured are protected and so on. Regev claimed Israel was making maximum efforts to get civilians out of harm's way. 800,000 had gone south. When it was pointed out to him that the south was being bombed, he answered "not in the same way" as the north, which must have been an enormous comfort to the victims. Israel had to distinguish Hamas fighters from civilians, something no sane observer could discern. To the observation that the UN office for human rights had declared Israel could be guilty of war crimes, he asserted Israel was staying within the law. Look at how the US and the UK had behaved in Iraq. He had sat in meetings with the US and UK military and the IDF compared well. This was the one point on which it was possible to agree with Regev. In the 2003 assault on Iraq, international law was thrown aside like a used rag. As ever, the US doctrine was belief in the rule of law and democracy only in so far as they serve US interests. It's the ideology of *The Man Who Shot Liberty Valance*. We're nice guys till you tread on our toes, then our hard men come out of the shadows and blast everyone to hell.

Francesca Albanese the UN special rapporteur on the Occupied Territories claimed humanity had been lost. The 2-States idea had been around for decades, yet nothing had been done. The Palestinians were being systematically dehumanised. Israeli leaders were making clear calls for genocide. Marwan Bishara dismissed US "humbug" regarding the protection of civilians. Israel could do nothing without American weapons, advice, money and training.

All this is perfectly in keeping with evidence and eminently reasonable, Yet, to say it shifted nothing. There was no shock expressed by Israel, the US, the EU or the UK at the idea that "humanity" had been lost. Of course, the humanity of people like the Palestinians was lost long ago and it is taken for granted by the doctrine of progress that lesser peoples have to be sacrificed. The idea has been expressed so often it is part of the air we breathe. Thousands were being killed in Gaza but since 1996 some six million have been eliminated in the Congo so the rich countries can have the cobalt needed for mobiles, laptops and electric cars. The need for cobalt should be a bonanza for the Congolese. There is estimated to be eight million cubic tons of the metal on the planet. The Congo has about half. Yet far from making the Congolese prosperous, the neo-colonialism of the US, the EU, Israel, China, ensures a desperate struggle for control with the inevitable ensuing violence and sickening exploitation. It goes without saying that most citizens of the fine democracies know nothing of what is going on in the DRC. Why would the slavish media inform people their mobiles are produced at the cost of millions of lives? Consumerism must prevail.

The Congolese are expendable. They have black skins and fuzzy hair. Liberal Europeans who would baulk at the idea of being racist enjoy their luxuries at the cost of the lives of children of a lesser god. The logic that kills people in the DRC was also laying waste to the Gazans.

Nor is it anything new to point out that the Americans fund and give ideological support to slaughter. It is always justified, simply because the assumption reigns that America is on the side of virtue. Whatever it does can't be evil. It is angelic by nature and this derives from its status as god's chosen land. Just as the genocide of the Native Americans was beyond criticism (how else could Manifest Destiny have been realised) so whenever the US resorts to violence, which is very often, it is beyond moral examination.

Francesca Albanese is right, but humanity hasn't been lost in Gaza since 7th October, it was lost when the notion first took hold in our minds that killing for gain is not only admissible but glorious. No doubt this happened during our pre-history, but the conditions didn't permit it to become a prevailing culture. That has happened most significantly over the past half millennium. However, there is a stark distinction between the north and the south. In the global south, revulsion at Israel's actions is widespread. People who have been on the receiving end of colonialism aren't so easily fooled. This is where hope lies. The global north will go no further than lip service to universal values, but for the global south they offer the chance of liberation.

As people in Europe began to protest, governments revealed their profound respect for democracy by trying to prevent them. Imagine for a moment Jewish civilians, besieged bombed and starved and German citizens descending into the streets to demonstrate. Is it feasible their government would seek to ban their marches? Yet Scholz attempted to ban those defending the humanity of Palestinians. It's important to understand that many of the protesters, in Germany and other European countries, were not overtly political; they were moved by humanitarian sentiment rather than ideology. They included, of course, Jews of conscience. Yet Scholz's response, like that of other European leaders, implied the marches were malicious.

At the same time, Benny Gantz spoke of heavy IDF losses: nineteen had been killed in Gaza City. Thirty-six journalists had already been killed by the IDF. Thousands of Palestinians. Gantz was giving obvious expression to the Israeli State view of the relative value of human lives; the simple name for that is racism, perhaps more accurately supremacism.

A hundred and thirty-six Palestinians had died in nightly raids on the West Bank. These, of course, didn't begin on 7th October; but have been a long-standing feature of the Israeli torment of the Palestinians, for being Palestinians. On the Israel-Lebanon border, Kiryat Shmona was hit by a dozen rockets. The town's name means The Town of Eight, being named after the eight Jews killed in 1920 during the Battle of Tel Hai, often thought of as part of the France-Syria war. Joseph Trumpeldor, the Zionist activist, was wounded in the fighting and died as a result. Idith Zertal has said the battle "marked the dramatic initiation of the violent conflict over Palestine." Three Hezbollah fighters died in Israeli shelling.

Elias Farhat, retired Lebanese General, commented no one could predict what Israel would do next. There would be repercussions in the region if Israel entered the

Gazan tunnels, probably a regional war. Surrounding Gaza City would be easy but getting into the city and the tunnels would involve close fighting and would entail many casualties. It would be similar to the battle of Bakhmut in which twenty thousand died.

Biden announced that seventy-four US dual-nationals had escaped from Gaza. Blinken was on his way to Israel, which, of course, would reassure no one. John Kirby spoke of isolated breaks in particular locations. What was the endgame? Blinken, it was claimed, was focused both on today and "the day after". Just what would precede this day was never specified, but no reasonably objective observer could doubt it was going to be hell for the Palestinians. There must be two-States for two peoples. Civilian life must be thought of. Aid must be admitted. The usual flummery, disguising the fact the US was being pushed around by Netanyahu and was refusing to use its unquestioned leverage. Of course, allowing Netanyahu to have his head was in keeping with US standard foreign policy: US interests come before all else. The lives of a few tens of thousands of Palestinians is a bagatelle. After all, the US has played dice with the survival of the species for decades.

Not at all surprising then that the word from the Pentagon's Patrick Ryder was there would be no ceasefire. Refugee camps may have been targeted but Israel was obeying international law. Hamas was to blame. Once more Article thirteen was invoked. There was no proof at all Israel was doing anything wrong.

On 3rd November the leaders of Burnley and Pendle councils called for Starmer's resignation because of his comment that Israel had the right to deny Gaza food, water and fuel. Shortly after, the council leader Afrasiab Anwar and ten others resigned. Labour councillors in

Oxford also stood down, causing the party to lose control. Starmer's position mirrored that of the Tory government, unsurprisingly. He was for pauses to permit humanitarian aid but opposed to an outright ceasefire. As was frequently pointed out, this was a policy of giving the Gazans something to eat before killing them. Starmer had a dismal record over the factitious allegations of antisemitism in Labour. Before his election as Labour leader he commented: "My wife is Jewish. We live this every day." Just what was he living? Jews thrive in the UK. His wife was hardly doing badly. A curious feature of the supposed antisemitism within Labour was that most of its alleged victims were successful, in the vulgar sense. Margaret Hodge, who claimed risibly being in Labour during Corbyn's leadership made her realize what it must have been like to be Jewish in Nazi Germany, was a multi-millionairess. Lousie Ellman who whimpered as if the Gestapo was her on her tail had been a Labour M.P. for decades. Even poor old David Baddiel could claim that as he was Jewish he didn't count. Jews have been seriously discriminated against in many places over a long period. That isn't something to toy with. The discrimination drove many of them into poverty and alienation and in its worst manifestation slaughtered them like cattle. How can you claim anything similar is happening to you when you're enjoying wealth and status? Trivialising real suffering in this way is bound to backfire. The UK is not a significantly antisemitic society. There are no legal barriers and few if any considerable cultural ones. Yet Starmer fell in with the distorted Zionist narrative. Did he genuinely believe what he said? It's unlikely. Rather, he knew the difficulty of facing down the Zionist manipulations and his ambition, the one thing about him which is never in doubt, drove him to take the easy route. He would cleanse Labour of antisemitism, no difficult task as it barely existed, but under cover of ridding the party of racists, he expelled the troublesome who had rallied to Corbyn's promise of transformation. These are usually lumped together as the "left" but that's inaccurate: many of them were barely more radical than Harold MacMillan. They differed from Starmer, however, in one particular: they believed it was right to challenge the supremacy of the rich. His rapid alienation of UK Muslims was pitiful but also dangerous when Islamophobia was being used by demagogues.

Anthony Zurcher, commenting from the US, said the casualties were becoming intolerable. The US was very worried about a regional war. There was one simple way to prevent it, but that, of course, was the one thing Biden wouldn't do.

Tom Tugendhat, Tory MP, stood by Sunak's support of Israel's right to defend itself, a right it amply disposed of prior to 7th October and which it signally failed to take seriously; forewarned, Netanyahu, failed to prevent Hamas getting away with an incursion. Yet none of those who staunchly propped Israel's right to defence saw fit to mention Netanyahu's appalling failure to keep his people safe. The Palestinians were suffering but the UK was doing what it could to alleviate. The RAF had delivered twenty tons of aid. James Cleverly supported a pause to permit trucks to enter. This was very different from Hamas which had no care for Palestinian civilians and was using aid to support what was going on in its tunnels. The law was clear. Israel took lawyers advice. Hamas targeted civilians. Military targets must be hit by the IDF. The UK was working incredibly hard to get Brits out of Gaza. As for the protests, the Israeli ambassador had commented that London was now less safe than Israel. It was a moment of great concern. Three million pounds had been given to the CST. Was the Home Secretary right to speak of "hate marches"? It was all well and good to have differing views but there must be no harassment. There had been a hundred arrests. The police were taking things very seriously. It was a highly contentious issue and the hard left was exploiting it.

A highly contentious issue? Hardly. The Israeli State, with the unstinting backing of the US had oppressed the Palestinians for decades. There had been an attack by Hamas, explicable in the light of the Palestinians' fate. In response, Israel was laying waste to Gaza and slaughtering innocents. Nothing was contentious. The root cause of the issue was the Israeli State's occupation, its supremacism, its brutality, its repeated refusal to accept UN resolutions. As for hard left exploitation, sixty-six per cent of the UK population supported a ceasefire, but as usual, that had to be ignored.

Jeremy Bowen, speaking on Radio 4 on 3rd November wondered what the response of the Hezbollah leader, Nasrallah would be to the increasing casualties. Hezbollah had some hundred and fifty thousand missiles. US warships were in region to deter, but their presence was aimed principally at Iran. The Houthis in Yemen were launching missiles. Lebanon, Bowen reasoned, didn't want war but Nasrallah didn't care. Iran, of course, is always cited by the "West" as the great threat to peace in the region, as a lunatic State run by irrational clerics, an anti-democratic regime which can't be trusted, wants nuclear weapons and risks world conflagration. It's worth pausing for a moment. Iran had a democratic government until 1953 when it was illegally overthrown by the UK and the US. Mossadegh had the temerity to want to audit the Anglo-Iranian Oil Company, to ensure the due royalties were being paid to his country and also to secure proper control of Iranian oil for Iran The AIOC refused to co-operate. In response, the malicious Iranian parliament voted to nationalise the oil industry. The response of the UK was to initiate a worldwide boycott of Iranian oil. This was during the Attlee government which had nationalised coal, rail and steel and introduced the NHS. What did Attlee object to? Clearly not nationalisation, just nationalisation by ragheads. The Labour Party's stance was plainly supremacist. Attlee held off from sending in the military, but once Churchill was in power he and Eisenhower decided the only way to deal with disobedient Arabs was to rob them of democracy and give them a good dose of authoritarianism. They backed a coup by the Iranian Army which brought the Shah, Mohammad Reza Pahlavi, to absolute power and kept him there for twenty-six years during which his secret police SAVAK had virtually unlimited powers. Churchill is lauded in the UK as a defender of democracy, the man who stood up to Hitler's fascism. His view of fascism, however, was wavering: while it wasn't right for foreign fascists to threaten the UK (even though as late as March 1939 he was praising Hitler) it was virtuous for the UK and the US to impose fascism on "backward" nations which didn't do as they were told. Amnesty International estimates that during the Shah's reign some 25,000 to 100,000 political prisoners were held in Iran. Attlee, now leader of the opposition, raised no serious objections to the UK's role in the overthrow, perhaps not surprising given his description of himself prior to his conversion to socialism as a result of seeing the appalling poverty in the East End when he worked as volunteer with young people, as a typical, imperialist conservative. Old habits die hard.

The rule of the Shah laid the ground for the Islamic Revolution of 1979. It wasn't principally a religious uprising, but the clerics provided the only united force in the country powerful enough to challenge the Shah's State. The real grievances of the Iranian people had little to do with religion: they wanted self-rule, an end to the brutality, free elections. Thus, with its customary efficiency, the "West" brought into existence exactly what it claims to oppose. We will never know how Iran might have developed had its democracy been allowed to function but we can be fairly sure it would have avoided a conservative clerical regime.

We now have a constant drip of anti-Iranian propaganda which never mentions the sordid history of UK and US intervention. Rather, the casual observer would assume the country is somehow simply imbued with madness, impervious to reason, wants war, hates democracy and therefore, is ripe for invasion. This is how the US ensures its world domination and the UK tags along, as always, the obedient poodle.

In American universities there were protests to which Jewish voices responded by saying they no longer felt safe. Odd that whenever people protest for a cessation of Israeli State aggression some Jews claim they are quaking in their boots. Privileged students on American campuses complained about their safety while innocents in Gaza were being massacred. There were no reports of concerted violence against Jewish students though it was reported that a student putting up a poster had been assaulted. Universities responded by clamping down.

Dr Amal Saad, of Cardiff University, pointed out that Hezbollah was not merely a fighting force but also a social services network. It had a hundred thousand fighters, long-range missiles, and was hybrid military actor, more powerful than the Lebanon army which would remain armed as long as Israel existed in its present form. In 2006 it effectively defeated Israel in the sense that the latter's aims weren't met. Its activity had increased since 7th October and its rules of engagement changed. Dr Saad is a thoroughgoing expert who has written extensively about Israel-Lebanon and Hezbollah. Unsurprisingly, she takes apart the "West's" simplistic view that Hezbollah is a mere instrument of Iran and its inexplicably vile plan to conquer the region, if not the world. Something, of course, the US would never dream of.

MIND YOUR LANGUAGE

Speaking to Johnny Diamond on Radio 4's *World at One* on 3rd November, the Lebanese ambassador to the UK, Rami Mortada, said there was a risk of regional war. The Lebanese government was trying to avoid it. The 7th October attack didn't justify Israel's assault. It was necessary to curb the level of violence. Israel must clarify its position. There were ten thousand dead and four thousand under the rubble, who was responsible if not Israel? The region was unusual. Israel had been in breach of UN resolutions for seventy-five years. The region needed to be treated as an entity. All regional actors should be involved in resolving the crisis and bringing peace. It couldn't be left in the hands of one party. Lebanon was a poor country whose population didn't want war.

Mortada's comment about the unusual nature of the region was right. Israel, like the US, is exempt from international law. It has the world's greatest military power on its side ostensibly because it's the "only democracy in the middle east", which it wouldn't be, of course, if the US hadn't diligently pursued a policy of shutting down democracy in the Arab States. The US likes to deal with compliant autocrats. It has no taste for what the Arab street may think. Inevitably, there is a gulf between the opinions of the people of the Arab States and their rulers, which serves the US's interests. Lebanon, which in spite of its poverty has welcomed one and half million Syrian refugees while rich countries like the UK wax hysterical about immigration, gets it in the neck.

One hundred UK citizens, including Hamza Yousef's family were let out of Gaza. The Israelis were permitting only UN and MSF vehicles to move and people were stuck. It was reported their names were kept on the list of those to be released for only seven days. The BBC knew of nineteen on the list who couldn't get out. IDF tanks were firing on civilians.

The area around the Indonesian hospital, in Bait Lahia, northern Gaza was attacked. The gates of the Al Shifa hospital in Gaza City were targeted as people left; dozens were killed. Ambulances were destroyed. In the hospital, dead bodies were everywhere. Ice-cream vans were commandeered as morgues. Palestinians were taking the perilous journey south along the two available routes. Al Rashid Street was littered with dead bodies. Fuel was in short supply. Ibrahim Fraihat, professor of International Conflict Resolution, accused Israel of deliberate escalation. Civilians were being killed on the street. Blinken had said that how Israel conducts its war mattered. Fraihat's message to Blinken was that Israel doesn't listen. It will do what it likes. It was on a rampage and everyone was a target. Western policy made it complicit in the mass murder. Israel had descended into madness. The US administration couldn't continue in the way it was behaving. Palestinians were being given food and then bombed.

Meanwhile, Blinken, with his customary dutiful boy-scout demeanour spoke of "concrete steps" to minimise civilian deaths. Once more he feebly invoked international law which he said must be observed in the West Bank too. Aid would increase. Foreigners must be able to leave. There had to be pauses in the fighting. Of course, there were no details. The picture wasn't coloured in. What exactly were the concrete steps?

While Blinken paltered, Netanyahu declared Israel would continue to go "full force".

At 5.05 on 3rd November an ambulance convoy leaving the Al Shifa hospital was attacked killing fifteen and injuring sixty. All in a day's work for the IDF. Mads Gilbert declared it a war crime, which the whole world knew. What happens when a system which advertises itself as respecting law permits force to triumph? The world takes a big step towards fascism, whose essential characteristic is power over law. Millions watched on their devices as the IDF attacked a medical convoy and nothing was done. Israel later claimed the attack was necessary because Hamas fighters were part of the convoy. They might as well have claimed it was IRA volunteers, or members of the ANC or Mandela himself. Their capacity for invention makes Walter Mitty look reasonable. People can't live in a world where such things happen without it changing them. It undermines their confidence in justice and reason. It sends the simple message that if you've got the weapons you can do what you like. Then kids stab one another and everyone wonders why.

Pressure was put on Sisi to open the Sinai, ostensibly a humanitarian move, but more likely to lead to another mass expulsion of Palestinians. Biden was opposed to permanent expulsions, yet like the rest of the US's response, there was no willingness to twist Netanyahu's arm. It was impossible to see what was happening and not conclude the Israeli State wanted all Palestinians either dead or out of Gaza. Blinken wittered about the impossibility of a return to the pre 7th October status quo. Hamas governing the strip was unacceptable. The question was, if Hamas was excluded, who was the "partner for peace"? Some entity needed to be built up. Of course, some entity imposed by the USA. What was never said in official circles was that the Palestinians should be permitted to decide for themselves. The common people of Palestine. The world order is dominated by the notion that elites must rule. Democracy can be permitted only in so far as it serves the ascendancy of elites. The idea that people can decide and act for themselves is from outer space. Hence the head-scratching about who should govern Gaza "the day after".

Nasrallah praised the 7th October attack. It was a "seismic quake" with "profound strategic and existential repercussions" which had revealed Israel's "stupidity and ignorance". If Hamas were to fall, Hezbollah would be the main front. If the US didn't exercise restraint, there would be a regional war. There is much to say about Nasrallah, his desire for an Islamic State, for example. An Islamic State can no more be a democracy than a Jewish State. A democracy must provide equality before the law for all. What matters here though is the impact of this intervention. The problem is that if we criticise Israel for its defiance of international law, we can't forgive others the same fault. The Palestinians, as an occupied people, have the legal right to resist, but that doesn't include taking civilian hostages. Had 7th October been a fight between Hamas and the IDF, the former would have been on safe legal ground. Nasrallah's statement was a gift to the Israelis and their supporters. Of course, when people have been cruelly oppressed for a long time, it's easy to sympathise with their revolt; but when the ANC put burning tyres round people's necks, how were they helping the cause of justice and peace? When the IRA blew innocent folk to kingdom come in Birmingham pubs did they expect the people of the city to hail them as heroes?

Marwan Bishara argued that Hezbollah wouldn't declare war. There would be skirmishes. Hezbollah was steadfast but not suicidal. The message being sent to the US by Lebanon and Sunni moderates was that Iran wasn't their patron. They were masters of their own decisions. However, Nasrallah did pledge allegiance to Iran. He was trying to warn the US to remind them of 1983 when they were forced to pull out of Lebanon. He was telling the US that if Israel was to start a pre-emptive war, Hezbollah was ready.

There was another IDF attack on Jenin, bulldozers destroying the water, sewage and electricity system. Israel claimed they were after militants. One hundred and forty-six had been killed in the West Bank since 7th October. In Rio de Janeiro a bodies on the beach protest took place. There were protets in Accra and Yemen. Blinken piped up: the attacks on people in the West Bank must stop. Of course, they didn't. Blinken looked more and more like a neophyte teacher failing to control the most unruly class in the school last thing on Friday.

Jeremy Bowen reflected that things were still in the early stages; Israel was angry and felt "as insecure as in the years after the Nazis". Israel intended to destroy Hamas and Islamic Jihad. Retired Major General Noam Tibon said "Gaza is going to suffer". Nice chap. As for civilian casualties: "It's a tough neighbourhood." Gaza was being turned into hell, said Bowen. No one knew how it would finish. The US had two carrier strike groups in the region for deterrence. Would Hezbollah and Iran get involved? They would certainly derive what they could from the debacle. Netanyahu was committed to no ceasefire. The US had hinted Israel might reduce its air strikes. There was no good news for civilians in Gaza. The south wasn't safe. There were many still in Gaza City. Israel simply told them to get out.

The idea of Israel being as insecure as in the wake of the Nazi genocide is stunning. This is a nuclear-armed State with what is thought to be one of the most powerful militaries in the world. Leaving that aside, it has the grotesque might of the US behind it. The Nazi genocide wasn't carried out against Israel. Its victims were Jews, many of them poor and powerless and mostly from Germany and central Europe. Hitler didn't vilify the Jewish State; when he began his propaganda campaign, there was no such thing. Hitler made "Jew" the repository for his irrational hatreds. There was no logic to his actions. Jews weren't in any way responsible for the problems of the Weimar republic. Hitler was right in arguing that the Versailles Treaty had humiliated Germany. Not all his thinking was wayward. Aldous Huxley points out that the sections of *Mein Kampf* dealing with propaganda are noticeably lucid. Hitler was astute in recognising the Germans were a defeated, diminished people, looking for an easy remedy, just as Trump is astute is seeing that US decline has hit the people at the bottom hard while people like himself have sucked in wealth. What made Jews insecure in Europe in the 1930s was economic failure, and that was simply an effect of the accepted cycle of "boom and bust" which permits "investors" to extract wealth during the good period and punishes the rest during the bad. Hitler was a common demagogue, if a particularly good one, whose demented rhetoric allowed the disgraced Germans to climb back to a phoney dignity over the corpses of innocent Jew, Romanies, homosexuals, artists, Polish Catholics and so on.

Destroying Hamas and Islamic Jihad was an impossible aim and Netanyahu knew it. By linking the two he was suggesting conflation. There is a lot to be said about the differences, but crucially what happened after its election victories in 2006. Hamas's was quite distinct from the PIJ's position. Netanyahu from the outset has deliberately blurred these kinds of differences in order to suggest the PIJ, Hams, Isis are all one ie mad terrorists bent on the elimination of Israel and unwilling to compromise. It hardly needs pointing out that Bush made no reply to the Hamas offer. As for the status of Israel, in its present iteration as the occupier of the West Bank, its existence is opposed by almost the whole world. To argue Israel must pull out its settlements and retreat behind the 1967 borders is not to propose its absolute disappearance. Yet that is what is always implied by the Israelis. The obvious debating point that Hamas is an idea which couldn't be destroyed militarily has been made repeatedly. It is nonetheless true; and if Hamas were destroyed, who would Israel have negotiated with over the release of the hostages?

Tibon gave straightforward expression to Israel's desire for vengeance. As if Gaza hadn't suffered enough. There was no hint Israel might respond to what the Palestinians were asking for. The assumption of Israeli virtue was as firm as ever. The "West" conspired with this from its own identical assumption. Hamas were terrorists, all Palestinians were associated with them, thus punishment of the most cruel kind was correct. As for the "tough neighbourhood", leaving aside that it's a cheap, glib comment, who was responsible for the ingrained violence? Comments such as these are made only by the winners. Those who are on the receiving end of the "toughness" don't accept its existence with such alacrity. Tibon's vile comments condensed the essence of the "West's" long-standing doctrine: we are angels, they are lesser creatures, if they get in our way we visit hell on them. Tibon is an educated man, so are they all,

all educated men. The role of intellectuals in upholding the worst most brutal injustice is a true wonder.

Bowen's comment that no one knew how it would end was somewhat naïve: it was quite obvious by early November that Israel was intent on maximum punishment of the civilian population, that tens of thousands would die in attacks, Gaza be razed and in all likelihood many more die from hunger and disease. Equally apparent was that the only force on the planet capable of preventing this was going to refuse to use its power. The catastrophe would have been avoided if international law had been adhered to. Its systematic breach by the State of Israel over decades was the assertion that power rules in its place. The entire debacle emerged from that proposition which is the fundamental rule of fascism.

Sir Stephen O'Brien, former UN Under-Secretary for Humanitarian Affairs and Tory MP, argued a ceasefire wasn't close. Moving forward was a delicate matter: diplomacy fails till it works. There was no equivalence between Hamas, vowing the destruction of Israel, and the democratic State it had attacked. Perhaps there could be a "lull", a "pause", aid could be brought in and people allowed out. Talks in the UN were fraught, especially regarding the Palestinians. A ceasefire would have suggested Israel should pull back from defending itself against terrorists.

Diplomacy is delicate, yet when the "West" decides what it wants, there is hardly delicacy. Bush and Blair's war on Iraq wasn't something that failed till it worked. It never worked, in any rational sense; but it succeeded in killing hundreds of thousands and laying waste to the country, presumably to make George and Tony feel better. When the poor or the oppressed need to be helped, diplomacy is a tricky, slow matter. When they need to be slaughtered, things move fast. O'Brien's lazy characterisation of Israel as a democracy was propaganda rather than thinking. At best, Israel is a limited democracy, a partial theocracy with democratic knobs on. For some sections of Israeli society, democracy works well, but a society which reserves full citizenship for people of a specific faith, falls short of democracy in any sensible definition. What O'Brien was doing was sanitizing the Israelis and demonising the Palestinians. His claim that Israel had the right to defend itself glossed over its recidivism and its clear defiance of international law in its campaign in Gaza. O'Brien is typical of those public school, Oxbridge, smooth, smart-suited, highly successful careerists only too willing to side with evil. By doing so they make it respectable. Look, highly educated, articulate, well-read, people who have risen to the heights in their field and are respected in elevated circles agree with this, so what gives you, the common folk the right to question? How would Mr O'Brien respond if his well-heeled, sweet Tarporley was being bombed, his family starved because Russia had managed to gain the upper hand in international affairs and decided Cheshire was a hotbed of terrorism? What we return to again and again is simply the unfounded assumption that the "West" is virtuous and therefore justified in using maximum violence.

Andy Burnham said that his call for a ceasefire along with ten other north-west councillors was not a defiance of Starmer. However, he repudiated the phrase "from the river to the sea" saying it wasn't language he would employ. This wasn't, he said, an internal Labour matter. People must be careful with language. He was trite in the latter. People who were as loose-tongued as a drunk when it came to immigrants or the poor or striking workers or despicable people dubbed "woke", pleaded for restraint about anything which the Israeli lobby might find offensive. Given this lobby takes umbrage at the idea that Palestinians are their equals, it's somewhat alarming we are supposed to walk on egg-shells to protect their sensitivity. The commonplace language of the political right is a consistent insult to those struggling most with the effects of the economic system they support, yet no one ever suggests evincing concern for their injured feelings. Did anyone ever say people should be careful what they utter about Jeremy Corbyn? He was traduced by a vicious, dishonest propaganda system celebrated as "free speech" by the very people claiming to be disturbed by a slogan whose meaning, to all but a few tendentious supporters of the Israeli State, is obviously that all people between the river and the sea should enjoy freedom. A shocking idea, of course, to the advocates of supremacism.

BOMBING THE BAKERIES

On 4th November five people were killed when the IDF attacked the entrance to the Al Nasr children's hospital in northern Gaza. The IDF also bombed the solar panels at a facility for the elderly, a sure-fire way to degrade Hamas. Blinken declared the hospital attack justified because it was a military target, a claim for which he adduced nil evidence. The Al Fakhoua school in Jabaliya refugee camp was hit and Israeli gunboats struck a Gazan fishing port. Dr Tanya Haj-Hassan, a paediatric specialist who had worked in Gaza and the West Bank for a decade and is the co-founder of Gaza Medic Voices, said "The world is watching and the viewers are silent. Worse, they are complicit." This was true, of course, of the spectators with power, in particular, Biden, the one person in the world who could end the horror; among the common people, however, especially those in the global south plenty of noise was being made. As usual it was ignored by the governing elites. In Berlin, for example, in spite of the government's efforts to prevent it, there was a big demonstration for peace. Schultz remarked that Israel's security was Germany's "reason of State." A huge crowd gathered in London, rallying in Trafalgar Square calling for an immediate ceasefire. There were protests in Sydney, Seoul and Taz (Yemen).

The Foreign Ministers of Egypt and Jordan called for an immediate ceasefire, promptly rejected by Blinken who claimed it would leave Hamas in place. The only viable solution was 2-States. Discussion was needed to find meaningful and practical steps. Ayman Safadi, the Jordanian Foreign Minister said the US bore a great responsibility. It was the right of everyone in the region to live free of the current horror. Alan Fisher, Al Jazeera's correspondent, called this a diplomatic snub to the US. The Arab nations didn't accept the US's view. The problem for Mr Safadi and other Arab leaders was, naturally, they were Arabs. Netanyahu responded to their calls for peace by refusing even humanitarian pauses. In keeping with this kindly response, the Israelis opened Salah Al Din Street, the main road from Rafah to the north between 11.00 a.m. and 2.00. p.m..

A hundred and eighty-three thousand houses, about forty-five percent of the Gaza Strip's stock had been damaged and twenty-eight thousand destroyed. Sixteen out of thirty-five hospitals were no longer working. Just how this was aiding Israel in wiping out Hamas wasn't explained. What was clear, after nearly a month of unrelenting assault, was Netanyahu's supposed aims weren't being fulfilled. On the one hand he claimed all his concern was to demolish Hamas and release the hostages, and the US backed him unreservedly. On the other, it was obvious to any minimally objective observer that the aim was to kill as many Palestinians as possible, whether with bombs, bullets or starvation and to force out those who didn't die. Why couldn't Biden see this? Because he chose not to. As Ahmet Goksun of Columbia University commented: wherever there is injustice in the world, the US is behind it. It might seem an outlandish claim but since 1945 the US has been far and away the most economically, politically and militarily powerful State and its cleaving to the Monroe Doctrine and Manifest Destiny render Goksun's comment pertinent.

A demand was raised for a flotilla carrying aid from Turkey. In Iraq a protest called for a boycott of countries supporting Israel. In Kuala Lumpur a convoy of protest vehicles called for a ceasefire and an end to the occupation. In Argentina, crowds displayed their support for Gaza, a ceasefire and Palestinian autonomy, in spite of both Presidential candidates supporting Israel.

Salam Marouf, head of the Gaza Health Ministry, reported that in Al Shifa twenty-eight people from the same family had been killed. A hundred and fifty medical staff and forty-six journalists had been injured. A hundred and fifty medical facilities, three university premises and eight thousand five hundred residential units had been damaged. Eighty-eight government buildings, two hundred and twenty school buildings, three churches. and fifty-five mosques had been destroyed. Bakeries were being targeted (presumably because Hamas fighters were partial to croissants). The green light was given by the US. Misinformation was rife. The claim that fuel provided to the UN was being passed to Hamas was a lie. All roads had been cut off. People couldn't get to the so-called safe places. There were calls for a general strike in the West Bank. The Arab countries should cut the supply of oil to Israel and the US.

Marwan Bishara pointed out there were thirty thousand staff at the State Department and the CIA but no proof of Hamas fighters in or under schools and hospitals. Claiming the fighters were in the tunnels was quite different from claiming they were in the facilities: the latter implied doctors, nurses, administrators, teachers were deliberately concealing them, making them complicit. Blinken, the Imperial Emissary, was giving the green light for the slaughter of civilians. Russia, China and Africa were giggling. The USA was giving worldwide sanction to attacks on civilians if a plausible excuse could be adduced. Israel and the US would pay a heavy price. He had never seen a Secretary of State hand over the right to kill civilians in this way. The US was speaking out of both sides of its mouth.

The right to kill civilians if they stand in the way of US interests has been a long-standing policy. It's estimated in excess of fifty thousand civilians died as result of US bombing in Vietnam. Bishara's point is a good one: if you set out to design a policy to make you reviled by the global south, the majority of the world's population, you couldn't do better than Israel and the US in Gaza; and if you wanted to provide the grounds for Putin or Xi to launch murderous wars, here they were. The way to undermine dictators and their expansionism is to uphold international law and democracy. Here was the indulgent father, the world's greatest military power, handing its spoilt brat the right to kill at will and expecting the world to applaud. Such a numbskull policy can derive only from too much power exercised for too long.

The water pipes from Israel to Gaza had ceased to function. UNRWA reported children falling ill with diarrhoea, fever and vomiting. Tanya Haj-Hassan of Médecins Sans Frontières spoke of "a new law in an unending stream of unconscionable violence." In Edinburgh, Waverley Station was brought to a standstill by protesters. Jonathan Sacks, Chief Rabbi of the UK condemned protesters, claiming they were marching alongside extremists, a logic which leads straight to a total ban on demonstrations. In Senegal there was a protest at the central mosque in Dakar. The following day, 5th November there were protests in Iraq, Iran, Yemen, Turkey, South Korea, Jakarata, Islamabad and Washington D.C. Mahjoob Zweiri of Qatar University said the US was under pressure to change. Its image was being damaged and there was a fear of the war widening. Yet Israel was allowed to get away with whatever it liked. Meanwhile, it was reported that the olive industry was almost at a standstill. Eighty percent of olive oil produced by the Palestinians was exported but permits had been blocked for groves near illegal Israeli settlements. The olive tree had provided a living for people for thousands of years.

Blinken met Abbas in Ramallah and suggested a humanitarian pause. Netanyahu refused. In a major escalation, Hezbollah hit four military sites. Nasarallah declared that if civilians were hit there would be retaliation. Forty-six journalists had been killed by the IDF, communications were down There was heavy bombing of central Gaza. Maghazi refugee camp was hit. Hamas announced that sixty hostages had been killed in IDF air strikes. The main hospitals were on the verge of collapse. The WFP declared there was "nowhere near enough aid". People were finding it impossible to evacuate from the north. Cars and ambulances were fired on. There was no shelter. UN centres were hit. The population in the south had doubled. Two thousand were buried under the rubble. Safe passage was a sick joke. The IDF was moving from east to west in its effort to isolate Gaza City. Cindy McCain of the WFP said people were starving.

Mark Regev, however, told a different story: there was no restriction on food or fuel entering the Strip. Hamas's military machine had missiles in the tunnels. They had stockpiled fuel. Israel was getting aid to the people but had to stop it getting to Hamas. A week earlier, he claimed, fuel was stolen from a UN depot by Hamas. The UN was forced to submit to Hamas. Lyse Doucet of the BBC said she had checked with the UN and no fuel had been taken from any warehouse by Hamas. David

Satterfield, the US Special Envoy for Human Rights in the region, said there was no evidence Hamas was stealing fuel or abusing humanitarian aid.

Hamas declared it was willing to accept international observers to verify hospitals weren't being used to hide weapons or fighters. The hospital "tunnels" turned out to be service ports. No retraction was provided by Israel. It was reported that six times as many children had been killed in Gaza than in Ukraine. Of course, the heartfelt support of the "West" for Ukraine and its unfettered condemnation of Russia flowed from the supposedly unprovoked nature of the Russian attack. There was no doubt Putin had breached international law in an act of State terrorism, far and away the world's most common form. Yet the notion that the intention to line up US missiles on the Ukraine-Russia border wasn't a provocation takes some swallowing. Twenty were killed as Bureij refugee camp was struck. In response to the Gaza massacres, Al Qassam rockets reached Tel Aviv in an attempt to overwhelm the Iron Dome system; ninety-five percent were caught. Some shrapnel fell on the city. It was announced the CIA director Bill Burns was to visit the region.

Marwan Bishara detected a change of tone. Arab foreign ministers were rejecting the US argument that Israel's action was self-defence. They were unhappy with the suggestions for "the day after" and wanted a ceasefire. There was anger on the Arab street and deaf ears on both sides in negotiations. The US was shielding Israel by providing arms on the one hand and ineffective diplomacy on the other. Blinken was a waste of time, talking of peace and keeping the war going. He was turning serious diplomacy into a beauty pageant. What kind of two-States agreement was he suggesting? He was engaging in fantasy. There was no partner for peace in Israel. The imminent intervention of Bill Burns was an indication of how Blinken was failing. It was obviously an attempt to wheel in a seasoned, respected figure, a man for big dossiers. Something was brewing behind the scenes with the real work possibly being done by Sullivan and Burns. The window was closing on the US as far as defending Israel's war crimes went. Across the world the common folk were showing their commitment to democracy. For them, Palestine was a symbol of justice and freedom. Western public opinion wasn't ready for another regional war. People were sick of it. Biden had promised to end "eternal wars". Now there were two US aircraft carriers in the eastern Mediterranean. Public opinion in the countries supposed to support Israel was becoming allergic to war. They remembered the false pretences on which the 2003 war in Iraq was fought and believed they might be seeing the same again. Israel was failing to make inroads in Gaza in spite of indiscriminate bombing and climbing casualties. The window to end the war was getting smaller. By the end of the week Gaza City might be decimated. The Palestinian resistance wasn't understood by the "West" which didn't appreciate how they were trying to free themselves from occupation. Hamas had a gruesome aspect and wasn't the legitimate representative of the Palestinians, but Hamas fighters were capable. They were holding their own after a month of vicious onslaught. They were willing to either force a ceasefire or die. The IDF were paid soldiers while Hamas was fighting for freedom. It was necessary to resist by legitimate means as that points to the ends aimed at. Occupiers are unjust by definition but resistance needs to be principled. The Palestinians had been under siege for more than seventy years. They would give in only when they were all dead. There would always be sons and daughters to take the struggle forward. You can't kill an idea. Israel had murdered many Hamas leaders but there are always new ones to take the place of the assassinated. The Palestinians will resist until Palestine is free. The Israeli Minister for Heritage, Amichai Eliyahu, was floating the idea of using nuclear weapons. The question at issue wasn't Jews, Muslims, Christians but the occupation. The Israeli cabinet contained fanatics and fascists because that is what the occupation was turning people into. Ending colonisation and apartheid was the only way out. The occupation had to be expelled if there was to be peace.

Bishara is a consistently fierce critic of Israel, but no glib friend of Hamas. His point is important: those resisting injustice are called on to operate at a demandingly high moral level. The danger of resistance is of being dragged down to the level of the oppressor. There is also a romanticism at work here. The Byronic hero going to war for justice, a posturing which all too often results in death and defeat. Milan Kundera writes about this: the appeal of glorious failure. The uplifting excitement of revolution, of taking to the barricades or hurling the Molotov cocktail, blinds to the sober assessment of the chances of success. Living to fight another day seems like cowardice and compromise. The corpses in the street in the June days of 1848 or the dead of the Paris Commune are testimony. Hamlet's hesitations are not without reason. The corruption in the court of Denmark needs to expelled, but is a stage strewn with bodies the way to do it? Those who face overwhelming odds from their oppressors need something of the mentality of Figaro: outwitting your opponent is crucial.

Bishara is right that ending the occupation is the only way to peace, but the question that hovers is why Herzl proposed a Jewish State as the solution to whatever he saw the problem of being Jewish to be. Persecution of the Jews, a despicable historical reality, was unlikely to be solved by herding them into one country where they alone would enjoy citizenship. Even in 1897 it must have been obvious to anyone who thought about it seriously that the answer was universal human and democratic rights. Of course, the ingrained supremacism of the European elites was in full flow. It would gain expression in the Balfour Declaration, drafted because Balfour wanted rid of the Jews who, he claimed, had done enough damage to Britain. Herzl, who was an enthusiast for German culture, especially its concept of Bildung, and who as a law student joined a nationalistic Burschenschaft, effectively gave up on the effort to defeat antisemitism: "I recognised the emptiness and futility of trying to 'combat' antisemitism." Instead, the Jews would have to "avoid" antisemitism, and the means to do this was an exclusively Jewish State. Suppose someone had suggested that homosexuals should renounce the struggle to end prejudice against them and proposed an exclusively homosexual State. The defeatism of Herzl's position went hand in hand with a wild vision of "a wondrous generation of Jews". In 1897 he wrote his famous article, *Mauschel* (*Yid*), in which he typified Jews who rejected his vision as "despicable". Herzl, in short, didn't believe in a world without antisemitism. On the contrary, he required it for the justification of his project. If it wasn't true that the world was incorrigibly antisemitic, there was no need for a Jewish State. If antisemitism could be defeated, the Jews could live anywhere. This is Herzl's inheritance. It is what informs the ideology of the State of Israel today.

The State of Israel, like Herzl, requires antisemitism. It has to be true that it is an incurable, universal plague. The only response to it has to be Zionism, a State for Jews alone in which they will become a beacon to the rest of humanity. If the world can shun antisemitism and Jews can be granted equal rights before the law, what is Israel for? The occupation exists because of Zionist defeatism and delusion. Antisemitism hasn't been eliminated in the US, Europe, Canada, Australia, Latin America, but in many countries Jews live without fear of persecution. In the UK they flourish, by any measure. When did you last hear of an American Jew being killed by having a policeman's knee on his neck for nine minutes? Are US prisons bursting with Jews? In the UK, are Jews under-represented in the media, parliament, the arts, sports, academia, business? It makes no sense to speak of prejudice unless there is clear evidence of its effects. Norman Finkelstein's questions are pertinent: what would you rather be in the US today, Jewish or poor? Jewish or black? Jewish or disabled? The startling and appalling truth is that Palestinians were being killed like cattle because of the defeatism of a confused man of moderate talent who thought he was the great liberator of the Jewish people. His ideology, that antisemitism can't be faced down and therefore the Jews must live separately from the rest of humanity, is part of the origin of the bloodbath and the shredding of international law we are witnessing in Gaza.

FROM GAZA TO DEARBORN

On 6th November thirteen Burnley councillors resigned from the Labour Party. Starmer seemed little moved by what was clearly a deep mistrust brewing among the Muslim population; somewhat surprising given the size and tilt of the Muslim vote. On Radio 4's *Today* programme, Jeremy Bowen reported that four hundred and fifty targets had been hit by the IDF in twenty-four hours. Perhaps Starmer failed to make the connection between that and the events in Burnley. The strikes were very heavy. Gaza City was surrounded. Communications were cut and ambulances didn't know where to go. The US had, Bowen stated in a fine example of litotes, "a certain amount of influence". Blinken was saying what his audience wanted to hear. The US was trying to deter Iran and other possible regional actors.

John Casson, the ex-UK Ambassador to Egypt, on the same programme, criticised the lack of breadth and depth in the debate. It was similar to 2003. The notion of a comprehensive policy was vilified. Britain was fully behind Israel but it was a posture not a policy. What was the "exit strategy" (the euphemism for "how do we get out of this hellish mess"). Why couldn't Britain be a critical friend? There was no military solution. The UK could take a leading role in peace-making. A ceasefire was not a policy. The fighting must stop. As for two-States, there was reluctance. In reality, it was an excuse not a solution. Who was going to govern the Gaza Strip needed to be stated. How could Israel do it? The settlement activity in the West Bank needed to be reversed and we had to jump past military logic. In 2003 military logic took all other possibilities off the table. We needed to serve the Palestinians better then we did the

Iraqis. There was rising hate. We were following Israel rather than working out a position.

Casson's view was significantly more rational than most of what was heard from UK politicians, especially the leading figures in the Tory and Labour Parties who were joined at the hip on the issue. He was by no means the only person to point out there was no military solution but the observation goes much further than the assault on Gaza: there is no military solution to the Zionist claim Palestine belongs to them. The belief has been imposed by force, prior to 1948 by a prolonged campaign of vicious terrorism, much of it against the British, and subsequently by the ethnic cleansing, oppression and imprisonment of the Palestinians. The primary Zionist justification is that god gave the land to Abraham some three thousand years ago. Zionists have a perfect right to believe that, but no right to claim it's a fact or to expect anyone else to believe it. There is no military solution to the difference of view between Zionists and those who don't share their beliefs; the only solution is compromise. There is no absolute reason why Zionists can't share their society with Muslims, Hindus, Christians, atheists, merely the far less than absolute reason they refuse to do so and insist their beliefs must prevail. In short, the notion they have the right to impose their will by force, the essence of fascism.

Casson was right too about the government's and opposition's absence of policy. Their response was redolent of a playground fight with kids coming running to spectate and cheer on their chosen combatant. It wouldn't have been out of place to hear Sunak or Starmer chanting, "Come on Israel!" Policy needed to address the complexities; for Tory and Labour alike the matter was reduced to a mindless simplicity: Israel is always right, the US is always right, all other considerations are extremism.

Reports were coming in from Dearborn, Michigan, that Biden was in trouble with voters of Arab heritage, fifty percent of the electorate. "He's lost our vote," local Muslim leaders were quoted by the press. Dearborn has the highest proportion of Muslims of any US town. Michigan has a Muslim population of about quarter of a million. In 2020, Biden won the state by a margin of about a hundred and fifty thousand. The state accounts for sixteen electoral college votes. Minnesota has a Muslim population of some hundred and fifteen thousand and Biden won in 2020 by a margin of about two hundred and thirty thousand, picking up ten electoral college votes. He gained three hundred and six college votes compared to Trump's two hundred and thirty-two. Toying with the votes in Michigan and Minnesota puts Biden only twenty or so college votes ahead of his rival. This is not to argue for foreign policy driven by electoral calculation rather than moral principle (when will we see that?) but to stress how slavish is the American will to serve Israel's needs. The indefensible actions of Zionists have become praiseworthy because of the insatiable US desire for power. History provides us with many examples of the limitless appetite of power. The gods are always thirsty; but few regimes can match America in its Gargantuan greed for control.

The Gaza Health Ministry accused Israel of war crimes. The occupation was deliberately killing the wounded. Eight hundred critically ill patients couldn't be evacuated for appropriate treatment. Israel was targeting hospitals, the Red Cross, the information system, people trying to bring aid. The crimes must be referred to the UN. Al Shifa had to be protected. Without it, medical services would collapse. The entire world was responsible. Gaza was forgotten. There was no genuine effort for peace. Something atrocious was in preparation. There was nothing standing between Israel and the annihilation of the Palestinians.

Tamer Quarmout of the Doha Institute for Graduate Studies agreed that Al Shifa was central to Gaza'a medical facilities. He was horrified. Israel's actions were insane war crimes. The Palestinians had been failed over and over. An investigation of Israel's fake accusations was called for. Sixty thousand people were sheltering in Al Shifa. In Gaza City the population of four hundred thousand was crammed into a small space. An attack would be a massacre. Israel was responsible. The Strip was in its hands. Assaults by settlers in the West Bank had tripled in a month.

Ahed Tamimi was arrested, again, in Nabi Salih, accused of an Instagram post in Hebrew, in which, her family protested, she doesn't write, calling for the extermination of West Bank settlers and mentioning Adolf Hitler. Tamimi, who saw her uncle and cousin killed by the IDF, was world-known for her slap of an IDF soldier who was arresting her brother. She and her family were practitioners of non-violent resistance, a particularly problematic form for the Israeli State which requires all Palestinians to be violent fundamentalists.

Two Israeli police officers were stabbed in East Jerusalem. Stabbing of a human being is a distressing matter, but this is a tiny degree of tragedy when set beside the rapidly escalating toll of Palestinian deaths.

Blinken in Türkiye failed to attain agreement. He was for a pause, the Turks wanted a ceasefire, or to put it another way they wanted the killing to stop, he wanted the IDF to take a breather and then return to the massacre. Some international mechanism was needed to guarantee peace. Of course, such a thing was impossible while the US called the shots.

At 17.00 local time on 6th November there were big air raids on northern and central Gaza. The death toll was now ten thousand. Not bad for a month. The Israelis were going for a place in the Guinness Book of Records. Solar panels on hospitals were targeted, a clear sign the IDF was using precision attacks on Hamas fighters. Fifty-six UNRWA schools had been hit and eighty staff killed, one more indication of the Israeli's fastidious intent to go after only Hamas combatants. Israeli Special Forces, disguising themselves in a civilian vehicle, killed four in Tulkarem in the West Bank. Demolition of homes in the West Bank increased too.

Eighteen UN agencies and humanitarian organisations called for a ceasefire as Antonio Guterres called Gaza, "a graveyard for children", which must have been very pleasing to Yoav Gallant, who made Herod look a cissy.

Marwan Bishara reflected on Biden's reiterated rejection of a ceasefire. He was shielding Israel. There was no commitment to justice, merely an intent to destroy Hamas at all costs, a classic case of ends and means. The Middle East was seething with anger but Biden was blindly following Israel. The US was less responsible than Israel. Israel's war and US diplomacy were identical. Biden had effectively regressed to gunboat diplomacy. The Arabs were in no mood to accept his logic. What was going to give? Egypt had a special relation to Gaza. Many Palestinians had studied there, there was symbiosis. Egypt should behave in a sober manner, one month into the genocide, it should step in to provide food, medicine and shelter through the Rafah crossing. Egypt had much to gain, it would be helpful for its future status to behave responsibly today. Once the dust settled, the Egyptian president could have a big role to play.

Bishara's point about the relationship of present behaviour and future status is a truism, yet history is littered with the follies of those who imagine posterity will never find them out. Many of the supposedly great figures of history are people whose names are forever associated with moral depravity. Yet somehow, Henry VIII, Rasputin, Napoleon,

Robert E, Lee, Hitler, Stalin, Pol Pot, Richard Nixon, failed to see how they would become figures whose actions are beyond moral justification. Famous men we are forced to revile.

The UN Security Council met in camera but couldn't find an agreement.

In Khan Younis on 7th November fifteen were killed when their home was bombed. On the same day, Netanyahu declared he would be in charge of security in Gaza. While Gallant said Israel had complete freedom of action and it would bomb children's hospitals, a leaked US diplomatic memo called for a ceasefire and more criticism of Israel.

Marwan Bishara argued that the US does not support forced repatriation but Israel favoured ethnic cleansing. Blinken had "got an earful" from the Arab States. The Palestinians had gone through seventy-five years of trauma. Israel didn't know what it was doing. It was "heavily armed and terribly lost". There was going to be a long campaign and Israel was defending the occupation, which was the essence of the problem. Israel was a garrison State and refusing to take US advice. Obama may have provided billions of dollars to Israel but to some degree he uncoupled the prevailing mindset. Biden was hooked to Netanyahu, who was a reckless loser. The US is a super-power but Biden was making it a slave of Israeli policy.

Bishara's view of Obama's attitude to Israel is somewhat generous. He showed no willingness to put pressure on Israel to withdraw the West Bank settlement or even to significantly reduce the scale of their spread. As for the US being Israel's slave, the submission was necessary, ironically, to maintain and expand US power.

The UN called for an end to collective punishment. In Islamabad there was a rally demanding a ceasefire. In the Muslim countries there was disappointment in the leadership. The Street was in conflict with the Elite. There was a growing consensus that Israel was engaged in genocide. In Sri Lanka hundreds rallied under the banner of Humanity First. This was not a cricket match. One dead was too many. The rainbow culture declared We Are One. There was a rally in Tokyo where demonstrators complained that the G7 had done nothing. The Japanese government called for more caution. They condemned Hamas but said a humanitarian pause was needed.

Jawad Anani, the Jordanian economist and politician claimed it was impossible to change the minds of Israel's leaders. Netanyahu was a staunch defender of the occupation. Blinken's diplomacy wasn't encouraging nor was that of the EU. Arab leaders were due to meet soon, they should withdraw all co-operation with Israel. Biden had the election to think about. He should recalculate. Was it in the interests of the US to be so supportive of Israel. There was a real chance of the conflict spreading. The longer the fighting went on the more likely it would drag in other States. There was now mayhem beyond control. Only a ceasefire could bring back order.

Maleeha Lhodi, the Pakistani diplomat and political scientist claimed the tide of global opinion was moving against Israel. Protests were becoming more intense. There was a changing dynamic. US blind support for Israel was a problem. Israel would respond to the US. There was a fourth attempt in the Security Council to secure a vote for a ceasefire. The gridlock was unfortunate.

Global opinion had long been critical of Israel, though, naturally, the "world" is usually defined as the US and its allies. Support for Israel had reached dismal levels in the global south for the straightforward reason that people on the receiving end of colonialism aren't convinced by its apologists. As for gridlock in the Security Council, once again, the power of the US ensures the "world" behaves in the way it likes. China, France, Russia, the UK and the US are permanent members and have the veto, a ludicrous arrangement: is Latin America of no importance, is Africa? The world changes and the creaking architecture of the UN remains unaltered. Why shouldn't consensus prevail? Why shouldn't the veto be removed?

Kealeboga Maphunye, the South African academic, said his country was impelled to withdraw its ambassador from Israel because of attacks on civilians. During the years of apartheid, the ANC had received support from the Palestinians; reciprocal solidarity was logical. In the diplomatic sphere, the African Union had a strong message of condemnation. Other African nations would follow suit. The occupation was the issue. As for the Hamas attack, the underlying issue was Palestinian self-determination. As a student of political science he was used to the stuck record of agreement-flouting by Israel and back to square one. During apartheid, powerful States listened to the South African liberation movement. A solution depended on Israel being willing to listen.

Netanyahu reinforced his determination that there would be no ceasefire until the hostages were home. The White House complained only five hundred trucks had entered the Strip in a month. WHO claimed amputations were being carried out without pain killers. The Israeli PM, however, asserted there was no humanitarian crisis, no lack of food or water, a declaration Faris Al-Jawad of MSF was alarmed to hear. He reported the situation in Gaza as "horrific". Netanyahu was out of touch with reality. The fighting needed to stop at once. A substantial number of the casualties were children, many suffering burns and crushed bones. In triage, the choices were gruesome. The most seriously injured were left to die. Two hundred babies were being born each day, but there was no food for them. The daily roll out of statistics concealed the truth that each death was a human tragedy.

Was Al-Jawad right that Netanyahu was out of touch with reality? Perhaps he was all too in touch with it: if the war ended, his political career was over and he was on his way to court and probably jail. What constitutes "reality" isn't a settled question. From Al-Jawad's perspective, that of most of the world's population, the reality was thousands of deaths of innocent men, women and children. From Netanyahu's, the Palestinians were a less-than-human threat and the survival of his ego more important than theirs. The Palestinian struggle to have their humanity recognised and their right to govern their own society granted is part of the broader struggle to elaborate a "reality" shared by the whole of humanity. Not very long ago, in historical terms, no one knew about DNA. Now, even those who wish to deny it depend on the science which revealed it. DNA is a reality which defines our common humanity, but we need much more than that to overcome the contending "realities" which deny it.

FANCIFUL AND FARCICAL

The White House asserted its opposition to an Israeli occupation of Gaza, something Netanyahu didn't appear to hear. In response to claims that the London demonstrations were making Jews afraid to leave their homes, some of them, it was claimed, going so far as to flee the country, Ben Jamal of the Palestine Solidarity Campaign explained the organisers had asked for a route which avoided the cenotaph on remembrance weekend. The protest would be held on Saturday while the main remembrance event was on Sunday. The Israeli assault on Gaza had quickly led to calls for peaceful demonstrations for a ceasefire to be banned, an indication of just how thin is the commitment to democracy of the British right.

Marwan Bishara dismissed those prosecuting and defending the assault as "absolute morons". It was "utter madness". Israel was repeating its failures. The US interventions were clumsy, they were boxed in, parroting the Israeli line. It was all humbug. The US talk about the "day after" was "fanciful and farcical". They weren't advocating even a twenty-four hour pause never mind a serious path to two-States. American credibility was in tatters and the Palestinians in Gaza were paying the price.

On 8th November, Lt Colonel Peter Lerner speaking on Radio 4 said Israel had miscalculated about Hamas, assuming it wasn't suicidal. The IDF had a good grasp of how Hamas functioned. They had been planning for a long time. They were hiding in kindergartens and mosques. They had some four thousand weapons. Thirty-two IDF soldiers had been killed. As for civilian deaths, every one was a tragedy. The protests may have been well-intentioned but they gave succour to the Hamas butchers, which was moral bankruptcy. A hundred thousand people marching through

London were supporting what was done by Hamas. Images of the placards from the demos showed what they were about. When people chanted "from the river to the sea" they were questioning the existence of Israel. People were clamouring for humanitarian aid, but what kind of humanitarian conditions were the Israeli hostages enjoying? Netanyahu had suggested Israel should stay in Gaza. Hamas must be removed from the realm of existence. It would be best if Palestinians could determine their own destiny. Israel needed a new security regime. The IDF had to improve. Before 7th October, he had been critical of Netanyahu. There might be dissatisfaction with the internal politics of Israel but the country was united in defence of its existence.

Lerner's claim that the protesters were Hamas supporters, his implication that anything but unconditional support for Israel was tantamount to terrorism, had become the glib line of Israeli State apologists. What never raised its head in this debate, however, was the well-documented and despicable history of Zionist terrorism. No one asked who killed Lord Moyne or Folke Bernadotte; no one mentioned the sinking of the *Patria*; no one reminded those who claimed Israel was a victim of terrorism but had never been its perpetrator, of Deir Yassin; no one invoked the bombing of the King David hotel, an outrage carried out on the orders of Ben-Gurion; and no one bothered to enumerate the Israeli Prime Ministers who had belonged to terrorist outfits. The terrorism which gave birth to Israel is the right kind of terrorism, like that of the US in Vietnam. Terrorism is condemned by the so-called "free world" only when it's perpetrated by the oppressed. The speed with which the political right hung the label of terrorist around the neck of everyone who wanted a ceasefire or spoke up for Palestinian rights is indicative of the fascism which bubbles beneath the thin veneer of democracy. Even Jews who took to the streets to call for peace were reviled as Hamas advocates. None of this is surprising to those who are clear-eyed about how the world order rests on violence carried out by the rich and powerful as they glibly mouth their belief in democracy, human rights and peace.

Perhaps Lerner's most astonishing comment, however, was his assertion that the best outcome would be for the Palestinians to control their own destiny. That would have been a simple matter of Israel getting off their backs. Lerner reached the apogee of double-speak with this comment. Such self-delusion is merely funny when we see it on stage in a play by Molière, but terrifying when it comes from a man with deadly weapons at his command.

On the same day on the same radio station, Jeremy Bowen reported the Israelis had no idea where the Hamas leader was. They didn't even know, he claimed, what was due to happen on 7th October. The world needs to know what the State of Israel knew and when.

Imran Hussain, Shadow Minister for Employment Rights, resigned his government post in protest at Starmer's refusal to call for a ceasefire. Hussain had been a Corbyn supporter, ironic as the chickens of the antisemitism scam were now coming home to their blood-soaked roosts. Had Corbyn's policy towards Israel-Palestine prevailed, there would have been no 7th October and the hundreds of thousands protesting on the streets were rejecting the view that led Margaret Hodge to call Corbyn a "fucking racist". Presumably the sixty-six percent of the UK population in favour of a ceasefire were all antisemites, along with the hundreds of millions in the global south.

Bridget Phillipson, Labour's education spokesperson, said more aid needed to get to the Gazans and that we all want to see an end to the killing, a somewhat curious observation when it was obvious Boris Johnson, Suella Braverman, Nigel Farage and all their followers were not so clear. She called 7th October "sickening acts of barbarity" but had no comment about the barbarity of the West Bank settlements, the imprisonment of two and half million people in Gaza or the ethnic cleansing of seven hundred and fifty thousand Palestinians. She called for pauses in the fighting not a ceasefire. As Starmer had said, to freeze the conflict would give Hamas a chance to regroup. The Labour Party's position was in line with that of the US. Principle may dictate international law must be observed, she did understand that, she was moved, but we were in a political crisis. What was needed was a viable Palestinians State and a safe and secure Israel.

She was moved. Maybe she'd been taking syrup of figs. Phillipson is the typical politician produced by a system of representation in which ambitious careerists compete for place on the political ladder, while the electorate is conceived of as their route to success: opportunist, not very bright, glib and morally feeble. A viable Palestinian State was exactly what Hamas proposed after it won the 2006 elections. It was rebuffed by Bush. The EU withdrew funding. Blair said they shouldn't have been allowed to stand. And then you get 7th October.

Sunak was putting pressure on Sir Mark Rowley over the 11th November London protests calling them "provocative and disrespectful." Provocative of what and disrespectful to whom? The demonstrations were overwhelmingly peaceful in every sense. The Prime Minister, all the same, asked for information as to how order would be kept. Someone should have told him the protesters ensured it. Rowley would be held to account by the Prime Minister. Rowley defended his position by pointing out he had to stick to the facts and the law. It wasn't lawful to ban people who turn up to rally at a protest agreed with the police. If they were banned, the response would be a judicial review. Only two minutes of silence was intended on the Saturday and the march would stay well clear of the cenotaph. It's interesting that the leader of a party which claims it dislikes the interference of the State and believes in the "freedom of the individual", tilts towards hysteria when a hundred thousand individuals express their freedom by taking to the streets and remaining remarkably well-behaved, without any need for the State to tell them to. Whenever the common people show any sign of real autonomy, the putative State-haters reach for the truncheon, the riot shield, the water-cannon and ancient statute.

John McDonnell, who signally failed to stand up to those who claimed Labour was riddled with antisemitism, telling Chris Williamson he should apologise to his local synagogue, joined the debate. Williamson, it will be recalled, had commented that Labour shouldn't be coy about its record on resisting racism. McDonnell also described Margaret Hodge as "a friend" after she foul-mouthed Corbyn. His failure to understand the nature of Zionism, the doctrine of the "new antisemitism" and his foolish belief that constant forelock-tugging before those lying monumentally about Corbyn and Labour antisemitism would make them back off, played no small part in Labour's defeat in 2019. McDonnell said there must be no intrusion by the demonstrators on those at the cenotaph, but the protest was justified given the scale of the loss of life and the need to bring pressure. The hostages needed to be released and there should be no delay in calling for a ceasefire. The Met and the organisers were working in concert. It was important not to politicise the police. Rowley was in a difficult position. Calling the protests "hate marches" was counter-productive. He had been on the marches alongside Jewish people. A ceasefire was inevitable. There needed to be pressure on Hamas as well as Israel. Starmer was showing his inexperience in not calling for a ceasefire. To show true leadership would be to do exactly that.

This was McDonnell in full liberal, humanistic, rule-of-international-law mode. His comments were rational and balanced; but when he was tested by the vicious, unprincipled attacks of the followers of Herzl who lie and distort (and much worse) to ensure they get their own way, he showed himself inept. He responded to them as if they were simply Jews, as if they were well-meaning, honest people genuinely concerned to defeat racism and stand for justice. He was simply not attuned to their level of nastiness, as if Ben Gvir can be reasoned with or Smotrich able to see the Palestinian side of the argument. What lies at the core of the project practised by the State of Israel since 1948, is the defining feature of fascism: the rule of force rather than the rule of law. Being complaisant towards the likes of Netanyahu, Ben Gvir and Smotrich is akin to bending over backwards to accommodate Stalin.

James Cleverly disagreed with Blinken, who asserted Israel would not occupy Gaza and called Israel's security "transitional". The UK Home Secretary opined that an Israeli presence in Gaza was certain for a while. What he meant by "presence" and "a while" are worth speculating over.

Jack Keane, Vietnam veteran and retired General accused Hamas-Iran of a brutal attack on 7th October. They wanted a violent response. They were tyring to undermine Israel security and achieve its international isolation. They wanted to scupper the Abraham Accords. Hamas had to be finished off, its extermination would be good for the Palestinians. Hamas was their oppressor and its guarantor was Iran. The US was one hundred percent behind Israel.

From the start, Netanyahu's aim was to pull the US into a war with Iran. Keane was falling into the trap by associating

Iran with the 7th October attack. There was no convincing evidence Iran was involved in the planning. That Iran backs Hamas is uncontroversial, but as we've already noted, so did Netanyahu. It was elemental to his strategy that Hamas must command significant Palestinian support. A rift between Hamas and the Palestinian Authority was vital to hold two-States at bay. Netanyahu never spoke in favour of the Palestinian National Initiative. A serious Palestinian body led by a highly principled and intelligent figure and committed to non-violence was exactly what Netanyahu didn't need. He was an active promoter of the violence he claimed to oppose because it served his overriding aim: the avoidance of Palestinian autonomy.

Keane's claim that Hamas wanted a violent response is contemptible. Did Mandela want violence from the South African State?; did Michael Collins want violence from the British State?; did Archbishop Makarios?; and did the American revolutionaries themselves when they rose up against the British? To suggest people resisting colonisation, demanding their autonomy, are inviting violence from their colonisers is despicable. Keane was right, however, about the Abraham Accords: every rational Palestinian would have wanted to undermine them as their aim was to grant enduring power to Israel and compliant Arab States thereby marginalising the Palestinians forever. When Blair was asked about what the accords meant for the future of a Palestinian State, he said it was finished. This was Sykes-Picot, the McMahon-Hussein correspondence and the Balfour Declaration revisited: the powerful carving things up and putting their boot on the neck of the weak. The mantra of the "West" is that the 7th October attack was unprovoked, but the Abraham Accords were a nasty provocation and perhaps the final straw.

Keane's statement that finishing off Hamas would be good for the Palestinians is straightforward colonial arrogance. Imagine if Hamas declared that finishing off the Republican Party would be good for Americans; would anyone see that as reasonable? There is a perfectly sound, evidence-based argument that the Republican Party is a danger to the American people, in fact to humanity. Yet isn't it taken for granted that if Americans choose to elect a President who believes drinking disinfectant may be a good way to cure a virus they should be free to do so? Why then shouldn't the Palestinians be permitted to make their own choices. Why should an octogenarian, American ex-General be permitted to decide what's best for Palestinians?

Keane's invocation of Iran as the power behind Hamas was, of course, a repetition of the standard line implying the Palestinians were unable to think and act for themselves; they were mere pawns in Iran's wicked game; they hadn't resorted to desperate measures because they were at the end of their tether but were incited to action by clerics looking to dominate the region. Like Netanyahu, many Republicans wanted a war with Iran. Keane was joining in with their distraction technique: divert attention from the real issue: the occupation.

While Keane was free to spread his glib supremacism across the airwaves, Rashida Tlaib was censured by Congress for criticising Israel and supporting Palestinian rights. The censure resolution was brought by Rich McCormick, ensuring his place in history as a malicious nincompoop. He claimed Tlaib was "promoting a false narrative" about the 7th October attack and "calling for the destruction of the State of Israel". In addition he claimed she defended the "beheadings" of the day of the Hamas assault. There is no evidence of beheadings. Her use of the phrase "from the river to the sea" doesn't imply the disappearance of Israel as an entity, simply that it will cease to oppress the Palestinians. As for false narratives, McCormick belongs to a party many of whose members still assert that Trump won the 2020 Presidential election. That's not so much a false narrative as insanity. Twenty-two Democrats voted for the censure. This sordid little episode indicates just how far from democracy the representative assemblies of the powerful nations are: you're allowed to debate so long as you don't tell the truth about how power works.

Ione Belarra, Spain's Social Rights Minister, was a rare voice of reason and consistency. She called for Spain to break off diplomatic relations with Israel on the grounds her country should have nothing to do with Netanyahu, a war criminal. Israel was engaged in "planned genocide". The EU was sunk in hypocrisy, reacting swiftly to Putin's illegality but being slovenly about Israel's decades-long breaches of international law. Israel enjoyed total immunity because it had US backing. There was much that could be done. Sanctions should be imposed. If Israel was allowed to get away with this is would be a "threat to global democracy" because inflicting genocide on the Palestinians implied Israel could do the same to anyone. An immediate ceasefire was required.

Listening to Belarra was like hearing the voice of a sane person in a madhouse. Her point about what this meant for Israel's capacity to act in the same way to others was the important one. In its defiance of international law and its obvious war crimes (we will see later how influential figures were unequivocal about this) it was asserting its right to ignore all agreed norms and protocols, to decide for itself how to use violence and against whom, to define its interests without reference to any other agency and to treat anyone who stood in its way as expendable. To express such a view is usually dismissed as anti-Jewish conspiracy theory, something akin to the Nazi blaming of the Jews for all troubles. The evidence since 1948 is clear. Israel has used extreme violence to impose its will, and post 1967 has had the US as its ever-willing thug. It has treated the Palestinians as less than human and its spokespeople have often given direct expression to that very idea. One of its leaders explicitly claimed Israel is universal ie where there are Jews, that is Israel. If Israel is willing to define others as sub-human and to use violence against them because it perceives than as such, and if wherever there are Jews is Israel, then Belarra is absolutely right.

She made her comments on 8th November. Had what she proposed been implemented, tens of thousands of lives could have been saved, the destruction of thousands of homes prevented, hospitals and schools saved. The opposite happened because power prevailed over reason. Biden, Sunak, Macron, Scholz, all the leaders who refused Belarra's rational proposals were complicit in the death and destruction, but worse: they empowered the vile megalomania of Israel's unprincipled leaders.

Qatar was negotiating the release of the hostages in return for a ceasefire. It was suggested up to fifteen hostages could be freed for a one or two day pause. Civilians were making their way to the south of the Strip on foot. According to the International Committee of the Red Cross, there were thousands on the road, including the elderly and handicapped. They had neither food nor water. The Japanese Foreign Minister said there should be no forcible displacement of Palestinians, no Israeli occupation of Gaza, no use of Gaza for terrorism, no reduction in the size of the territory, no terrorism from the West Bank. The G7, he claimed wanted a pause not a ceasefire. Japan was in favour of Palestinian self-government.

The assault on Gaza produced an endless supply of comments which were denied by what the Israelis like to call "events on the ground". The Japanese Foreign Minister said there should be no forced displacement as hordes of displaced Palestinians were forced south. That was ethnic cleansing. The Israeli excuse was its desire to protect civilians but as people moved they were shot at and bombed and the south in which they arrived was under attack. On 7th October there were three hundred thousand residents in Rafah. By the time those cleansed from the north had arrived there were one and half million. Population density had risen to eighteen thousand five hundred per square kilometre. Across the "West" leaders were chirping "no forced displacement" as the forced displacement happened, and the people who mattered lacked the imagination, principle and courage of Ione Belarra.

The death toll among children now stood at four thousand two hundred and thirty-seven with one thousand three hundred and fifty of them still missing. Sixty percent of Gaza's medical facilities were shut down. Antonio Gutteres commented that the high death rate showed there was "something wrong" with the Israeli campaign. On the contrary, it was doing exactly what Netanyahu intended. There would have been something wrong had he been genuinely concerned to protect civilians, but everything was going to plan: the Palestinians were being slaughtered, made to run around like insects in a jar and terrorised.

MUGS

By 8th November ten thousand five hundred had been killed. There was fierce fighting in the streets of Gaza City. The dead were deprived of coffins or funerals. Mass burials became the norm. Bill Burns, having been to Egypt was on his way to Qatar, Jordan and the UAE. He was the ex-US ambassador to Jordan and on good terms with the king. Viewed as the US's best stealth diplomat it was speculated he was being sent to bring success where Biden had failed. Marwan Bishara pointed out that legally, as head of the CIA, Burns wasn't supposed to reveal his whereabouts, but his intervention showed how Biden understood his diplomacy was inadequate. His role should go beyond the matter of the hostages. There were three variables in play: the captives, the length of any ceasefire and the Palestinian prisoners. Hamas wanted many of them released. Blinken was in possession of the G7 communiqué. The US had been cowardly. It was shameful that it couldn't achieve even a two-day pause. The G7 position was alarming: no more ethnic cleansing, no reoccupation of Gaza, no more putting Gaza under siege or reduction of the size of the Strip. It was alarming to find this in the G7 document because it revealed that Israel intended these things. It was good that the G7 said no. The European public had seen enough. Ireland was angry. The US front was cracking. Israel was unlucky: when the Dutch were in Indonesia, the French in Algeria, there were no mobile phones. Now everything was recorded. Israel was a coloniser, the last colonial power which had engaged in seventy-five years of State terrorism.

Bishara was astute: the G7 communiqué did give the game away. Israel wasn't engaged in trying to disable Hamas; Netanyahu had gone to great lengths to strengthen it in order to divide and rule. The assault on Gaza was an attempt to wipe out or displace the entire population. Yet the G7, essentially recognising this in their wording, didn't rise to the moral outrage it demanded. Nor did they demand an immediate halt to Israel's campaign, which was the only rational response to a recognition of its aims. As ever, there was fuzzy, contradictory and hypocritical thinking: we support Israel, but would like to see fewer civilian deaths; we support Palestinian autonomy but are not prepared to force Israel to accept it.

Daniel Hagari said Israel had made gains. It was hitting Hamas targets and they had lost control in the north. Israel was opposed to a ceasefire and humanitarian pauses. There was domestic pressure on Netanyahu but he would make no deal until all the hostages were returned.

Netanyahu was simply making mugs of those who supported him. By insisting on the unconditional return of the hostages he was ensuring the war would go on. Had all the hostages been released, then, of course, the war would have gone on. He was getting away with this spoilt child behaviour for exactly the same reason as spoilt children: no one with the authority was willing to say, that's enough.

On 9th November, Jeremy Bowen declared Gaza a "wasteland".

As 11th November approached, the political right went on the offensive over the planned demonstration. Suella Braverman, who with every utterance added to her persona of an ugly-minded enemy of democracy, claimed the Met was biased towards pro-Palestinian groups. Naturally, she adduced no evidence. Sir Tom Winsor, inspector of constabulary for a decade, upbraided her: she should not do this. She was politicising the police. By talking about the police "playing favourites" and of "pro-Palestinian mobs" she risked creating huge problems. Her rhetoric would encourage far-right groups to turn up. She didn't understand the law. Dany Kruger, Tory MP and one-time advocate of "creative destruction" of public services, apologist for Johnson's rule-breaking during lockdown and irresponsible dog owner whose puppy caused a stampede among deer in Richmond Park, said the proposed protests showed "disrespect" and the police should intervene if people had masked faces (somewhat ironic given that Kruger was challenged for not wearing a mask on public transport during Covid). "Decent" people who joined the demo, he suggested, should question who they were associating with.

Sadiq Kahn pointed out that the Home Secretary had oversight but it wasn't appropriate to influence police decisions. Politicians don't instruct the police. The 1986 Public Order Act was enough. If the Home Secretary had intelligence about the demo, she should give it to the police. As for masks, everyone had an opinion. The right to protest was enshrined in law. If there were breaches of the law, the police would deal with them. The Met had lawyers from the CPS in the control rooms. What were the views of the head of the Met on the Middle East? It wasn't for him to know. The far-right were on the street too. It was important to unite communities. The far-right is violent and Islamophobic. It was important to support the police and to address fears rather than to whip them up. He was not at odds with Starmer, who had shown sympathy. They agreed on many points. Khan was for a ceasefire. They had a difference over that but they could disagree agreeably.

Khan's position was much more democratic than the hysteria in the tabloids and the dishonest increasing of the temperature by Braverman and her ilk, but its implication that the State can be impartial was naïve. The UK State was unequivocally behind Israel and therefore fundamentally racist towards the Palestinians and Arabs in general. What was being granted, effectively, was the right for British citizens who hold the wrong opinions to demonstrate. That those citizens constituted a majority, sixty-six per cent wanting a ceasefire, didn't alter the atmosphere of pat-on-the-head condescension. What was said by leading politicians and the media never granted that the views of the demonstrators might be as valid as those of the State. The calls for the protests to be outlawed flowed directly from the conviction they couldn't be. The message, as usual, was self-flattering: "Look how tolerant, we are. We permit even people as wrong-headed as you to protest". Of course, this kind of phoney tolerance has a short reach. If such wrong-headed people go so far as being on the verge of putting a radical in power, viciousness takes the place of tolerance.

As for the disagreement with Starmer, Khan was too important to be suspended or expelled, but many grassroots member had lost their place in the party for much less.

Abdelhamid Siyan of Rutgers, speaking of the Paris conference of 9th November said Macron had called for a ceasefire and the release of the hostages as soon as possible. The root causes needed to be addressed. There could be no *status quo ante*. There had to be unity around the humanitarian crisis. People were dying of thirst. Lazzarini was getting his act together. Cyprus was to establish a naval bridge to Gaza. Within two or three days there might be a pause. Disease was rampant. The Kerem Shalom crossing needed to be opened. An aerial bridge was possible. Aid was all set to be delivered. If it didn't happen it would be hell within days. That Blinken was in Tokyo was encouraging.

Of course, the fly in the ointment was Israel. Over and again rational and well-meaning people made sensible interventions, but reason and good-will are impotent when evil is given its head. Diplomacy didn't forbid Regan from evoking the "axis of evil". The rich and powerful can always call those fighting for their rights wicked: the ANC was evil, as was the IRA, EOKA, ETA and of course no official voice held back from dismissing Hamas as wicked; but it was out of the question to characterise the Israeli State as a possible evil actor, though this was the point which needed to be reiterated.

Since 7th October, one journalist per day had been killed in Gaza. *Reporters Without Borders* were submitting a complaint. *The Committee to Protect Journalists* evoked article seventy-nine of the Geneva Convention whose core provision is that journalists working in dangerous locations shall be treated as civilians. A somewhat ironic stipulation in Gaza where civilians were being murdered like ants. That the Israeli State was deliberately trying to silence its critics, to make serious reporting as difficult as possible, was as obvious as everything else denied by its apologists. Foreign journalists had been debarred from the Strip from the outset. Gazan journalists had to take on the burden and the risk. Israel's government had modified the old adage: it wasn't truth that was the first casualty, but journalists. Truth takes a battering because of what is called "the fog of war" but there was no fog here, rather a clear-sighted Israeli State determination to wipe out anyone who dared shed a glimmer of objectivity on the horror.

Dr Ahmed Mokhallalati, a plastic surgeon at the Al Shifa hospital, said the facility was collapsing. They had only small generators so the lights were out and the only lights available were from mobile phones. They had run out of anaesthetics. Children were being treated without pain killers. Ophthalmology services had ended. Israel was killing fifty percent of its victims directly and the other half through lack of treatment. A shortage of ICU beds meant patients had to be prioritised and those least likely to survive left to die. Sixty thousand were sheltering in or near the hospital. Sugar and vinegar were being used as dressings.

There were no antiseptics. Four hundred were waiting for plastic surgery. Operating theatres had no nurses. He was treating deep burns which became very quickly infected. There was evidence of the use of white phosphorous.

Few people fail to admire figures like Mokhallalati. Dedicated to a life-saving and life-changing profession he points to a model of citizenship. Everyone has skills and talents. We can all employ them beneficially. Yet here he is profiled against the background of sheer, unlimited ill-will. Only the ideologues who were willing to believe every Israeli State lie (which was more or less every official statement) and to excuse every outrage, believed the twaddle about Hamas fighters hiding under hospital beds. Every remotely dispassionate observer knew the IDF was delighting in killing. This was a return to savagery. On the one hand, the rational, skilled, morally viable Mokhallalati, on the other the morally bereft, lying, conniving narcissism of the despicable Netanyahu.

The international lawyer, Ahmed Abofoul explained that the Geneva Convention and the Rome Statute defined genocide. Israeli officials had made genocidal statements, going so far as to suggest the use of nuclear weapons. Israel, of course, did not subscribe to the International Criminal Court. Gaza presented evidence of a series of war crimes: for example forced transfer and starvation. The head of the New York office of the UN had resigned because not enough had been done.

Just as the contribution of a surgeon stands out as positive against the vile killing the Israeli State was engaged in, so the reasoning of a lawyer takes on a peculiar hue in the face of gangsterism. Israel was no more likely to support the ICC than Al Capone to believe in the FBI. If your intention is to get away with everything you can, to violate every norm in pursuit of your distorted aims, any agency demanding even minimal adherence to an agreed set of rules is anathema. This is what the world saw and heard over and again during the slaughter: a regime of gangsters and psychopaths being able to make a mockery of all impersonal standards and common rules because it was backed by the greatest military power the world has ever seen.

In Jenin, gunfights between the IDF and Palestinian fighters killed ten. The Emir of Qatar went to Egypt. Biden asked for a three-day pause and was said to be frustrated things were taking longer than expected. Such naivety in conjunction with such power. What else did Biden expect from Israel? Biden was like a father watching a wayward, spendthrift son eat through his savings, sitting passively, expecting frugality to kick in because of his fond indulgence of his offspring.

Colonel Elad Goren, head of Coordination of Government Activities in the Territories (double-speak for keeping the Palestinians in their place), interviewed on BBC tv said humanitarian aid to Gaza was more than adequate, instantly destroying the accepted meaning of the adjective. Terrorists were hiding among civilians. When Hamas began the war Israel told people to move south. Hundreds of trucks were entering the Strip every day. The IDF was assessing the civilian situation three times a day. When it was pointed out that prior to 7th October six hundred and sixty-five trucks a day were entering Gaza and there was now a shortfall of some two thousand, that twenty eight million litres of water per day were needed and that only ninety six trucks had arrived the previous day, he replied things were being coordinated with the UN, the US and Egypt. There was an information war. It was Hamas who started it. Civilians were part of it. Israel was doing all it could. As for the West Bank and the hundred and seventy Palestinians killed so far, terrorists were not only in Gaza. They were in Judea and Samaria too. Settlers were not trigger happy. They upheld law and order. The IDF did not harm children. In any case, a seventeen-year-old with a gun was not a child. To the question of who would run Gaza once the fighting was over, he said Israel was intent on winning the war not thinking of the day after.

The interesting question is whether Goren believed any of this tripe. People can convince themselves of almost anything when they have an interest to defend, but Goren's statements tilt into insanity. That Israel was doing all it could to protect Gazans was tantamount to claiming the US cavalry was protecting the lives of the Lakota at Wounded Knee. The silly comment that Hamas started it is at the level of a playground tussle: adults do not respond to every provocation, nor, in fact, do sensible children. The notions that the IDF does not harm children and that West Bank settlers uphold the law are too jaw-dropping to elicit comment. Goren was typical of official Israel spokespeople, as if they'd all been programmed by an algorithm. Perhaps a revised version of the Turing test would have been in order: when you converse with an Israeli State official can you tell you're not dealing with a rational human being?

Mike Noyes of *Action Aid* reported there were no basic services or supplies. He didn't understand what he had heard from Goren. There was utter destruction. There had been enough supplies for one day over the past thirty. He hadn't been able to get fuel. Israel's line was very worrying. There were rules to war: depriving civilians of basic supplies wasn't permitted. Babies were being killed, not seventeen-year-olds with guns. *Action Aid* was working in both the north and the south, in small teams and great danger. Though it wasn't one of their facilities, he could confirm a warehouse had been destroyed by the Israelis. Biden's three-day pause was better than nothing, but a ceasefire was required.

Who had the greater incentive to lie, *Action Aid* or Goren?

Mohammed Nabulsi, Syrian professor, claimed Gaza's infrastructure was destroyed which was typical of Israeli actions, reminiscent of Lebanon in 2006. Biden and Netanyahu were failing to comply with UN resolutions. Netanyahu, paradoxically was dependent on the Palestinian resistance. He had no exit strategy.

Ilan Pappe argued there was an Israeli consensus about the military action. Political decisions would bring a settlement but there was not one answer. Part of the Israeli government believed in the return of settlers to Gaza. Netanyahu was close to that position. He was contemplating tent cities in the Sinai and the annexation or control of the north. The Palestinian Authority might be allowed to take over and a buffer zone established. Israel does not learn from history. Did 7th October create doubt about how it was supposedly protecting itself? Instead, Israel engaged in talk about ISIS and Nazism while its allies provided immunity from criticism. There was an obvious military imbalance. The cycles of bloodshed would continue.

Vincent Fean, retired UK diplomat, (slightly unusual in not being privately and Oxbridge educated) evoked the UK's responsibility because of the Balfour Declaration. The UK's intentions were not clear. Gaza had been occupied since 1967. The Palestinian Authority had co-operated with western governments for thirty years. What was needed was Palestinian agency, they had to achieve self-determination. Blinken was drawing red lines but would Israel listen? Did the US have any real sway? In the eyes of the Israeli government, it owned the whole of Palestine. The Palestinians had a right to territory and a State. The western powers must tell Israel it could not have control. In the UK, civil society accepted this, it was the government which differed.

When Netanyahu visited the UK during Johnson's premiership, the latter proudly showed him the desk on which the Balfour Declaration was signed, thus paying tribute to a declared antisemite who wanted Jews out of Britain so they could inflict no more harm. Fean's reference to British responsibility was up against institutional forgetting. Balfour had been transmogrified from a Jew hater to a great friend of Jewish freedom. It's remarkable just how much distortion of the facts is possible by superficial thinking. Fean had no need to ask, however, whether the US had any influence: it was dancing to Netanyahu's tune, but only because of its failed policy and Biden's stupidity. The power to stop the fighting was no more than a phone call away. Biden was stuck up the blind alley of absolute agreement with Israel, which, of course, flowed from the US's belief it served its domination. Nothing could have been more pitiful than to see Biden feebly hoping for restraint from Israel but holding back from insisting on it.

DREAD DEMOCRACY

On 9th November the US hit a weapons facility in Syria. Martin Griffiths of the UN spoke of a "wildfire which could consume the region".

A big protest in New York called for a ceasefire. Students were being expelled from US colleges for pro-Palestinian comments or activity. Online speech and images were being doctored to make them appear antisemitic. The atmosphere in US colleges was tense. The ironies piled up. To defend the world from the Jew-hatred which was part of the totalitarianism of the Nazis, totalitarian measures had to be employed. Across the freedom-loving "West" leaders gleefully called for restrictions of free speech and the right to protest.

Marwan Bishara commented that pro-Palestinians were being terrorised. Was this stupidity or cynicism? Didn't these people know their history or did they know it and were lying? Israel had been created by the ruin of four hundred villages and towns and ethnic cleansing. Between 1947 and 1967 Israel had a military government. From the river to the sea, there was an oppressive system. Antisemitism had been rendered banal. Every critic of Israel was dubbed an antisemite. The two greatest antisemites of the moment were the Israeli PM and President. Implicating Israel in genocide was antisemitic. Netanyahu was engaging in criminality for his own gain. He permitted his country to be attacked. Those who implicated Jews in genocide were antisemites.

On 10th November, Jeremy Bowen reported that Israel was likely to attack the Al Shifa hospital, claiming it was a weapons store.

Braverman and the hardliners were pushing Sunak. She was after the leadership and being sacked might be good for her.

Her position was becoming untenable after her article in *The Times* claiming the Met was on the side of the Palestinians. Labour claimed the ministerial code had been broken. The chair of the 1922 Committee called her intervention "unwise". Miriam Cates, Tory MP and campaigner against non-existent "Cultural Marxism", a risible conspiracy theory which drags Adorno and Walter Benjamin into bed with antisemites, claimed Braverman's views were shared by many people. Gavin Stevens, chair of the National Police Chiefs Council argued the police needed "space to make difficult operational decisions." Steve Hartshorn, head of the Police Federation of England and Wales said if things go wrong, the police will get the blame.

Braverman and Cates, along with assorted far-right irrationalists, like the American republicans, had ceased to engage in democratic politics in any meaningful sense, and embraced instead an insurgency based on a fantasy to which they appended the name "Cultural Marxism". This phantom of the tortured minds of the far-right owes its history partly to Lyndon La Rouche who argued Herbert Marcuse and Angela Davis were involved in COINTELPRO. That there is not a scintilla of evidence goes without saying. The far-right has peeled away from parties of liberal capitalism out of the fear that over time democracy will bring transformation. In this they have some credibility: democracy is a threat to "the masters of mankind" as Adam Smith called them. It is the one way the common people have of making a difference. By voting, the majority have won health care, education, pensions, public transport. After the advances of the 1960s, when questioning of authority became commonplace, and matters like the decriminalisation of homosexuality and abortion threatened the control which repressive sexual moralism imposed, especially on women, the far-right pulled away from the mainstream with its commitment to liberal democracy.

Democracy had become the problem. Of course, the danger had been recognised long before. Walter Lippman had written about the need to keep the meddlesome masses out of politics in the 1920s. Post 1945 there was a difficulty: a bitter war had been fought against totalitarianism and the Soviet form was the enemy. The "West" had to look democratic. By the late 1960s, however, the far-right was in a panic: after all, if a hugely famous pop star could sing "give peace a chance" and make it an anthem for youth opposed to war, perhaps the masters of mankind really were in trouble. Enter La Rouche and his magazine *Executive Intelligence Review* (which called Obama's health reforms Nazi). By the early 1990s Michael Minnicino had intervened with his fanciful speculations in *New Dark Age: The Frankfurt School and Policial Correctness*. Apparently, the philosophers were seeding the overthrow of Christianity, the family and "tradition", in order to put socialism in its place. The theory is barmy precisely because it believes in a conspiracy and it has to because it can't accept democracy. If the people want to ditch Christianity and embrace socialism, why shouldn't they? Isn't that what democracy means? Failing in the democratic argument, the right had to summon up a bogeyman: European philosophers the common people had never heard of were plotting to fill the conduits of popular culture with subversive content. This wasn't democracy. The people were being hoodwinked and bamboozled. It wasn't possible to fight back through democratic means. Fire had to be fought with fire. There needed to be an insurgency because democracy itself was in the hands of the conspirators. It's a very short step to Trump denying he lost a free and fair election. Any outcome but victory for the right shows the corrupt conspiracy is winning.

The people, of course, were being hoodwinked and bamboozled, but not by Marcuse or Adorno. Edward

Bernays had explored in his seminal *Propaganda*, how advertising techniques could be used for political ends. The essence, as Hitler appreciated, was to narrow possible responses and to appeal to emotions. Elections today are run on lines set out by Bernays. Like Lippman, he saw the people as a threat which needed to be controlled for its own good. Invisible forces must rule the public mind. People must be herded into opinion pens. The aim, of course, was to serve capitalism. The propaganda system Bernays helped bring into existence has been stunningly successful, but power is never satisfied. There can never be enough conformity. That's one part of the explanation of the need for a wayward conspiracy theory. The other is that, in spite of the propaganda system, the people will insist on asking awkward questions. Democracy refuses to lie down and die. The irony for the far-right was that the assault on Gaza had awakened the democratic spirit across the globe. It required no intellectual sophistication nor great learning about Israel/Palestine to grasp the Israeli State was lying. The sheer brutality of its actions left hundreds of millions aghast. The claim that every criticism of Israel was antisemitic was shredded as the majority of the world's population opposed its lack of restraint and obvious war crimes. The entire right, from Biden to Trump, was shaken by democracy asserting itself. Israel's occupation was proving itself a stimulator of enormous democratic opposition to the accepted view of the "masters of mankind." The genie was out of the bottle and panic was starting to spread among the world's leaders.

Al Shifa hospital was hit by a missile strike and the IDF raided what it claimed was a Hamas facility nearby. Thirteen were killed.

Professor Sultan Barakat reported Palestinians leaving the north were being targeted. The IDF was trigger-happy but Israel always has an excuse. Biden was congratulating himself on have secured a pause (four hour pauses began on 10th November and a break from 24th to 30th November) but this was a sick joke: Israel would be further alienated and isolated by agreeing to only a short break in the assault. Israeli media were claiming the pause would apply to only certain areas. The UN was calling Gaza "hell on earth".

The death toll was eleven thousand and seventy-eight, four thousand and fifty-six children.

Marwan Bishara called the four-hour pauses "humbug". The Israeli war cabinet had dubbed the Palestinians "animals" and threatened to "bomb them back to the Stone Age". Israel had no regard for international law or the advice from the US. For Israel, it was business as usual. The US was trying to tell the world Israel was obeying international law which was a cover for its inability to impose anything on the Israelis. Pauses simple meant more war. We stop killing you for four hours, then we come back with a vengeance. Only a ceasefire could end the killing.

Yahya Sinwar claimed Palestinians were public enemy number one. Netanyahu was a dead man walking. Dozens of Hamas leaders had been assassinated but the resistance continued. Israel's aim was total destruction of the Strip.

Like Hamas in Palestine, Hezbollah in Lebanon was stubborn and formidable. Both were born of the occupation. Hamas had its origins in a sports club. It was radicalised in tandem with the occupation. The logic was simple: end the occupation, end Hamas. However, the usual colonial trick of divide and rule was applied. The US referred to the recent history of Israel/Palestine, but it was the US and Israel who brewed the coup d'état after Hamas won the 2006 elections. Those who preach democracy didn't like it when it produced a result they disapproved of. They did what they always do, set democracy aside and resorted to force.

Bishara's final point is the important one. If democracy prevailed the world would be very different. The discrepancy between what the people in the putative democracies support and the policies they get is much studied and the conclusion clear: the interests of a few billionaires have far greater influence than those of the voters. How this happens is also subjected to scrutiny. The propaganda system, the education system, the entertainment business, the advertising business, all work to propose a very narrow view which mustn't be questioned. The extent to which shibboleths like "the free market", "social mobility" or "the need to grow the GDP" are accepted as truths universally acknowledged is remarkable and at odds with the notion of open democratic debate. If discussion runs outside the narrow, designated tracks, the switch from democracy to force comes rapidly. In the self-proclaimed democracies, it isn't so easy to bludgeon those who won't conform, but propaganda takes the place of the truncheon, and if your ability to earn a living an feed your kids depends on not saying what the ruling ideology forbids, mass obedience is common.

In Mombasa there were pro-Palestinian protests. President Ruto spoke out in defence of the Palestinian cause. There had been one thousand two hundred and eighty-three complaints of Islamophobia in the US since 7th October.

Author Mitchell Plitnick of Jewish Voice for Peace argued Islamophobia was the flip-side of categorical support for Israel. Arabs were depicted as anti-US and anti-West. The Americna people wanted a ceasefire but members of Congress were either cheerleaders for Israel or silent. There was a disconnect. Among young Jews there was no longer knee-jerk support for Israel.

At Al Shifa hospital, snipers were firing constantly. Its generator had been hit. Staff were intimidated. The IDF was encircling. Anyone trying to leave was a target. There was no evidence the hospital was a weapons store or hideout for Hamas, but for the IDF it was a symbol.

Marwan Bishara called this a "strategic fiasco". The hospital had been bombed in 2014. Such strikes were usually exceptions but here they had become the rule. The green light had been given by the US. The claim the hospital was part of Hamas infrastructure was ludicrous; there was no one there but doctors, nurses and patients. Israel's intention was to harm civilians. It was engaged in revenge. Its strategy was to commit war crimes. There was a failure of international law. Since the end of the Second World War, the victors had never paid the price for any breaches of law. It was the losers who paid the price. Israel was not part of the ICC but if it had nothing to hide, it would join. The 2014 case against Israel in the ICC had brought no result. Israel's continued impunity was part of the reason for what was happening in Gaza. The double standard at work would hurt Israel's allies. Israel had already lost the battle for public opinion. The claim that all criticism was antisemitism was simply a cover for war crimes.

Much of this is obvious, but was Israel concerned to win the battle for public opinion? The reason Israel was necessary, according to Herzl, was because Jews could never be safe among non-Jews. Hatred of Jews is taken for granted. This strain of non-thinking runs deep. It isn't, of course, without historic cause. Antisemitism has been an enduring and vicious phenomenon; but the adoption of a status of permanent victimhood is a mistake, unless you see it as source of power. The privileged condition of victim is perfectly well-known and the manipulation it involves a despicable trait. Yet if your assumption is that all the world is against you, only you know what justice is, no one else can be trusted, you are forever on the verge of being annihilated, why would you want to gain the approval of a public you believe is beyond persuasion? Hence the adoption of the view that every criticism is motivated by irrational hatred. For Israel to try to win public opinion to its side would involve accepting that the world isn't intrinsically antisemitic, but for the hard-line Zionists, that would be giving away their advantage.

Also, is there a double-standard at work? Isn't it rather a single standard: the US is always right and its use of violence to get its own way an expression of virtue. This standard has been around a long time, since at least 1823 when the Monroe Doctrine was recklessly cast into the world. Underlying it is a false belief which still grips the American mind, and many others: humanity is composed of higher and lower "races" and the former have the right to use, abuse, exploit, brutalise, rob and murder the latter in the name of "progress". This ostensibly innocuous little word has done enormous damage. It is an imprecation. Utter it and no horror is forbidden. It is because America wrongly believes that Israel is a "progressive" society, that it is composed of people drawn from the higher "races" while Arabs are lesser and therefore regressive, that people were being massacred like vermin Gaza. So it will continue until these falsehoods are swept from the human mind, never to pollute it again.

ARAB SOLIDARITY

Mustafa Barghouti of the Palestinian National Initiative wasn't prominent in reports from those countries whose leaders supported Israel. The Israelis have tried to assassinate him more than once, he's an Arab, after all. Barghouti is a problematic figure for Israel and its apologists because he rejects both fundamentalism and violence, which makes characterising him a terrorist slightly difficult; not impossible, of course. Millions of people across the globe protesting for peace were agents of Hamas, according to much of the "western" media. Yet it's dangerous for those who must create a caricature of their opponents as backward, uncivilised, ignorant, sunk in superstition, addicted to violence to give prominence to a highly educated, cultured, civilised, balanced articulate medical doctor who can incisively nail the lies which keep his people oppressed. Founded in 2002, the PNI is relatively small but as a force campaigning for democracy and unity among the Palestinians, distancing itself from both the corruption of Fatah and what is sees as the extremism of Hamas, is very dangerous for the powerful. Hence its not being embraced and celebrated by the US, the UK, the EU and all those who claim they pine for democracy and unity in Israel/Palestine. Biden is quick to hug Netanyahu, a gangster running a cabinet populated by fascists, but shows no such affection for Barghouti. Were democracy and peace the true aims of Israel's supporters, they would carry Barghouti on their shoulders.

On 10th November Barghouti argued Arab countries should expel Israel's ambassadors, send aid to Gaza and seriously challenge Israel. Further, they should tell the US, the UK, the EU and others they would no longer be supplied with oil from Arab countries and imports from those places should be stopped. The alternative was the continuation of the killing. In 1948 the Palestinian's land was stolen. At that time, Palestinians owned eighty-two percent , now it was three point five. Netanyahu clearly wanted to occupy Gaza. He wanted to forcibly displace the Palestinians and find some other entity to look after them. His intention was to expand the occupation and end all talk of two-States. The killing of Rabin was illustrative: Netanyahu had stirred up ill-feeling. Netanyahu had always hated the idea of two States and was happy to be supported by a fascist like Ben Gvir.

Why didn't the Arab countries follow Barghouti's suggestions? Had the decision been with "the Arab Street", they might well have, but very wealthy elites rule in some Arab countries and for them money comes first. Why would Mohammed bin Salman have been interested in a democratic Palestine? The shared Sunni faith might have inclined him to support the Palestinians, but his rule and exorbitant wealth rest on a denial of democracy. The so-called "Abraham Accords" between Israel and the UAE and Bahrain signed on 15th September 2020, were effectively part of Trump's ludicrously misnamed "peace plan", a barely disguised attempt to isolate the Palestinians, grant respectability to Israel and scupper any hope of them attaining autonomy. Naming this scam after Abraham, commonly recognised as a forbear by both Islam and Judaism, was a clumsy attempt to use religion as a cover for a cheap political sleight-of-hand. People have a perfect right to believe in Abraham, just as they have to belief in fairies, but there is no archaeological or anthropological evidence for his existence. Evoking commonality when the underlying intention was to send the Palestinians the same way as the native Americans was a shabby, dishonest manoeuvre. Barghouti's call was high-minded and principled, but the leaders of most Arab States were unfortunately neither. People defending wealth and power never are. In November 2021 Israel, the UAE and Jordan signed a letter of intent for the sale of six hundred MW of electricity per year, from Jordan's solar farms, to Israel. The solar farms were built by a company owned by the UAE State. In return, Israel would provide two hundred cubic metres of desalinated water to Jordan each year. Being Arab was not enough to prevent leaders in the Middle East supping with Israel with a very short spoon.

Netanyahu denied his coffin and hangman's rope protest had suggested he supported the assassination of Rabin. Yigal Amir, the gunman cited *din rodef*, the Jewish law which exhorts action to stop those who intend harm to Jews. In Amir's far-right view, the Oslo Accords did just that. Netanyahu was a prime mover in opposition to the Accords, modest though they were. Edward Said thought them a Palestinian Versailles. Barghouti was right. Netanyahu was significantly responsible and the murder was a great success. The Oslo Accords would have at least recognised the validity of the 1967 borders and granted the Palestinians a degree of autonomy. It's important also that they were made possible by secret negotiations between Israel and the PLO, in Netanyahu's view, an inveterate terrorist organisation with which talks were impossible. They are all terrorists until they become statesmen aren't they?

Marwan Bishara asked if Israel was contemplating external guardianship for Gaza. Netanyahu was improvising. There was no agreement about where things were leading. The US warned re-occupation was a mistake. The G7 said there should be neither occupation nor siege nor shrinkage of the territory. How could Netanyahu cross these red lines? The Arabs had leverage, not least through their huge influence in the oil and gas markets. If they used their influence, US policy would change. Macron had complained about the injustice of slaughtering women and children. This might be an inflection point, time to put Israel on notice.

The first reports arrived of mass graves for Palestinians.

On 11th November, Macron called for a humanitarian ceasefire. It's worth asking what the difference is between that and a ceasefire. The underlying idea was, Israel had a perfect right to its violence against Gaza, but there was a need to protect innocent victims. However, if "Israel" embraced the occupation of the West Bank and the decade and half siege of Gaza, on what grounds was there a right to violence? When the mantra of "Israel's" right to defend itself was reiterated, didn't that mean the entity which was in breach of one UN resolution after another, an entity in daily breach of international law? How can such an entity be granted the right to defend itself when that very right depends on acceptance of the rule of law? Israel, Macron declared, must stay within international law, somewhat like arguing money-launderers must respect the banking system. Too many children, women and old folk were being killed, said Macron, suggesting he'd have been happy if a few less could have been slaughtered.

On BBC radio Nicholas Soames, grandson of Churchill, widely regarded by female MPs as the most sexist member of the Commons during his time there, the man who accused Diana Spencer of "paranoia" when she claimed her husband was having an affair with Camilla Parker-Bowles and, according to comedian Mark Thomas,, was claiming tax relief on the grounds some of his furniture was open to public view, called for a ceasefire. Grant him his due, he did upbraid the US for endorsing Israel's Golan Heights Law which defied UN Resolution 497. That even Soames couldn't stomach Israel's wayward violence indicates just how unhinged it was.

The 11th November pro-peace, London demonstration was estimated by the police to be three hundred thousand strong. If five people marched down Oxford St, the police would say there were three. No one can be sure of the number, but it may well have been nearer a million. There were one hundred and twenty arrests ,ninety-eight far-right counter-protesters. Few would lift an eyebrow if the police took in a hundred and twenty on cup final day. The protest was solidly peaceful and attended by a charming variety of folk. In the manipulative mentality of Braverman and her ilk, they were united in hate, but a cursory glimpse at the footage from the day shows they were united in a desire for peace, which for the masters of mankind is a very dangerous idea. A world of peace is one in which the rich can't prevail. Trace the threads back, and what is the source of concentrated wealth? Violence. This is not because violence is a necessary condition for prosperity, which is perfectly compatible with peace and equality, but because it is a necessary condition for economic and social injustice. The masters of mankind are intensely sensitive about their status. The super-rich see any threat to their wealth as tantamount to the end of the world, which is why they are willing to end the world to protect it. The Palestinian protests were particularly galling because if the US and its lapdogs are no longer permitted to eliminate, oppress, imprison, dehumanise and abuse backward peoples who stand in the way of "progress", the game is up for the billionaires. What the protesters were saying was, to the defenders of huge wealth, truly disgusting: we care more about human life and about justice than we do about money. That's why Braverman was foaming at the mouth. That's why the UK media ran headlines about the "antisemitic mob".

Israeli tanks were twenty metres from Al Quds hospital. Volker Turk condemned Israel for the attacks on hospitals. Israel, naturally, responded with contemptuous silence.

Mads Gilbert pointed to two aspects of the horror: the hospitals were surrounded by snipers. A nurse had been killed. Thirty-eight neo-nates had been moved. There was no electricity. Babies were lying on the floor. Three neo-nates had died. The more serious matter was the one and a half million displaced without food and water. This was a massive failure of international humanitarianism. People were sleeping outdoors. Who could say how many? He had never seen any sign of Hamas in hospitals during his three decades of time n Gaza. The IDF was without moral standards. Bombing medical facilities was standard Israeli practice. Biden should be asked if he supported the shooting of nurses and doctors. The US was to blame and the EU complicit.

Simon Moutquin, ecological MP in the Belgian parliament, called for sanctions on Israel. On the other hand, Lindsey Graham claimed the people of Gaza were the most radicalised in the world while Nikki Haley proclaimed "finish them off". Interesting that Graham shows no inkling of understanding why the people of Gaza might think and feel as they do; nor did he seem to appreciate that "radicalised" could apply just as well to the Republican Party. Thinking of its meaning of going to the roots, that was perfectly true of Haley. She revealed she had been competently brain-washed in the doctrine of US supremacy and the joy of genocide.

The Toronto journalist and author Pacinthe Mattar was alarmed by the "abject silence" over the deaths of journalists. It was necessary to be able to report with clarity. She had worked at CBC for ten years and conducted hundreds of interviews, only one had been spiked: an Al Jazeera journalist. It was a stark example of how the media were shutting down on fair reporting.

Mattar was right, of course, except examples of a similar nature were easy to find and had been, indeed, the stock-in-trade of the media for decades. Pick virtually anything you like: Vietnam, Bay of Pigs, Afghanistan, Iraq, Ireland, Grenada, Chile; take a look at the reporting. Objectivity isn't greatly evident. People are used to it, so they don't notice it, like a bad smell. That's the technique: get people accustomed to tilted reporting; they won't have the time, the expertise or the inclination to dig out the truth. There has always been propaganda, but the past century has seen the perfection of a propaganda system. Gaza has caused a spike in the dishonesty and obfuscation for the reasons cited above: there was risk the masters of mankind could be deprived of some of their wealth and power. The system went into overdrive and became hysterical. Hysteria is always present in the propaganda system but the more ostensibly educated outlets try to appear calm. That more or less disappeared. Of course, for the Israeli State anything remotely close to dispassionate reporting was terrorism. Hence the targeting of journalists.

A kindred point was made by Mark Owen Jones of Hamad bin Khalifa university: the Palestinians were discriminated against by marginalisation. The *Daily Mail* had featured Gaza on its front page for fourteen days but there was no mention of Palestinian deaths. The liberal *Guardian* wasn't much better commonly using terms like "brutal" in relation to the Palestinians but writing of "precision strikes" from the Israelis.

On 22nd October, twenty-one members of Ahmed Alnaouq's family were killed when their home was bombed. Alnaouq is the founder of the *We Are Not Numbers* collective which trains Palestinian journalists to write in English. He pointed out that the media reported he had "lost" his family. Everything he said was subjected to intense scrutiny, the suggestion being he was lying. On the other hand, the lies of the Israeli State were circulated without scrutiny. The implication was always made he was a Hamas supporter.

On 12th November attacks on hospitals intensified as Netanyahu declared there would be a ceasefire and Gaza would be demilitarised. Israel would be in control. Tubas in the West Bank was attacked and one person killed. Two thousand people from the West Bank had been taken into "administrative detention". Donkey carts were replacing cars. What might the response be if people in New York, London or Paris had to get around by donkey cart? Al Quds hospital had shut down. Al Shifa was out of power. Three premature babies at Al Shifa had died. Anti-tank missiles fired from Lebanon killed six Israeli civilians. In Khan Younis four residential buildings were bombed and dozens killed.

President Herzog declared Al Shifa without problems. The hospital, he claimed, had electricity. The tv footage showed the opposite. The BBC claimed it was difficult to know given the "fog" of war; curious when it was the medics who were reporting the absence of power. Jake Sullivan said he was "uncomfortable" with reports of gun battles around hospitals. Difficult to imagine such a word being applied if shooting was taking place around hospitals in Washington or Tel Aviv.

In Paris there was a demonstration against antisemitism, attended by Marine le Pen. She, of course ,had to kick her dad out of her party in her search for respectability. In 2021 he was on trial, again, this time for comments about the singer and actor Patrick Bruel. When told Bruel's background was Jewish, Le Pen commented: "I'm not surprised, next time we'll do a whole oven batch." His daughter has swung to ostensible support of France's half million Jews against what she perceives, along with many right-wing politicians who see an opportunity in Islamophobia, as a Muslim threat. Of course, the massacre in Gaza was only very tenuously linked to religion and many Jews were appalled by Israel's actions, some orthodox Jews publicly burning their passports. It was convenient for right-wing ideology to reduce the matter to a religious conflict. In doing so, the right-wing figures were pushing to its logical extreme the general tenor of reporting. Muslim versus Jew was a much easier matter than autonomy versus colonialism and a neat way to cloud matters for the lazy-minded. It had long been true that many had absorbed the media presentation of the Israel/Palestine matter as a "conflict" in which it was six of one and half a dozen of the other. The fact of the "West's" supremacism imposed by violence had to be hidden.

Sabri Saidam, a senior Fatah official who lost more than forty members of his family in the slaughter, said Israel was engaged in a war against all of Palestine, a war to destroy the Palestinian people. It was a stain on humanity. Netanyahu was talking about "the day after" but an immediate ceasefire was needed. A Palestinian national consensus was required. People couldn't wait. Only a collective effort would prevail.

Many are aware of Joe Biden's personal tragedies: his daughter from his first marriage, Naomi Christine was killed in the same car accident as her mother in 1972 and in 2015 Biden's eldest son Beau died from brain cancer. Biden has spoken publicly about these losses. A "western" political leader suffers the death of close family members and it's treated with dignity; it's a tragedy; we are expected to empathise with the grief. But a Palestinian sees more than forty members of his family wiped out and who knows or cares? In this way, a more or less invisible supremacism enforces itself. The message is seldom spelled out but it is always there: the lives of these people are expendable. They don't grieve like we do. They don't have the same emotions. What was truly remarkable was the restraint and poise of people like Saidam when they made media appearances. It is a cliché that the deepest hurts are the least expressed, but it's what we should remember.

WOE TO THE VANQUISHED

The Palestinian Health Ministry reported one thousand seven hundred children buried under rubble, eleven thousand killed including one hundred and ninety-three medics and forty-nine journalists. Twenty-eight thousand two hundred and seventy had been injured. Attacks were focused on hospitals. Al Shifa was established in 1946. The IDF was Nye Bevan in reverse. There were two hundred and forty-one schools in the Strip, sixty-one had been destroyed, as had seventy mosques and twenty-five percent of agricultural land. Someone needed to put a leash on Israel.

Who could, other than the US?

The founder of the Shaikh Group, a Middle East consultancy, Salman Shaikh reported that Gaza City was being trashed. Israel was proving that might is right. International law was the north star which should guide everyone. Without a long-term ceasefire there could be only escalation. Biden's resistance was a mistake. He was losing support and his fatal error was leaving him behind the curve. The coming phase would be much more escalatory. The Arab States needed to do more. Their summit was weak. There was no military solution. The Arab street was incensed and Arab leaders would lose the support of their populations for generations to come. If the UN Security Council couldn't secure a vote for a ceasefire, there was a chance of regional war.

The idea of might is right has ancient origins. "Woe to the vanquished" was first recorded in Livy, but the idea was expressed by Homer and also in Hesiod's *Works and Days* in the parable of the hawk and the nightingale. Socrates challenged the notion, Lincoln reversed it. Crucially, the Enlightenment belief in the rule of law is its dismissal. The entire rhetoric of politicians in the representative democracies is drawn from its rejection. Democracy is thoroughly incompatible with the notion those who can seize power by force are bound to rule. Yet the world watched as the Israeli State regressed several thousand years. It is commonplace to hear defenders of Zionism castigate Enlightenment values. By definition such values scupper their project: basing your ideas on evidence, recognising the limits of cognition, upholding the rule of law, these are poor principles for messianic doctrines. Yet it was clear those who gave support to Israel were brimming with childish excitement at the thought of "might is right" establishing itself as the norm; except of course, when it came to Putin or China. Then they became, once more, dutiful believers in the rights of the common folk, adherents of peace, and the rule of law. It was a circus spectacle to make bears laugh, except tens of thousands paid the fatal price.

Al Shifa hospital had ceased to work. There was power only in the emergency section. Five had died there on11th November. The head of the WHO demanded a ceasefire. Alice Rothschild of Jewish Voice for Peace said Israel's violations of law were morally indefensible. Al Shifa had been a life-support before the war. It was an appalling catastrophe. The staff were exhausted and traumatised, diseases were rampant, including sepsis and gangrene. There was a simple choice for many people: a quick death or a slow death.

Al Shifa was hit by drones firing in all directions. Mahdi maternity hospital, housing many of the displaced, was hit.

Meanwhile, Jake Sullivan declared the US didn't want "firefights in hospitals" but did want the US hostages brought home.

This is interesting. When the US didn't want the North Koreans to get away with invading South Korea, a breach of international law, they didn't restrict themselves to a few pleading statements and a little low octane, in-the-shadows diplomacy; they provided ninety percent of the forces that fought the war. There's no doubt the northern invasion was a crime, but what was the division of Korea along the 38th parallel at the end of the Second World War if not a big-power carve up which left the Korean people, long subjects of Japan, without control of their own society? On 8th March 1965 US marines landed at Da Nang, an invasion of South Vietnam not agreed with its government. On 25th October 1983 the US invaded Grenada to get rid of Hudson Austin, a rebel leader they disliked. The list goes on. Yet Israel was bombing hospitals and sniping at doctors and nurses and the US could do nothing but say they didn't like it. Sullivan and Biden could have told the IDF to stop. The reason they didn't was their supremacism: these were Arabs being killed. Who cares about them?

There was real urban warfare under way and in spite of the alarming death rates, Israel was not fulfilling its aims. Hamas was launching hit and run attacks on Israeli tanks which were less mobile than the fighters emerging from the tunnels.

The Emir of Qatar was in talks with Blinken, asking for a ceasefire, the opening of the Rafah crossing, and serious moves to two-States. He pointed out that Qatar had hosted an Hamas office for years at the request of the US.

Mark Regev, whose media appearances were as convincing as Lady Macbeth's feigning innocence, claimed it had been proven Hamas had an HQ under Al Shifa. Seventy thousand Gazans had moved voluntarily, in spite of Hamas trying to restrain them at gunpoint. Israel was doing all it could to safeguard babies while Hamas was using them as human shields. It was hard for Israel to speak of these things while the fighting was ongoing.

The only surprise was Regev didn't claim he was the messiah.

Fikr Shalltoot the programme manager for Medical Aid for Palestinians, said the hospitals were in a catastrophic state. Israel might be saying it was doing what it could but in fact there was nowhere to take patients. All hospitals were overwhelmed. Ambulances were finding it impossible to move. Tjada McKenna, head of Mercy Corps, bemoaned the lack of basic necessities. Israel was making unilateral announcements that were no use. Its insistence Hamas must agree to ceasefire was correct, but Israel was negotiating in bad faith. Her organisation was trying to save lives. Aid had to be admitted. Prior to 7th October there had been five hundred trucks a day, only eight hundred had entered in the past month. There was no safe place in the Strip. What was the US doing? There needed to be advocacy at all levels.

Interviewed on Radio 4's *Today* programme on 13th November, James Heappey, Minister of State for Defence, admitted he couldn't confirm schools and hospitals were being used by Hamas. Mishal Hussein challenged him: the BBC's correspondent, who knew Al Shifa well and had worked in the region for years, said it was impossible to conclude one way or the other. Heappey responded it was impossible to trust anything Hamas said and Israel's self-defence was legitimate.

Why did no one say it was impossible to trust a word Regev, Netanyahu, Ben Gvir or Smotrich said and Palestinian resistance legitimate?

Exactly as she had wished, Suella Braverman was sacked by Sunak for writing a piece which criticised the police, among other sins. Braverman studied at the Sorbonne and is said to be a Francophile; not something she foregrounds in her bid for votes from the fearful, the prejudiced and the bamboozled. Like Lady Macbeth, she was fully aware what she was doing was wrong but she did it for the same reason. She is an outstanding example of how ambition can strip people of all moral restraint. Her technique was banal: cause as much trouble for the leader as possible, then he'll have to sack me, then I'll be in the headlines, then I can make more outlandish statements, suggest blasting immigrants into outer space, win the support of the wealth-and-power press and significantly increase my chances of becoming Tory queen and PM. Braverman had reached that point, so easily attained by politicians on the make, at which adherence to truth or facts had been swept aside in favour of appeal to whatever misguided, ill-informed, bigoted opinions might lift her on the swelling tide of desperate frustration. Right-wing politics thrives on the latter. Meet people's needs and they are far less prone to irrationalism. Braverman was perfectly aware there was enormous frustration and disaffection over promises not met and the simple sense of kiltering down to ever worse general conditions. Like a good right-winger, she didn't seek to find solutions, but to play on negative emotions for personal advantage.

Her characterisation of the Gaza protests as "hate marches" was a classic piece of political double-speak. She didn't believe it. She knew full well thousands of Jews were on the marches, as she knew also that many of the protesters belonged to the "Guardian-reading, tofu-eating wokerati" she dismissed for being soft and cuddly. The madness which seizes the minds of those hooked on power was well advanced. It's curious we have "drugs czars" and get into a lather about people addicted to nicotine or alcohol or gambling, yet say not a thing about the far more dangerous and pathological addiction to power.

David Cameron, he of Greensill, was made a lord (a lesson to our young people: bend the rules and you'll get big rewards) and appointed Foreign Secretary. Cameron has an urbane façade, once again reminiscent of Macbeth (*There's no art to find the mind's construction in the face*), but is a ruthless and unflinching defender of the rights of great wealth. Apparently emollient, he was to prove himself a low-minded friend of Netanyahu and apologist for unhinged massacre.

On US college campuses students began to exert pressure for a ceasefire, a harbinger of what was to arrive in May 2024.

Not much was reported about the effect of the murder in Gaza on the Israeli economy, but gas exports were down some seventy per cent. Egypt and Jordan were big recipients of Israeli gas. Israel provided about 0.5 percent of the global gas market. Its own energy needs were secure for the moment but Egypt was significantly hit and was buying liquid gas on the international markets. The recent surge in gas prices was partly due to the events in Gaza. Needless to say, the Israelis who were taking a hit for Netanyahu's ambition were the poor, but try to find reports about that in the UK media. The Israeli economy shrank by about 20% in the last quarter of 2023. There was bound to be pain for years; the poor would get it in the neck.

Netanyahu was seizing twenty percent of the land in northern Gaza, said Professor Sultan Barakat. It was becoming no man's land. What he was aiming at was total control to be followed by further incursions. It was too early to say how Netanyahu saw things working out. Fifty per cent of Israel's housing stock had been destroyed. The refugee camps were decimated, education had come to a halt (while parents in the UK fretted about GCSE results). Unemployment levels were appalling. Communication with the rest of the world was being cut. Israel's claim aid was being diverted to Hamas, that much of what was being brought in had dual-use, didn't stand scrutiny. The same claim had been made ten years earlier when influx of aid was supervised by the UN, the EU, the Palestinian Authority. Every piece of equipment was tracked, slowing the process enormously and making it ten times as expensive. The Arab summit had missed a chance: it should have passed economic sanctions.

Tamar Qarmout argued the international community's help to the Palestinians was largely wasted because since the Oslo Accords, Israel had behaved like an occupier. Israel never paid the price for its actions. The peace process was a failure. Israel was unaccountable. Hamas had taken the democratic route in 2006. Donors can't pick and choose. There should be no discrimination when it comes to humanitarian aid. The outcome of the Arab summit was no surprise: the Arab leaders put their interests before Gaza.

In response to the killing by Hezbollah of a civilian in Dovev, northern Israel, Gallant said only one tenth of the IAF was deployed in Gaza and could easily retaliate, turning Beirut into a second Gaza. Dovev, with a population of about five hundred, is a moshav, a community, agricultural collective of the kind established by Labour Zionism between 1904 and 1914. It rests on the site of a Palestinian village, Kafr Bir'im and is named after David Bloch-Blumenfeld, a leader of the Zionist Labour movement. The moshavim never attained the status of kibbutzim during the Labour years. Both have suffered since the success of Likud post 1977. They have needed Palestinian workers for many years. There is an irony here: apparent commitment to equality and co-operation along with a belief in supremacism. At the core of the Labour movement is the belief in a common cause: those who do productive work share an interest in seeing its fruits equitably distributed; just as those who profit from the work of others have an interest in seeing their wealth stay in few hands, those of the "masters of mankind" in Adam Smith's phrase. Labour Zionism is a contradiction in terms. The latter is a messianic political doctrine born, in its Herzl version, out of a belief in the impossibility of defeating antisemitism. The Labour movement, leaving aside its Marxist chiliastic theorizing, is the response of employees to the moral injustice of employment. Workers had no need of Marxist theory to see where their interest lay, rather, he had need of their spontaneous action as the root of his theory. Labour Zionism proposes co-operation between Zionists, but exploitation between Zionists and non-Zionists. Being Jewish isn't enough to benefit from Labour Zionism, because to reject its supremacism makes a Jew "self-hating". It's a great historical irony that a State founded on the expulsion and murder of an indigenous population could embrace the doctrine of those working to eliminate exploitation and join humanity in its common endeavour of productive work. A short-lived irony, however, as the hard-line capitalists of Likud took control in Israel.

Turkey set sail a ship to establish hospitals as soon as possible. The question was how to transfer patients safely.

Diana Buttu, a Palestinian-Canadian lawyer and former spokesperson for the PLO said Israel ties to make the illegal, legal. They were propounding the same allegations as in 2008, 2012 and 2014, but were, as ever, unable to substantiate. The onus was on Israel to provide evidence for its claims. They were involved in a clear attempt at genocide.

It's a truism that proof has to be adduced to prove a claim; but one set aside in the case of Israel. Such is the purblind adulation of the fawning "West" for this State founded on racism and terror and maintained through oppression and violence, its outrageous assertions are treated as holy writ.

Palestinian farmers were denied access to customers in Palestine. Prices were falling steeply. Huge detours had to be made because of the checkpoints and to avoid settlements.

One hundred and eighty-eight had been killed in the West Bank since 7th October. In Hebron, a sixty-six year-old taxi driver was shot in the head during an Israeli raid. Five of the seven thousand Palestinians in Israeli prisons had died in custody over the same period. One hundred UN staff had been killed. At its peak, there were thirteen thousand UN workers in Gaza, now there were five thousand. Netanyahu must have been delighted.

The UN was in a cleft stick, Marwan Bishara argued. The veto wielded principally by the US prevented the UN blocking war crimes. The UN could unite humanity. Its flag was issuing a clear message: stop the madness. On the other hand, Israel's Ambassador to the UN was claiming the organisation had been infiltrated by Hamas. Israel had peddled its lies for decades, but they still worked because international diplomacy was willing to recycle the untruths. The US parroted Israel's distortions.

Cornell West, the veteran US civil rights activist, declared: "We do not hate Jewish brothers and sisters, we hate the occupation." A distinction so simple a five-year old could grasp it. Bring Joe Biden a five-year-old. Loving the Palestinians was nothing to do with hatred. The US was morally bankrupt. The lies had to be shattered. We had to rise above hatred and revenge. The Democratic Party had lost its way and was supporting genocide. In the US, there was fear of the ADL and AIPAC. It was necessary to speak without fear. There had to be a commitment to truth like that of Martin Luther King and Malcolm X.

West was right about the Democratic Party, but not that it had lost its way over Gaza. It had supported extreme violence, ignored human rights, given succour to dictators and spurned movements of the common folk for decades. It was fully signed up to the moral bankruptcy West diagnosed because it could never put principle before US interests, which means those of the rich and powerful.

Cameron had been grabbed, Marwan Bishara commented, because the Sunak government lacked a statesman. The ex-Prime Minister was supposed to bring a bit of heft. The UK was at the centre of the storm, acting as the eyes of the US. Cameron, however, was the politician who fatally misjudged the EU referendum. The UK was now suffering for being outside the EU. It had lost some of its privileges. As for Braverman, she was somewhat scuppered by the fact of a relatively effective democracy in the UK. Her accusations against the police were divisive and unwelcome. Would she ever lead the UK? It was highly doubtful.

Britain had a special responsibility in relation to Gaza given the Balfour Declaration and what followed. At the end of the Second World War there were a hundred thousand UK troops in Palestine, but they were driven out by Zionist terrorism. Presumably, after six years of war, Attlee didn't have the stomach to stay and fight the terrorists who had assassinated Lord Moyne, Folke Bernadotte and created so much mayhem and anguish during the Mandate. The partition of Palestine was as much a crime against the Palestinians as that of Ireland against the Irish. It wouldn't have happened if Truman hadn't bought delay to allow Resolution 181 to be passed by the UN. In this, there is a great irony: Israel owes its existence to a resolution by the body it now routinely excoriates and whose decisions it has ignored for decades. The Zionists were enthusiasts for the UN when they could use it to further their messianic aims, but loathe it when it defends the rights of those they oppress.

The Archbishop of Canterbury called for a ceasefire, saying he didn't know what the military or political solution might be. The latter was easy: Israel should remove its illegal settlements and end the siege of Gaza. As for calling for a ceasefire, what took him so long ?

GENOCIDE JOE

By 13th November Hamas was ready to release seventy hostages in return for a five-day truce. Given one of Netanyahu's main aims was the return of the captives, he might have been expected to respond enthusiastically. Further, if Hamas was willing to offer this, what other offers might it make? Wouldn't it have been sensible to at least explore the possibility of an enduring ceasefire in return for the release of all the hostages? Those who were starting to protest in Tel Aviv were astute: Netanyahu was playing his old political games: the hostages were mere pawns. He couldn't see beyond his ambition. We've all read Macbeth. We know murderers lie as we know they must wear a false face to hide their false hearts. The more Netanyahu expressed his concern for the captives, the clearer it was he didn't care if they lived or died.

Attacks on southern Gaza intensified. Residential areas were flattened. The W.H.O. declared the condition of the hospitals "dire and frightening". Biden appeared to concur when he said hospitals must be protected by which he meant, he explained, Israel's actions should be less intrusive. He might as well have suggested the prohibition of rain. While he continued to treat Israel as the world's spoilt child, the State which can do no wrong and the eternal victim and therefore beyond accusation, Netanyahu's war cabinet was going to continue to snub its nose at the world.

Every time talks were about to achieve something, Israel scuppered them, claimed Osama Hamdan, Hamas politburo member. Hamas was willing to exchange fifty hostages for five hundred Palestinian prisoners. (The figures tell the story.) Israel's tactic he said, was to add more conditions just when agreement might be reached, citing the demand for the names of the hostages. None of the trucks going into

Gaza under the supervision of UNRWA, the Red Cross or other agencies were delivering anything to Hamas. Qatar was doing its best to get the hostages out. Israel was the problem. It goes without saying, Hamdan was ignored by the "West". He was a terrorist. End of story.

Eleven thousand two hundred and forty had been killed four thousand six hundred and forty of them children. Twenty-seven thousand had been injured. How many Hamas fighters had been killed? In spite of Israel's claim they were hunting down Hamas, they were extraordinarily coy in revealing how well that effort was proceeding. Regev commented that the crisis was "manufactured by Hamas". Heavy rain contributed to the risk faced by the Palestinians. There were huge Israeli strikes on southern Gaza, and the central area was bombed. A mass grave was uncovered in the Al-Shifa hospital. There were four active fronts in the north of the Strip. Hamas claimed Israel was stalling on the release of the hostages.

The Israeli government had nothing to say about the possible five-day ceasefire. The US and the UK wittered about protecting hospitals and reducing civilian deaths but Sunak at the Lord Mayor's banquet talked about stopping "extremist violence". It's hard to be sufficiently scathing about a world order in which a Prime Minister associates violent extremism with people marching through the streets for peace while simultaneously giving moral, diplomatic and military support to a regime massacring people wholesale. In such a context, truth is mangled, all objectivity refused and the most morally despicable positions defended because they tally with extreme, benighted self-interest.

On 13th November, Defense for Children International-Palestine filed a case against Biden, Blinken and Austin, aided by the Centre for Constitutional Rights, a New York based human rights agency, on the grounds of aiding genocide in Gaza. As the major supporter of Israel since 1948, they argued, the US bore a major responsibility. The law's delay, of course, might have driven Hamlet to suicide. The Palestinians needed rapid relief, and that wasn't going to arrive from a court case destined to drag on for months. The law can't act precipitately because it has to consider all the evidence and arguments, hence the tactic of fascists: facts on the ground. It has been the Zionist way of doing things since the founding of the State of Israel: use violence, get what you want, then claim to stand for the rule of law. It was, of course, highly unlikely the US court system would find against its President, Secretary of State and Secretary of Defence. No doubt, tucked away in the constitution is some proviso which gets them off the hook.

When polls showed eighty per cent of Democrats and sixty-six per cent of Americans wanted a ceasefire, Biden claimed the young were dismayed by the events. The cleavage between an old-school hack like Biden and the young who had learned to question the slavish obedience of the US to all things Israeli, was pitiful. Here was the opportunity for the Democrats to follow the opinion of the bulk of their supporters and use their leverage to bring peace, a move which may well have boosted Biden's chances in the November election. Instead, Biden hung the label of "Genocide Joe" around his neck and alienated millions, especially among the young.

Forty US government agencies called for a ceasefire. Four hundred US officials signed a letter in support of a ceasefire and effective aid. Three leaked State Department memos challenged Biden's policy.

As Israelis protesting Netanyahu's policies and calling for the hostages to be released marched from Tel Aviv to Jerusalem, Biden declared; "Hang on in there, we're coming". He was referring to getting the captives set free but it was somewhat alarming to hear him suggest the US hadn't yet arrived: they were propping up the Israeli war cabinet diplomatically, politically and militarily. The hostages weren't released because the US was behind Netanyahu's hopeless approach. Those seized could have been released on 8th October if Israel had simply been willing to swop them for thousands of Palestinians in Israeli prisons.

Al Shifa had no fuel for incubators and respirators. The UN was running out of fuel too and was finding it difficult to pick up aid. Jake Sullivan helpfully commented Biden thought a ceasefire would help Hamas, though the notion of Biden being able to think was somewhat far-fetched.

Lula da Silva, who exhibited a far greater capacity for logic and reason said: "If Hamas committed an act of terror, Israel is committing several." Israel was born from terrorism, just like most States. Is there an example of a State which wasn't brought into existence by violence? That doesn't imply the State can't be transformed into a peaceable, beneficent agency, but most of the States that matter in the world are armed for annihilation and deny their people services on the grounds of lack of funds while they can always find billions for killing; and if people's needs were met, what would be the likelihood of conflict?

The US, Sultan Barakat argued, had been pulling back in the region for two years. Over the past twenty, there had been an economic change: the US was now the largest exporter of oil and gas which diminished its need to be in the area. The US public was tired of war. The real reason for US heavy involvement was the survival of Israel. The US had been in a dilemma over Iran since 1979. It was using Arabs as proxies but worried about their commitments to causes it didn't support. Hamas was forced to turn to Iran. It had embraced the need to govern only because of the failures of the Palestinian Authority. The Arab Street couldn't bring change. Hope came from Europe, the US, South America but it was the global population which could really bring change and that included Jewish movements like Not In Our Name.

The idea the global population might take things into their own hands must have been terrifying for the political elites, the corporates, the super-rich. There's the rub: reflex support for Israel was supposed to be the guarantee the global population couldn't do things for itself. Israel is iconic because it's a militaristic, oppressive, supremacist State. Therefore, the message it transmits is: if this can be done to them, it can be done to you. Standing by Israel is intended to send a message to the global population that it had better know its place. What was taking place in Gaza reinforced the doctrine: dare to resist and you'll be massacred by, of course, the most moral armies in the world.

A big pro-Palestinian protest was held in Manila. The Filipinos have good reason to dislike colonialism, as the novels of José Rizal show.

The Palestinians, apparently, had no right to defend themselves, argued Marwan Bishara. The much-repeated Israeli right to self-defence was a right to occupation. The Palestinians in Gaza were being driven from one place to another while Israel spoke of voluntary movement. Gaza was unliveable. Netanyahu's idea was to keep going in the hope the Palestinians would leave the Strip. Israel didn't know how to shut up. They were unfamiliar with *L'art de se taire* (Abbé Dinouart's famous 1771 sideswipe at those who write or talk too much or too thoughtlessly). International lawyers were talking about the possibility of proving intent to commit genocide. Could it be proven? Yes. What else could be meant by the comment that there were no innocents in Gaza or the suggestion of using nuclear weapons.

Smotrich was promoting the notion of the voluntary emigration of Palestinians as the "right solution for Palestinins and the region". Netanyahu had lobbied the EU to push for Palestinians to be accepted in the Sinai.

Al Shifa hospital was under fire between 7.30 and 9.30 GMT. It was attacked by a hundred commandos. A direct hit on the fourth floor left a half metre wide hole. The place was surrounded by tanks, snipers and drones. Snipers were aiming at medical staff. Andrew Mitchell called for hospitals and civilians to be spared. David Lammy said Israel's *modus operandi* needed to change. Mitchell, who describes himself as a "reformed establishment lackey", is best known for his work in international development where he has been relatively benign; relative, that is, to the worst of his Tory colleagues. He is, however, as has been often observed, an Establishment caricature. At Rugby, he was known as "Thrasher" for his nasty authoritarianism and even his decent work is marked by paternalism. To his credit, he has previously offered mild criticism of Israel's actions in Gaza. That he saw fit to make this intervention, however, is indicative of just how exorbitant were Israel's breaches. As for Lammy, his belated conversion was expected, given his diligent greasy-pole climbing.

Dr Ahmad Mokhallalati of Al Shifa, said there had been no water for five days. Israel was refusing permission for burials in the area. Their behaviour was totally inhuman. The world was waiting to see the Palestinians die one by one. Six neo-nates had died over the past few days. They were killed because they were Palestinians.

Mokhallalati was wrong, of course, that the Israel actions were inhuman. They were all too human. No society has ever operated without rules. Government and the State aren't necessary, but rules are. Without rules the atavistic impulses can run wild. The purpose of culture is to educate the emotions to prevent exactly that. The notion that it is intrinsically human to be fair, kind, generous and peaceable is as contentious as believing the opposite. It is living by agreed rules which limits the expression of the negative potential of our nature. Israel's actions were in keeping with the human in so far as they were permitted to live beyond the rules. Diplomatically the question of their breach of the rules of war or of international humanitarian law was moot; to any ordinary, objective citizens, they were obviously guilty.

Perhaps it's worth noting another feature of human nature: we are capable of getting on with our lives, attending to petty details, cleaning the kitchen, keeping the garden neat, while the most horrendous, hellish violence is taking place a few hours away by plane. If people in Manhattan or Paris had to go five days without water, it would be viewed as a shattering catastrophe. It can happen to Palestinians because we have failed to create a culture which properly recognises our common condition. We still make the fatal mistake of dehumanising our enemies.

Meanwhile, an Israeli spokesman said Gaza's hospitals were at risk of losing their protected status and Biden observed, dim-witted as ever, that Hamas was using hospitals for cover. Hagari asserted the hospitals were military facilities.

A raid on the Tulkarem refugee camp left seven dead. Israel claimed it was engaging in counter-terrorism.

Smotrich's rhetoric, argued Dr H.A. Hellyer of RUSI, blurred the line between civilians and soldiers. A leaked document from the Israeli Ministry of Intelligence indicated a policy of expulsion of the Palestinians. Israel was sleepwalking to this kind of policy. History showed that when Palestinians were forced to leave, they didn't return. The US was spouting fine words but doing nothing serious. It had plenty of muscle but wasn't using it. Brett McGurk was on his way, but what did that signify? Israel takes one thing into account: the price it has to pay; so far, it had got off scot-free. There was no cohesive policy in the Israeli war cabinet. Was the Palestinian Authority going to have a role in Gaza? The policies were half-baked.

The Yemeni Houthis fired five missiles at Israel. Three were injured in Tel Aviv by rockets fired from Gaza.

On 15th November Regev claimed the Israeli attacks were "as surgical as possible", which leaves you very glad he didn't train as a surgeon. Hamas argued Biden must have given the green light for the attack on Al Shifa. Martin Griffiths said he had never heard of anything similar. A hospital was not a war zone. Israeli rhetoric did not alter the well-established principle of the protection offered by international law. A ceasefire was needed for humanitarian obligations to be met. A day or two would be no good. It needed to endure. Gaza was in a parlous state prior to 7th November. Palestinians had nowhere to go. the plight of children in Gaza was the most distressing element. Love of our children should unite us. War had become a thinkable option but we seemed to have moved away from peace as the same.

Michael Howard, speaking on Radio 4, defended the 11th November march and the sacking of Braverman. Howard, hardly a friend of the Palestinians, was a voice from the Tory past, before it had begun to imitate Trump, turning itself from a serious political party into an organised insurrection. His concern was not so much for the lives of the Palestinians, as for the danger to his party from Braverman's style of unhinged rhetoric. He was right, as the elections of May 2024 were to indicate.

Mads Gilbert described what he had seen in Al Shifa as beyond his wildest fantasy. It was "medical apartheid". What was happening to babies in Gaza wouldn't befall white, blue-eyed, blonde-haired babies. Those in Al Shifa could be saved. They were being killed by racism, by "reheated colonialism". The world's leaders were "lame". Nor was what was taking place new. The Israelis had acted in the same way in Beirut in 1982. Israel's impunity was total. The IDF was shooting at everything that moved and Biden was shielding them. He could stop the killing immediately. The morality of the world was collapsing. Rules that make life possible were being destroyed by Israel. Israel was out to kill everyone in Gaza.

Gilbert's point about Biden was made over and over. He was behaving as if the Israelis had some power over him. Rather, the reality was a Kafkaesque distortion in which the power he granted them came back to render him impotent. He was intellectually and morally incapable of taking the small step of recognising that Israel was engaging in sheer gangsterism. They were no more targeting Hamas than Trump won the 2020 election.

Dr Omar Abdel-Mannan described Al Shifa as absolutely horrific. Babies had the appearance of rats. Many were doomed to die and those who lived would suffer life-long deficits. The Israeli war machine was engaged in a systematic attack on medical facilities. There was blood on the hands of the Israelis who failed to speak out. Al Shifa was a cemetery inside a concentration camp. Sunak was turning a blind eye. Infections were bound to spread. It was a man-made disaster. Doctors were heroes. They acted according to the Hippocratic oath. They would rather be bombed than leave their patients. Israel's arrogance was the result of its impunity.

The doctor might have specified it was a Zionist made disaster. What became progressively clearer was the alarming extent to which the Israelis had fallen for their own propaganda. It was hard not to conclude, as ordinary citizens expressed casually views which would have been commonplace among some of history's worst regimes, that the Israelis were a brainwashed people: the Palestinians couldn't be lived with; they were the enduring problem; we have tried everything; there is nothing for it but to be rid of them one way or another. Change Palestinian for Jew and, hey presto. Yet the psychological blindness of the people promulgating these opinions was stunning. We are angels. We have never done anything wrong. We are incapable of doing anything wrong. They are the evil which must be expunged. They were the doctors rightly described as heroes. It's alarming to think Israelis can know about doctors risking their lives rather than leave their patients, and still cling to the idea they are inferior because they are Arabs. Of course, the Israeli media made sure the people had a thoroughly distorted perspective. That's how democracy works: the rich and powerful peddle lies through the media they own and when people vote accordingly, they claim it's a free choice.

Both sides were guilty of war crimes according to Geoffrey Bindman. The IDF was in complete control of Al Shifa. Staff and patients were being questioned room by room. All the same Hagari commented no harm was being caused to civilians. Just what Orwell warned us about.

Geoffrey Bidman said there were war crimes on both sides, a view which would come into its own in May 2024 when Karim Kahn issued his call for arrest warrants. The Hamas attack on 7th October was a war crime as was Israel's bombing of Gaza, deprivation of water, food and fuel. There were not only war crimes but crimes against humanity. The number of civilians killed and the high toll of children could not meet the criterion of lawful warfare which requires proportionality and protection of civilians. Trials were possible. The ICC was investigating. Netanyahu might face arrest. The evidence was on everyone's tv screen.

The burden placed on those fighting for freedom from colonialism, occupation or oppression is enormous. They have been subjected to violence. In every case, violence is the means colonisers have employed to gain their ascendancy. Yet to use violence to resist brings the charge of war crimes. History has moved on a little, but not far enough. The Rome Statute, effectively bringing the ICC into existence, came into force in July 2002. By then, Israel had been abusing the Palestinians for fifty-four years. The Geneva Conventions were operative from October 1950. Long after the Zionists had bombed, murdered and lied their way to power. The same phenomenon is repeated at large in the "advanced" economies: capitalism established itself by force; by the time democracy was permitted, as an afterthought, the common people were already at a great disadvantage. Thus, the disadvantaged and oppressed are required to meet a moral standard their exploiters and tormenters have never reached. On the one hand, this is a crushing weight, on the other an opportunity. The Palestinians, given their plight, have behaved with remarkable fortitude and restraint.

Oxfam's Bushra Khalidi said the Palestinians were helpless. The borders of Gaza had been closed for sixteen years. The condition of the Palestinians was utterly demotivating. There was no fuel. No access for aid. People were trapped and starved. The Strip was uninhabitable. International law was clear: there was a duty to protect civilians. There had been serious breaches of international law.

Israel claimed the Gaza tunnels constituted a city beneath a city. They existed under every building. As with their assertions about hospitals being rife with Hamas fighters, they were unable to adduce serious proof.

From Al Shifa, pictures were beamed around the world of men aged sixteen to forty forced outside and onto their knees in their underwear. Obvious protection of civilians.

Hasan Barari, of the University of Jordan and the Washington Institute argued the forced removal of the Gazan population was Israel's aim. The US was unable to control Israel in spite of American public opinion trying to shift Biden. Israel had the green light from the US. It could kill civilians at will. It wanted a deal on the hostages by the Palestinians caving in.

On 15th November, the first fuel truck since 7th October entered Gaza.

Cyril Ramaphosa met the Emir of Qatar and expressed the view that the two countries shared a deep concern. They were appalled at the horror and tragedy. Those with the power must stop the crime against humanity. The situation of the Palestinians was akin to that of the coloured population of South Africa under apartheid. A referral to the ICC was possible.

Those with the power? Who else but the US and therefore Biden; but why should he stop a crime against humanity? America was founded on a crime against humanity. This was the essential dilemma: the only person with the power to end the killing at once was an old school believer in the right of angelic nations to kill who they choose. Vietnam, Iraq, Afghanistan, they may have gone badly, they may have involved tactical mistakes, but the idea they were morally beyond justification was unthinkable. What was coming into view for those who hadn't seen it long ago, was the need to thoroughly rework the world order to ensure such horrors and tragedies could happen no more.

UBU ROI

The problem began in Europe, Yanis Varoufakis claimed. There had been centuries of antisemitism. Then there was the vile Zionist doctrine of a land without people. It was the old colonialist story: Britain in Australia, Kenya, all over the globe. There had been a very long effort to rid Europe of Jews. The only answer was the end of the apartheid system. Netanyahu hated the peace process and the idea of 2-States. As for the EU, who exactly did Ursula von der Leyen represent? She had cheered Israel's war crimes. She was playing Netanyahu's game by isolating Gaza. The calls for Hamas to surrender didn't answer the question of what would happen in the West Bank if they did. Israelis claimed to be offended by the chant "from the river to the sea" but that was Netanyahu's doctrine. He wanted Palestinians removed and a Greater Israel. Von der Leyen was his useful idiot. Europe bears the responsibility for the Nazi genocide. Europeans now looked down on Arabs like they had once looked down on Jews. They saw them as infinitely inferior. He had a Jewish friend in Berlin who had been arrested for making a one-person protest. This was a morbid form of antisemitism and pointed to the end of civil liberties. The Israeli Foreign Affairs minister called Al Jazeera antisemitic. The extremists were benefitting from the tragedy in Gaza, as they always do. He had grown up under fascism. Was being critical of that regime mis-Hellenist? The conflation of criticism of Netanyahu with antisemitism was a victory for antisemitism. In France, Le Pen's supporters were wearing Israeli insignia. The same was happening in Greece and worldwide. An extremist Zionist view, that the Palestinians were intruders in Palestine and must be removed was embraced by the far-right which had traditionally been the source of antisemitism.

Guilt over the Nazi genocide has poisoned the European mind. It's right to reject the Nazi regime as morally despicable and the slaughter of Jew, Romanies, Polish Catholics, homosexuals, trade unionists, socialists as one of history's most appalling crimes; but it's a terrible mistake to believe in the virtue of the victim. Virtue does not inhere in victimhood, it's a matter of choice. Victims are perfectly capable of behaving badly. The Zionists have done so by misusing the Nazi genocide to promote the empty notion that Judaism and Israel are identical, and to press on from there to the fascistic conclusion that any criticism of Israel is tantamount to Nazism. This is where the acute sensitivity in Europe arises: people fear being associated with the gas chambers if they criticise Netanyahu or Ben Gvir or Smotrich or for that matter Ben Gurion or Begin. Hence the profound irony that people give an easy ride to fascists out of anxiety about being thought of as fascists. People were being massacred in Gaza because they were Arabs, just like Jews died in the death camps because they were Jews. There was absolute identity. The Israelis found the excuse: all Palestinians are terrorists, just like the Nazis: all Jews are fat bankers who ruined the economy of the Weimar Republic.

In the common conception also, the State of Israel was seen as a reward to the Jews for their terrible suffering at the hands of the Nazis; but this is to exaggerate. Herzl conceived a Jewish State when Hitler was in short lederhosen. It was an act of defeatism and intrinsically antisemitic: all Jews are the same and they can't live with gentiles. Out of this confusion comes the stodgy notion that to defend Israel at all costs is to stand with the oppressed, the victims, to set your face against racism, and thus to take Israel to task is align yourself with neo-Nazis. Hence we have the obscene spectacle of precisely neo-Nazis, hiding themselves behind the shallow respectability of suits, soundbites and electioneering, waving the Israeli flag, while the Israeli right disdains the leftists and liberals who have traditionally faced down antisemites.

Martin Griffiths called for more UNRWA shelters in southern Gaza; improved humanitarian notifications to deconflict certain areas; more distribution hubs; civilians to be allowed to move to safety and to return to their homes; funding of $1.2 billion for immediate help and a humanitarian ceasefire.

Hearing such calls from people like Griffiths was always like imagining someone appealing to Stalin to spare the Kulaks or Pinochet to respect democracy or for that matter Trump to accept election results. Everyone knows how impossible it is to reason with a bigot or to keep a wilful thug from violence. That was what was being played out internationally: a small group of bigoted thugs who had control of a State because they had been woefully indulged by the "international community" for decades was deaf to every plea. Griffiths might as well have tried to cajole Lady Macbeth to recognise the moral depravity of murder. Yet, what else could he do?

Netanyahu visited a military base in southern Israel where he said there was no hiding place for Hamas. He had two sacred goals one of which was to annihilate all Hamas fighters. Gantz echoed his words, saying there was no sanctuary for them. Wherever Hamas operates, Netanyahu promised, it will be taken out. The families of hostage needed answers.

Beyond chutzpah. There were obviously plenty of hiding places for Hamas. More than eleven thousand Palestinians had been killed, according to the Gaza Health Ministry, but how much nearer was the defeat of Hamas? The IDF was a long way from killing all Hamas operatives, and that was merely in Gaza, a tiny strip of land. The notion that Israel had to capacity to hunt down and kill Hamas members anywhere in the world was fanciful. What would Netanyahu have done had some of them found refuge in South Africa? The bluster, braggadocio, arrogance and fantasy omnipotence of Netanyahu were straight out of *Ubu Roi*. As for answers for the families, Netanyahu was using them as pawns in a typically cynical political game. They could have been released on 8th October. While they were held, he had a lifeline. Even the Israeli public was coming to terms with Netanyahu's depravity.

Jordan declared Israel a terror State and Turkey, Hamas a liberation group.

Marwan Bishara said withholding fuel was collective punishment. Israel's grounds for keeping it back were feeble. Where was the UN? People were slow-walking around the fact of mass deaths. Hamas had offered to accept independent observers in Al Shifa. Israel knew its claims were a sham. The US was complicit in Israel's crimes. The attacks on hospitals, the killing of children were sanctioned by the US the UK and other Israeli allies.

The UN Security Council voted for a ceasefire, with, inevitably, the US abstaining. Israel ignored it. Gilad Ardan complained the resolution made no mention of 7th October. Hamas, he said, was starving its people and forcibly holding them as human shields in hospitals. Israel was doing all it could to improve the humanitarian situation. Hamas was solely responsible for the terrible events. Israel always obeyed international law. The hostages were its priority. This resolution would have no traction with the terrorists. Israel had no choice. Hamas was intent on genocide. If Hamas surrendered, the war would be over. Oh, and the dog ate his homework.

On the same day, the Dail defeated a Social Democrat motion calling for the expulsion of the Israeli Ambassador, Dana Erlich. Such a motion would have been unthinkable in the US Congress and more or less so in the House of Commons. Ireland, with its history of colonial oppression was aligned with the global south for whom the usual big power rhetoric of democracy and human rights rings thoroughly hollow.

Israel produced an image of what it claimed was military equipment in Al Shifa. It had he appearance of a squaddy's kit laid out for inspection by the sergeant major.

Defying their leader, who since his election to the position had sounded like a loyal member of Likud, fifty-six Labour MPs voted for a ceasefire. Eight front benchers either resigned or lost their positions: Jess Phillips, Afza Khan, Yasmin Qureshi, Paula Barker, Sarah Owens, Rachel Hopkins, Naz Shah and Andy Slaughter. The resolution, advanced by the SNP, was lost by two hundred and ninety-four votes to one hundred and twenty-five. A hundred and forty-one Labour MPs abstained. Two hundred and eighty-eight Tories voted against. Given that an abstention was a vote for the continued decimation of the Gazan population, nearly four hundred out of six hundred and fifty MPs voted for Israel to continue murdering civilians in spite of two-thirds of the population being in favour of a ceasefire. Such is representative democracy. A quick way to improve it would be instant recall. If all those Labour MPs, and some Tories, had faced rapid removal by their constituents, the result would have been very different. Parliament is a place where interest trumps principle.

Rachel Reeves, who once showed the depths of her anti-racism by claiming she didn't look like "a typical Jew", presumably a hooked nose, a fat cigar and pockets stuffed with lucre, remarked: "Sir Keir wants to act like a Prime Minister in waiting and that means aligning ourselves with the international community and taking practical steps to get support into Gaza whilst also putting pressure on Hamas to release the hostages." Ms Reeves seems to have been purblind to the "international community" being heavily in favour of a ceasefire. That includes, of course, the global south. Presumably what she meant was the US. Nor did she suggest any pressure should be put on Israel to release those held under "administrative detention" or to stop shooting people in the West Bank, or to remove the illegal settlements or to lift the blockade of Gaza or to create a link between the two. The Labour Party, having defamed and marginalised its most consistent anti-racist, was in the hands of a pair of sycophantic apologists for Israeli supremacism. In the name of eradicating antisemitism, the Party was fully supportive of a State whose essential doctrine subsumed all Jews to the same category and dismissed those who refused to conform as "self-hating".

Netanyahu declared, with typical modesty, "they said we couldn't and we did," an assertion of Israel's right to defy international law. Meanwhile, Biden declared himself "mildly hopeful" about the hostages, a significant step back from his previous confidence. John Healey, defence spokesman, citing no particular evidence, claimed weapons were hidden in hospital areas and there were "ammunition dumps amongst civilians" Lucy Willimason, reporting for the BBC, said she had been forbidden to speak to doctors or patients in Al Shifa. In the ICU the petty kit was laid out. Laptops had been found and the IDF was going to assess what they contained. Hamas had been there in the last few days was the assertion, but there was no proof. The IDF spokesman argued Hamas had taken most of their equipment away. Thus, the position was that because there was military equipment, Hamas must have been there, but there was very little because they'd removed most. It was now, apparently, hidden in tunnels. Boxes supposedly containing weapons were found to house medical supplies, the contents being marked on the outside in English. The fact was, the IDF was in control and was aware of and getting sensitive to criticism over incubators being out of use and food being held back.

Speaking on Radio 4's *Today* programme on 16th November, Obama's ex-National Security Adviser said there was some distance between the US and Israel. Embracing Netanyahu hadn't worked. He was a loose cannon. Private messages were no good. The US needed to withdraw some support from Israel. During the Obama years, Netanyahu had no confidence in the president. Nothing in the past fifteen years gave any reason to believe Netanyahu was willing to listen. He needed the war to go on. He presented himself as "Mr Security" yet had presided over a serious breach. The same was true of the far-right. When was the "day after" going to arrive ? Biden was backing the Palestinian Authority but Netanyahu wanted Israel to be in control. The US was supporting a possibly endless military operation. Embracing Netanyahu in public and trying to make him listen in private didn't work.

It was asserted many times that Netanyahu needed the war to continue but less often that he needed it to begin. Over a month into the massacre there had been no serious investigations into what Israel knew and when, nor into how many of the dead on 7th October had been killed by the IDF. It was, of course, obvious Netanyahu was unamenable to Biden's foolish strategy of praising him publicly while trying to persuade him behind the scenes: Biden was being manipulated by the arch-manipulator and was blind to it because of his arrogance and ignorance. His historic support of every Israeli move was indicative of his thoroughly sentimental, weak-minded view of how Israel came into existence and had maintained its position as the oppressor of the Palestinians. Biden was faced with thoroughgoing evil but was unable to see even the least fault due to his absurd parti pris. It was no exaggeration to say Netanyahu was willing to see tens and maybe hundreds of thousands slaughtered for the sake of his ambition, hardly anything new; but Biden was unable to see him in the same light as history's murderous monsters because of his Noddy and Big ears conception of Israel.

NO WORDS

At a fundraising event on 12th December 2023, Biden spoke of "indiscriminate bombing" and recounted his old saw about having inscribed a photo to Netanyahu: "Bibi, I don't agree with a damn thing you say." "That," he told his audience, "remains to be the case." The next day, unsurprisingly, John Kirby and Matthew Miller began to pick the thorns from the president's barb. The first mention of "indiscriminate bombing" came, however, almost a month earlier on 16th November. On that occasion, Biden muddied the waters after his remark by, apparently, claiming it had to be seen in the light of the evidence of Hamas fighters in Al Shifa.

Erik Fosse, surgeon and founder of the Norwegian Aid Committee who has worked extensively in Gaza, pointed out there was no gunfight when the IDF entered Al Shifa, hardly consistent with the place being wick with Hamas fighters. Throughout the Israel massacre, rational voices like Fosse were pointing up the obvious, reiterating truisms, demolishing with the most simple arguments the dispiriting Israeli lies; yet it made very little difference. The loud voice was the US and it had no concern for reason. Its business was power. From the most trivial domestic tiff to the most disastrous international conflict, the pattern is the same: power ignores reason, denies evidence and asserts what it likes.

The hospital's infrastructure was down, Fosse reported. The IDF were loitering in the hospital. There were more than six hundred and fifty patients. Israel had made the same allegations in 2008, 2009 and 2014. Fosse was there for one or two stints per year. He was able to move freely. He had never seen any sign of Hamas fighters, nor was there any evidence of the existence of a command centre. The IDF had targeted an oxygen facility. Hagari's claims couldn't be proven.

Jake Sullivan declared there would be no Israeli occupation of Gaza. To show they understood their American masters, the IDF began raising Israeli flags on Palestinian territory.

A Kayum Ahmed of Human Rights Watch pointed out Palestinians were using hospital as shelters. HRW contested Israel's view (making it, of course, a vile proponent of antisemitism). As of 10th November, eighteen hospitals had been forced to shut. Israel's alleged evidence needed to be verified. Even if it was, it didn't justify an attack on the entire health system. Israel's actions were disproportionate. The laws of might could justify shooting a sniper found in a hospital but not an attack on an entire hospital.

Thomas McManus, an expert in international State crime of Queen Mary University, London, explained hospitals could lose their protected status if the facts proved they were putting the opposing army at risk (which, of course, they were in Gaza as the survival of any injured child was obviously deeply antisemitic and an act of terrorism.) The principle of proportionality had to be respected. Israel was obliged not to attack hospitals but to keep them running. On 3rd November, ambulances had been hit by Israeli fire. Targeting ambulances was a war crime, as was stopping supplies. The facts on the ground were irrefutable. Israel was guilty. He wasn't hopeful.

Not being hopeful was a wonderful bit of litotes. No rational person could see what was happening in Gaza and not despair. The worst in human nature was on display. It could be stopped instantly by one phone call. The most powerful person in the world refused to make it. Not since Titus Andronicus served up his enemies to their mother in a pie had the world seen such unhinged cruelty. Shakespeare's villain is an example of a simple truth: we are capable of the most depraved violence, dishonesty and nastiness unless our emotions are educated towards civilised responses. What gets in the way is the moral pride of those who define themselves as virtuous, as the rich and powerful always do.

Israel bombed a desalination plant on 16th November. Presumably, Hamas fighters were beneath the water with breathing equipment. Josep Borrel called for the protection of civilians, somewhat like asking Herod to protect children. Lazzarini said UNRWA's operation was being strangled, which no doubt had Netanyahu dancing a jig. Yair Lapid made a feeble call for Netanyahu to be ditched; his majority was secure and there were no serious cracks in the administration. The World Food Programme said seventeen per cent of Palestinians in the Gaza Strip had potable water. The danger of starvation was imminent. Eleven thousand three hundred had been killed. Jabalia was bombed again.

Jeremy Bowen reported on 17th November that it was hard to know exactly what was going on because journalists were not allowed to work in Gaza. The IDF was still searching for evidence in Al Shifa but had found nothing convincing. What was supposed to be a tunnel entrance was a service pipe, there was nothing to support the claim the hospital was a command centre. Netanyahu simply says it is. The civilian death toll was so high it was causing concern to the US, which was the only power Israel worried about. The Security Council resolution of 15th November had passed without the US using its veto: twelve for, none against, and three abstentions (guess who?). The Elders, the group brought into being by Nelson Mandela in 2007 to work for peace, justice and sustainability issued a statement condemning Hamas but arguing that destroying Gaza did not make Israel safer. The calls for a ceasefire were steadily growing.

Netanyahu has grown so used to being able to make any assertion he fancies without the least supporting evidence, it's surprising he doesn't claim the earth is flat. This is what happens when people are exempt from conversation, which is the primary means by which those too big for their boots are put in their place. Our global political processes are inimical to conversation. The people are spoken at and the ways they are permitted to respond are stage-managed and empty. The Israelis are an extreme example of prejudice being free to flood all public space. No one would expect a child permitted to hit her siblings or friends without rebuke to turn out restrained. The child, Israel, born in 1948, has been woefully indulged with the inevitable result: Netanyahu saying whatever is convenient.

The US might have been the only power the Israelis worried about, but they didn't worry much. Why did they need to when the country was run by a moral half-wit and they could hope that by January 2025 it would be in the hands of a psychopath? There was a moral constituency in America, but it was nowhere near Congress. It was found on the campuses and among ignored communities. The US being the country where the propaganda system has been perfected, the ideas and feelings of the meddlesome masses are kept in severe check. To listen to the State's spokespeople, you would have believed the US populace was fully behind the Israeli slaughter. In fact, polling showed support for a ceasefire was consistently well above fifty percent.

What made the Elders believe Israel was pursuing safety? That was, of course, what it had to claim, but it had always sought peril as a proof of its status of victim and its claim the world was trying to destroy it. The path to security had been available to Israel for decades. It had refused to take it because there is no reason for a Jewish State if Jews are safe. The Zionist claim has to be Jews are never safe and if Jews and Israel mean the same thing, Israel must never be safe. Logically, if Israel devoured the entire world, it would then have to devour itself, because to face no existential threat removes its need to exist. Israel's desire is not safety, but power. Its aim is not peace but endless conflict. Otherwise, why not achieve peace and safety by sharing Palestine with the Palestinians in a democratic society of equal rights for all? Well, only because all Palestinians are terrorists who want to roast Jewish babies for breakfast.

Josep Borrell travelled to Israel where he met the families of the hostages. He was to move on to Qatar. Peace negotiations were in the balance. A peace process was vital. The Army couldn't guarantee security. The cycle of violence had to be ended once and for all. Peace negotiations had to involve the Palestinians. Gaza after the war could not be rebuilt on the basis of forced displacement, nor reduction of the territory, nor occupation, nor rule by Hamas. The Palestinian Authority must play a major role defined by the UN Security Council and supported by the international community. The Palestinian Authority needed to be stronger. The settler violence in the West Bank had to stop. The Arab countries must be involved, as must the EU, in rebuilding Gaza physically and politically. War has rules. Hospitals can't be attacked. There was a deepening humanitarian crisis.

Two tankers of fuel per day were arriving in Gaza providing sixty thousand litres, some six percent of the pre 7th October amount. Ben Gvir and Smotrich were opposed to even this petty provision, claiming it was giving life to Hamas. It was a wonder they didn't call for the sun to be shut down for the same reason.

Meanwhile, San Francisco State bridge was blocked for four hours by protesters as the Biden administration exerted pressure for fuel to be supplied. It was reported too that the IDF was getting worried about the spread of disease: there was a need for minimal sanitation if Israeli soldiers were not to be at risk. Palestinians dying of horrible infections was, of course, only to be expected. On 17th November, South Korean activists displayed two thousand shoes as a symbol of the Palestinian suffering. Twenty-five hospitals and two hundred and fifty medical facilities were out of service.

Abbas appealed to Borrell for the EU to do more. The EU was divided. Mohammad Shtayyeh, Palestinian Prime Minister, said it was a pity Borrell didn't see Gaza through the eyes of the Palestinians. Two hundred and fifty-one houses had been destroyed. The south of the Strip was a concentration camp. Water pipes were empty. Electricity was scarce. One thousand five hundred were buried under the rubble. Two hundred and three had been killed in the West Bank. In Hebron, the IDF had opened fire on and stopped ambulances. Thirty-six UN Special Rapporteurs had signed a declaration of the "failure of the international system."

On the contrary, the international system was functioning exactly as intended: the poor were getting slaughtered and the rich getting away with it. Evoking the "international system", what the SRs meant was acceptance of the rule of law and its equitable application. That has never been the international order since the State made its appearance. There has to be a pretence of such, just as all villains must claim moral legitimacy; because we are moral creatures by nature. This doesn't mean, unfortunately, we are instinctively and inescapably morally valid. Many creatures, though they may have some degree of choice and creativity, are forced to live within very narrow limits. Whales can't survive out of the water. The same is true of us to some extent. However, we have evolved to be moral, which means to make choices. If we couldn't behave badly we couldn't behave well. Were we locked into good behaviour it wouldn't be moral. There is no morality in the behaviour of a boa constrictor: it does what it must to survive. In that sense, a boa constrictor is always well-behaved, even when it squeezes the air out of you and makes you its dinner. It has no choice. Even psychopaths know choice is inevitable. Lady Macbeth understands she and her husband have to appear moral, as all dictators, tyrants and brutes. The international order, based on supremacism, violence and unprincipled pursuit of lucre, can't present itself as it is; it must claim it upholds a system of rules and applies them without fear or favour. When the US was dropping napalm on peasants in Vietnam it was virtuous because they were communists, or communist sympathisers or maybe just unlucky "collateral damage". The important point is the virtuous are allowed to use as much violence, as many lies and as much manipulation as they need. A person convinced of their virtue is dangerous, a State convinced of it is always threatening Armageddon.

The SRs were taking the notion of an "international system" seriously. A shoddy simulacrum does exist, but we have to think like Pollyanna to imagine it prevails. What rules is brute force and in Gaza, that was working marvellously.

John Entwistle of the Red Cross said he was running out of words. There was no fuel, bakeries were closing, water filtration was failing, there were no medical supplies.

Entwistle's point is a good one. Words poured out. Millions and millions. Calls for a ceasefire, for humanity, for aid. Many of them were diplomatic. Diplomatic language is based on a broad acceptance of the existing order. By definition, therefore, it can't gain much purchase. What needed to be said about Gaza required artistic means, a Sophocles, a Seneca or a Shakespeare at his best. The fate of

Oedipus doesn't make us believe there is a benign international order, nor does *King Lear* reassure us about universal human rights. If art has any power to change us, it might be through cathartic shock: Shakespeare doesn't let us off the hook. "This is what you are like," he tells us as we watch Gloucester's eyes being gouged out. Entwistle's frustration came from his position as an aid worker required to speak in measured terms. It isn't possible to be measured about the horror of Israel's persecution of the Palestinians. It is thoroughgoing evil and we should set it down than men may smile and smile and be villains.

There was a protest in Hebron and a rally in Amman. Some were allowed to leave the Strip by the Rafah crossing: the wounded, cancer patients and foreign passport holders. Ehud Olmert said there should be no Palestinian State because, "We have a different self-image of what we are as human beings," a remark whose depths of supremacism, arrogance and delusion can barely be plumbed.

Mustafa Barghouti accused Israel of invading West Bank cities. Two had recently been killed in Hebron, three in Jenin. The settlers were terrorising the population. Fifty-five communities had been evicted, two hundred and thirteen had been killed, nine by settlers. They were free to do what the liked. The West Bank was split into two hundred and twenty-four pieces, in other words Bantustans. The were six hundred and fifty check points. Movement was very difficult. The US was exerting no real influence. The West Bank was ruled by Smotrich and Ben Gvir. The options were leave, die or accept subjugation. The US was imposing no sanctions on Israel. Hamas had to be eliminated, in Israel and the US's view, but it was the PLO which represented the Palestinian people. It was important not to confuse resisting the occupation and support for Hamas. If there were an immediate election neither Hamas nor Fatah would win. The

Palestinians had a right to democracy but Netanyahu had spent thirty years wilfully destroying the Oslo accords. The attainment of two State required the fulfilment of an indispensable condition: the removal of the illegal settlements.

Being free to do what you like sounds marvellous. It is the one rule in Rabelais's Abbé Thélème: Do What You Like. Of course, Rabelais made an assumption: no one would have power over anyone else. That should have been his first rule. With that in place, the second is benign. In a world order based on the right of the rich to employ extreme violence, it's a disaster. Israel is unique. There have been many societies which have viewed themselves as angelic. It's a feature of power that it garlands itself with righteousness. Yet there may be no historical example quite like Israel: a society brought into existence by supremacism and terrorism and propped up by the most powerful nations which not only excuse its every crime but view them as proof of progress.

Leave, die or accept subjugation, these have been the options of the poor for centuries which is why Israel is so symbolic: if the Palestinians overcome their subjugation, is the game up for the rich? While Israel in its current iteration exists, the message to those who resist the power of super-wealthy, super-armed States is clear. The most powerful leaders who claimed to believe in two States were not willing to vote for recognition of Palestine in the UN, let alone twist Israel's arm to make it obey international law. The rule is very simple: we believe in international law, but not yet, in democracy, but not for you, in liberty, but not for those who don't agree with us. In other words, we believe in gangsterism, tyranny and thought-control.

AMALEK

Speaking on MSNBC hosted by Mehdi Hasan, on 16th November, Regev explained something about 7th October: ".. we'd over-estimated. We made a mistake. There were actually bodies which were so badly burned we thought they were ours; in the end, apparently, they were Hamas terrorists.". You might have expected the media to leap on this: Israel was admitting its claims about deaths on 7th October were wrong. Curious also that being badly burned meant that the bodies must be Israeli. What weapons did the Hamas fighters have which could have caused such damage? Hamas fighters were so badly burned they were almost unrecognisable, which meant they must have been hit by serious Israeli fire. How many of the dead were killed this way? How many of their own did Israel massacre?

The US had to play up the brutality of the Hamas incursion and the innocence of Israel to justify the unjustifiable. Not only was it important to begin history on 7th October, it was also vital to distort even that so the world could divide between the good guys and the bad guys. Just as in the old cowboy films the only good Indian was a dead Indian, so in the fantasy version of 7th October every Israeli was killed by the evil Hamas enemy and virtuous Israel was defending itself against an unmotivated assault. An interesting point was made some months later: when the IRA bombed the British mainland, the UK government didn't respond by flattening Londonderry. Were the Birmingham pub bombings acts of war or criminality? Did they come out of nowhere? Was it simply the ingrained evil of the perpetrators which explained the events?

Abu Obaida, spokesman for the al-Qassam brigades, claimed sixty-two Israeli tanks had been destroyed and

Hamas was ready for a long war. Music to Netanyahu's ears. Meanwhile, an Israeli defence official said it would be impossible to keep up the assault if there was an epidemic in Gaza. No doubt if a virus had taken hold, Netanyahu would have condemned it as antisemitic. Rockets were fired from Gaza towards Tel Aviv but, as usual were intercepted by the US-funded Iron Dome. The World Food Programme said only ten per cent of the food needed was getting through. Martin Griffiths said "without doubt there is a humanitarian crisis", it was "intolerable" the fighting had to stop.

Unfortunately, Griffiths was quite wrong. It was anything but intolerable. Not only was the massacre tolerated by Biden, the EU and other powerful leaders, it was celebrated in some of the most comfortable quarters on the planet. The US Republicans delighted in the cruelty. The UK Tories were quite happy to go on providing weapons, on the grounds they constituted a small proportion of the total, no doubt very comforting for the victims. As for the far-right on the march across the globe and particularly menacingly in Europe, they waved the Israeli flag with glee in spite of their historic association with antisemitism and the Nazi genocide. Every time people like Griffiths used words like "intolerable", and there were many well-intentioned who did it over and over, they were expressing their belief in a set of values which was being shredded in Gaza, at the behest of the world's most powerful military and with the collusion of most of the rich.

The WHO declared Gaza a crisis for the UN. There was an increasing incidence of diarrhoea, skin diseases. There were no words to describe the horror. Biden called the Emir of Qatar, a feeble intervention given the leverage he might have used, calling for release of the hostages and complaining the flow of aid was too slow. Think back to "shock and awe". Brown University estimates the war cost the US in excess of $1 trillion. Bush didn't make a few polite phone calls. Unhinged violence was unleashed because the US believed its interests were in play. All that was required in Gaza was the withholding of weapons and money and tens of thousands of lives could have been spared, but like the Iraqis butchered in 2003 the Palestinians had the wrong colour hair and eyes.

In East Jerusalem, water canon and tear gas were used against Al Aqsa worshippers. People were forced to pray on the street. Al Jazeera's camera team was tear-gassed, proving once more Israel is the only democracy in the Middle East.

A one-hour warning to leave Al Shifa was issued on 18th November. The IDF was questioned about the humanity of this by the BBC but offered no response. Journalists were not allowed to report. The IDF tried to recruit aid groups to assist in clearing Al Shifa. At least two thousand wounded and displaced were sheltering in the hospital.

UNRWA's Juliette Touma called Gaza a man-made horror-show. Only a tiny shipment of fuel had been received in the last few days. Humanitarian work was becoming impossible. Very late on the previous night communications had been restored. Living in Gaza without means of communication was terrifying.

The Al Fakhoura school in Jabalia was bombed and two hundred killed as Netanyahu quoted Samuel, Chapter Fifteen: "Now go and strike Amalek and devote to destruction all they have." Clearly, he believed he was involved in a religious war, but the idea is absurd. He was simply making use of the Bible to justify colonial occupation. To pretend a connection between today's Palestinians and the Amalek of the Bible is risible. There is no convincing historical or archaeological evidence for the existence of the Amelakites as Netanyahu is probably aware.

The Biblical story provides cover for bad behaviour, something everyone wishes for. Mostly, people want cover for minor misdemeanours: being lazy about the housework or spending too much on booze; but the trick is the same as with psychopathic behaviour. Did Netanyahu know he was lying? Of course, like every tyrant or power-grabber. It isn't possible to tell the truth and have power over others because authority which is consented to leaves potency with those who give consent. Power and lying go hand in hand. Netanyahu's grasping at a Biblical verse was the desperation of man sunk in evil. A composite text written hundreds of years after the event would be no prop for a rational mind. It was in Netanyahu's interest to pretend a religious war was under way: the angels on one side the devil on the other. Religion being a matter of faith, it has no requirement to rest on evidence: but the law is not a matter of faith. Whatever is written in the Bible or any sacred text, Israel was the illegal occupier and in Gaza was committing multiple war crimes and crimes against humanitarian law. Amalek was nowhere in sight.

Rabbi Alissa Wise called Netanyahu's comment an "unambiguous genocidal statement". Nadim Nahif, the digital rights expert, said social media were awash with observations of the same kind. A spokesman for the Israeli government on the other hand said there were no civilians, no innocents, only two and half million terrorists.

Thousands fled the Al Shifa compound heading south to the so-called safe areas. Homes were bombed in Khan Younis, designated safe. Sixty were killed. Biden opined that the West Bank and Gaza should be united under a revitalised Palestinian Authority. There must be no forceable removal of the population but neither should there be a ceasefire. As ever, his absolute refusal to blame Israel for anything meant there was no possibility of a resolution. A Reuters poll indicated sixty eight percent support for a ceasefire among Americans and an Ipsos poll that thirty-eight per cent thought the US should support Israel.

There were protests in Sidon, Paris, London, Santiago and Brasilia, in front of the US embassy.

Haaretz for 18th November published a piece arguing Israeli helicopter fire may have killed some of the revellers at the 7th October rave. Once again, something which might have expected to cause a bit of a media stir. However, as Gideon Levy, a leading Haaretz writer commented. Israeli media did not expose the people to the horror of Gaza. The lives of most Israelis were jogging along peacefully. Things weren't so bad.

Basma al Sharif, the Palestinian film-maker spoke of the protests at the start of the Amsterdam documentary film festival when the organisers banned the use of the slogan "From the river to the sea". As usual, the most far-gone interpretation was applied to the chant: all those who use it want to eliminate Jews from Palestine, and by implication from the world. Odd that people evoked the possibility of slaughter of the Jewish people while Palestinians were being butchered every day. This is not to play down the Nazi genocide or historical antisemitism, but where in the world in November 2023 were Jews facing annihilation? The Zionist misuse of the Nazi genocide to turn Jews into the eternal victim, ever able to demand special treatment, ever on the verge of disappearance was behind the misinterpretation. What people were demanding was an end to the violence and equality for Israelis and Palestinians. Had they chanted, "From our breakfast to our tea, Palestine will be free" the Zionists would have called it antisemitic.

The WHO called Al Shifa a "death zone". In Khan Younis there were multiple air strikes. The European hospital south of Khan Younis was bombed. Jenin was raided at 1 a.m.

Abbas asked Biden to stop the genocide. He had a special responsibility. He could awaken the world's conscience. Only the US could stop the killing, it was the biggest sponsor of Israel in every way.

Biden might have awakened the world's conscience, if he'd had one of his own. It would have required the most minimal moral reasoning to recognise the only way to act, having the power to do so, was to stop the fighting and start the talking. Biden's conscience was truly American; we pretend to uphold objective standards and impersonal values until our interests are touched, then we respond with maximum violence and ignore every restraint. What Biden couldn't grasp, lacking both imagination and the intellectual capacity, was that this doctrine had shaped the world for decades. Putin was applying it, but not with the ferocity of the US in Iraq. The Chinese were employing it, with a conflagration over Taiwan the likely outcome. Why shouldn't everyone employ it, as the world's greatest military power was setting the standard?

The US denied it had made an agreement with Qatar and Israel for a pause in order to get hostages released. Negotiations were ongoing. No deal had been reached. Biden published an op-ed in the Washington Post arguing Hamas had to go, its leadership had to surrender.

The US had to use violence to throw off British colonialism. I wonder if Biden believes his forbears should have surrendered.

Abdehamid Siyan of Rutgers commented that the standing of the US was very low in the Arab world. It needed to do something blatant. If it stopped the war, if there was a real pause, it's position might improve. Talk of two States had gone on forever. Resolution 1397 was passed in 2002 and we were still waiting (the resolution in question called for the Palestinians to cease attacking Israel and for the latter to end the occupation). The US had done nothing to bring two States nearer. It had no plan. Gaza was changing the whole world but the root causes were not being addressed. Only the US could dictate to Israel, but look what happened; the 1991 Madrid conference for example.

If you own a shotgun and are prepared to use it, while your neighbours are unarmed, why would you worry too much about how they view you, unless you're interested in friendship rather than power. Power is the US's drug and it has been an addict since the Monroe Doctrine. Further, a supremacists mentality so ingrained you don't need to think about it is unlikely to make you anxious about how your obvious inferiors see you.

Israeli historian Omer Bartov predicted that forcing Palestinians to the south of the Strip would cause huge congestion and was tantamount to ethnic cleansing which would in turn lead to genocide. A pogrom in the West Bank was under way prior to 7th October. Hamas's attack had been dubbed a pogrom by an American commentator. The IHRA definition of antisemitism had given rise to the Jerusalem Declaration. Antisemitism was being weaponised to defend the Israeli State.

The somewhat slippery meaning of pogrom permits its frequent misuse; but as a violent riot intended to remove or intimidate a particular population, it seems appropriate for the settlers' actions in the West Bank. Applying it to the Hamas assault of 7th October is more problematic: as a nuclear-armed State with a huge army, Israel wasn't seriously threatened by an incursion from a relatively small number of fighters, fairly crudely armed. The Hamas action was more akin to a criminal act than anything as comprehensive as an attack on an entire population.

Stephanie Fox of Jewish Voice for Peace complained that the use of "human animals" to describe the Palestinians was deeply dehumanising. 7th October had been caused by Israel's "system of violence". Many were calling for a ceasefire and an end to the root cause: seventy-five years of violence and emergency. Adam Shatz argued that from the start Israel had abused Jewish suffering. Jews were taught that the Palestinians were the rightful inheritors of the blame for the Nazi genocide and the Palestinian desire for autonomy was wrongly portrayed as hatred of Jews. Pastor John Hagee, one of the US's most powerful antisemites was now an advocate for Israel. Marjorie Taylor Greene had moved a censure motion against Rashida Tlaib on the grounds that a rally for peace she organised in Congress was incitement to insurrection and antisemitic. Members of the Anti-Defamation League were shouting down Jews calling for peace.

Omar Baddar argued Israel's fantasy was to be rid of the Palestinians in Gaza. The genocidal intent was clear. Soon, Gaza would be unfit for human habitation. If what was happening went on long enough, it would be genocide. Amos Goldberg claimed the IHRA definition was "catastrophic"; it was an intentional confusion about antisemitism. Playing with the definition of antisemitism was dangerous. Under siege Gaza effectively had no economy. It had no seaport or airport nor any right to trade freely let alone a right to defence. An Israeli source had spoken of "a unique and rare opportunity to evacuate the entire population." Whenever Israel attacks, there is an increase in antisemitism. Israel was less interested in fighting antisemitism than in advancing the Israeli State.

Everything genuine can be made phoney. Hence, genuine belief in democracy and opposition to violent insurrection can become Taylor Greene's utterly insincere claim. She knew she was lying. Honesty has no traction when power is at stake. In December 2022, in comments which she later claimed were mere sarcasm, Greene said if she and Bannon had organised the January 6th assault on the Capitol, they would have won and would have been armed. Thus, a woman who celebrates Trump's attempt to subvert a free and fair election claims a peaceful rally in support of ending violence is insurrection. You have to marvel at the mind's capacity for duplicity. Which raises the crucial point: as we are easily capable of radical dishonesty, there is a moral imperative to resist it; an imperative which exists only because the evil is possible. People convinced of their virtue are prone, by definition, to neglect their capacity for moral depravity, which explains the likes of Taylor Greene.

Mads Gilbert accused the IDF of killing patients in Gaza hospitals. Thirty-one premature babies were moved to the Emirati. There were two hundred and fifty critically injured in Al Shifa, unable to leave, most unable to walk. The IDF ordered evacuation. Israel failed to approve Red Cross movements across Gaza.

The Yemeni Houthis seized the Galaxy Leader, a ship owned by an Israeli capitalist but registered in Britain and Japanese-operated in the Red Sea on 19th November. Israel promptly blamed Iran. Four days earlier, the UN Security Council passed a Malta-proposed resolution calling for a humanitarian pause. The US, the UK and Russia abstained, the first two because it didn't condemn Hamas, the latter because it didn't call for an immediate and long-term ceasefire. In other words, because they couldn't get their own way. In Tokyo there was a pro-Palestinian rally, in Paris a silent march by the artistic community. France offered places in its hospitals for Palestinian children from Gaza.

Daniel Levy claimed the Israeli government had the US under its control. The US was working against a ceasefire. There was a trickle of aid and a flood of weapons. US leaders may ultimately face trial. Hezbollah was calibrating its response. A wider war was possible either by premeditation or happenstance. Israel was currently tied down in the north. It had a chance to draw the US further into the morass. There was no possibility of a return to the situation pre 7th October. Israel was trying to do the impossible. The US was in a trap of its own making, its stance was illogical, it was the enabler of apartheid.

Levy articulated what many had said: the US, supposedly the world's super-power, the State which prided itself on being pushed around by no one, was being dangled on a string by a pipsqueak country run by an arch manipulator in hock to far-right demagogues. It was pitiful to behold, like seeing a parent have their bank account cleared by a wayward teenager. Biden's pathological inability to see any fault in Israel led him to a position of utter weakness, while wallowing in the illusion he was in control. His power to force Israel to end the violence was beyond question as Israel's dependence on the US was enormous. He could have proved himself a statesman by quietly twisting Netanyahu's arm,ending the killing and bringing everyone to the negotiating table. Instead, he was committing slow political suicide as his poll numbers slipped and the young, especially the students who took the rational and principled stance he was incapable of, peeled away.

Levy was right too about Israel and the impossible. Israel is an impossibilist endeavour because it tries to be both a thoroughgoing democracy and a quasi-theocracy. John Kerry, as Obama's Secretary of State, pointed out Israel had to choose between being a democracy or a Jewish State. Imagine the UK declared itself a Christian State and denied full citizenship to all non-Christians. You can hear the howls of "antisemitism" from every Jewish organisation. They would be quite right. Yet Israel denies full citizenship to Christians, Muslims, Hindus, Sikhs, and atheists other than secular Jews and is simultaneously lauded as the Middle East's only democracy.

BRAVO !

H.A.Hellyer of RUSI argued there had been no decision to regionalise the fighting, but there was "high recklessness". The risk of quick extension wasn't taken seriously. Things could be out of control in no time. There were sure to be more deaths in the West Bank. Washington and the UK were behaving nonchalantly. There was dysfunction in their governments. The priority before 7th October had been "normalisation". Smotrich and Gvir wanted expansion of the West Bank settlements. It was easy to sleepwalk into escalation. Iran and Hezbollah might decide to raise the temperature, something not taken seriously in Washington and London. What was the US plan? Two States but no removal of the settlements? Would Hamas be destroyed? No, it wouldn't happen. Hamas would emerge from the carnage politically stronger.

Senior Fellow with Refugees International, Nicholas Noe said Israel's key leaders wanted to extend the fighting. They were restrained by the Pentagon. The Israeli military was in a precarious position. It needed US firepower to be able to fight on two or more fronts. It was hoping to hit Hezbollah while the US was in the region. Many wanted a huge confrontation. There was another angle, however: the US election. With only eleven months to go Trump was taking a hard line and some Democrats were supporting him. Key Israeli figures wanted to control matters. Biden had put himself in an impossible situation by tying himself to the Israeli right wing. Both the Pentagon and Biden liked what Israel was doing. They wanted Hamas destroyed.

The Yemeni military warned that all Israeli vessels would be targets.

Israel claimed it had discovered a fifty-five-metre-long tunnel under Al Shifa. There was, however no claim of evidence of a command centre.

Bravo! Declared Marwan Bishara, they had found one out of what were alleged to be hundreds. Where was the city under the city? Where were the one thousand three hundred kilometres of tunnels, supposedly forty to seventy metres deep? Maybe they might find a nappy. They've found a calendar. There was no evidence. It was Israel that was committing war crimes. It was the mother of all scandals. Public opinion in the US and elsewhere was changing. The seizure of the Galaxy Leader wasn't significant. It was theatre. It might even benefit Israel. The real issue was Gaza where there was genocide in plain sight. Biden had written an op-ed in the Washington Post and hadn't mentioned Iran. Both countries were pulling away from possible confrontation. Things were heating up on the Israeli-Lebanese border while the western media focussed on the captured ship and the threat from Iran. Israel was desperate to cover up its crimes, producing a bag from behind an MRI scanner as if it was evidence of Hamas presence. There was a pretence of a regional threat while the real threat to Israel was the testimony from doctors, evidence of its crimes and the effect they would have on public opinion.

Qatar's Minister for Foreign Affairs announced a deal on the hostages as more or less ready. There were minor challenges. He criticised the west for its double standards.

Edward Bernays understood propaganda is a form of advertising. It's characteristic of adverts to emphasise benefits and downplay, or usually ignore, faults. No product is without them and manufacturers know it; but no car company is going to tell prospective buyers that the injector bolt commonly snaps or the fuel gauge often becomes faulty or the clutch wears out quickly. Advertising is a form of dishonesty. Telling people about a product in objective terms is quite different, but that wouldn't fit the essential dishonesty of commercialism. Propaganda multiplies advertising's dishonesty but rather than selling products, it proposes a way of life and engages moral questions. All propaganda is dishonest. Political parties don't use it to tell people what they are going to do any more than advertisers tell the truth about products, but to convince people to support them. It's a form of cynical seduction which leads to inevitable disillusion. Israeli propaganda has always been stunningly distorted, but the depths reached during the Gaza assault were remarkable. While the IDF slaughtered people daily, they produced a calendar as evidence of the dastardly evil of Hamas. There is a further feature of propaganda: its purveyors often fall for it. Believing your own propaganda is perhaps the height of narcissism, yet to some extent, all propagandists do it. Propaganda tends to eliminate the scepticism which attends all knowledge and understanding. The Israeli leadership must have been aware of its dishonesty, while the public was systematically denied the evidence needed to form an objective view, yet at the same time Netanyahu and his cabinet looked convincingly lost in the labyrinth of their own mendacity.

The Community Security Trust reported a significant rise in antisemitism, a claim dutifully reported but never seriously examined by the media. Bodies producing such statistics should be expected to provide supporting evidence. Crucially, the CST could have been asked to show how they determine an act to be antisemitic. The media, still in a funk after the false accusations of institutional antisemitism in Labour, became merely the CST's conduit. Did the CST, for example, class the pro-Palestinian demonstrations as antisemitic? Did it do the same for every statement in support of a ceasefire? These questions weren't permitted:

Israel is an Angelic Nation and the CST an Angelic Institution.

Andy Burnham pointed out there had also been a rise in Islamophobic incidents. What is the Islamic version of the CST, which is a charity, receives government funding yet is known to have undertaken information-gathering about UK citizens? If such a body existed, would its claims have been broadcast uncritically? Was there a political party in the UK or Europe organising around antisemitism like the French RN, Geert Wilders, Giorgia Melone, the Afd and more were doing around Islamophobia? Neo-fascism, replete with closet antisemites, was acceptable, support for a democratic Palestine, the work of the devil.

The Israeli Ambassador to the US, Michael Herzog, talked of a prisoner exchange and a brief pause in the fighting while eight premature babies died and pictures of others, four to an incubator, appeared on our screens. Netanyahu, eager to see the region on fire, called the taking of the Galaxy Leader "another act of Iranian terrorism". Examination of Israel's evidence for tunnels under Al Shifa showed the putatively conclusive video had been edited.

Catherine Russell of UNICEF commented that children don't start wars but suffer in them. For Israel, children were an obvious target. No one asked why, if Israel was as concerned as it claimed to spare civilians, why didn't it offer temporary refuge to women and children in Israel. After all, it insisted it wasn't at war with the Palestinians but seeking only Hamas. It prided itself also on its high moral standards. What simpler way to confirm them?

Heavy rains caused floods in Gaza, some parts of the Strip were down to five or six days supply of flour. China's foreign minister called on the world to demand a ceasefire and for more aid to be provided. The world agreed, the US didn't.

Ibrahim Freihat of the Doha Institute of Graduate Studies argued China had historical links to the Arabs and had sought to help Palestine. The US-China duality was belied by the multi-polar world order. The US was utterly biased and a party to the war. There was a need for a third party and China, which had a rapprochement with Iran and Saudi Arabia was a possibility. Israel was well aware of China's economic importance.

What about the Chinese people? Freihat was evoking the Chinese State. While it was true the US was thoroughly tilted to Israeli interests, China was hardly a model of impartiality. The Chinese State, that is. Who knows what the answer might have been had anyone bothered to ask the Chinese people? What was not in doubt was that the people of the world were on the side of peace, but as usual, the State in its role as a supporter of the wealthy smothered their voice.

The Palestinian Red Cross reported a large volume of desperate calls from people who had dead bodies in their homes and were unable to bury them. A school in the Bureij refugee camp was hit killing thirteen. Overnight the Indonesian hospital in northern Gaza was struck depriving it of electricity, medicines and anaesthetics. Its doctors refused to leave without the guarantee of safe passage. The only broadcaster working from Gaza was Al Jazeera.

The dead unburied, schools bombed, hospitals devastated, doctors under siege and an almost total news blackout; this was how Israel "defended" itself, this was how the Middle East's great democracy conducted itself and this was how the US and its allies believed peace and two States should be brought to Palestine.

The Palestinian journalist and academic Taghereed El-Khodary regretted the failure of the diplomatic path. Gaza had been neglected by the influential for years. Human

Rights Watch, Amnesty International and organisations of their ilk were required in Gaza, how else could what was happening be verified? The genocide in Gaza was reminiscent of Bosnia. Killing children was being normalised. Biden's declaration, "I feel for the kids" was a joke. On October 17th Israel denied attacking a hospital, now the world accepted its story. As for the Israeli population, it was oblivious. There had to be third party investigations.

El-Khodary's high-minded adherence to third party objectivity was, of course, exactly what the Israelis feared. Power can't live with objectivity, which is why our common political discourse is unadulterated flummery. When politicians cite statistics, a quick check always reveals they are lies and damned lies. Selectively applied, they can support almost any argument. Israel isn't a fascist State but it is fascistic in its preference for power over law. The same is true, to varying degrees, of all the so-called advanced democracies. Mostly, the propaganda system is effective enough to permit relatively marginal bodies like Amnesty to function, but when it comes to war, and in particular when it came to Israel using 7th October as a pretext for annihilation or removal of the Gaza Palestinians, the first casualty was any form of independent perspective.

Antonio Guterres pointed out that in 2017-18 the highest child death rate in conflict was inflicted by the Taliban, followed by Syria and Yemen. The thousands killed in Gaza was "unparalleled". More civilians had been killed in Gaza than in any conflict since he had become General Secretary. Kristen Saloomey, the excellent Al Jazeera reporter, asked Guterres if Israel was committing war crimes and challenged him to call them out. Guterres brought El-Khodary's point into focus: diplomacy was more or less impotent. It depends on States being willing to listen to third parties and to compromise. For Israel, all third parties were antisemites and compromise betrayal.

Biden intervened usefully, shielding the Israelis from criticism and consequences by claiming the first war crime was committed by Hamas and reiterating his unfounded assertion of a command centre under Al Shifa. Of course, the first crime was committed by the Palestinians, as by the first people of north America: they had the temerity to exist.

Hezbollah hit an army base in northern Israel. There were no casualties. Netanyahu opined that the taking of the Galaxy Leader was a very serious, on a "global level". Araba in the West Bank was raided. There were clashes between Palestinian youths and Israeli forces. Twenty eight premature babies were transferred to Egypt. In Khan Younis a residential building was hit. Health services in northern Gaza were at a standstill. In the Bureij refugee camp an UNRWA school was hit. A refugee shelter in Jabalia was hit for the second time. Seventeen were killed including children who were torn to bits. The Indonesian hospital in northern Gaza was surrounded by tanks and armoured vehicles in a repeat of Al Shifa. In the compound of a clinic, doctors from MSF were fired on. Qassam rockets were fired at Tel Aviv. There were no casualties.

Biden declared a hostage deal near. John Kirby said the details were being worked out. The hope was for a pause and the delivery of aid. Amos Hochstein, born in Israel and having served in the IDF, was in the land of his birth as a senior White House adviser. Imagine if a "diplomat" on the Palestinian side had been a member of Hamas; would it be likely the media would present him or her as a typical "honest broker"? No mention was made in media reports about Hochstein's time in the Israeli military. As he was representing the US, he must be impartial. Hochstein's mission, apparently, was to prevent the opening of a second front in the north.

Jewish Power, the party led by Ben-Gvir declared its slogan: Life First ! The focus must be the families and the hostages. The government wasn't going to get them released. Meanwhile, Hamas called for the release of women and young girls from Israeli prisons. Lapid said Israelis were losing faith in Netanyahu. Ben Gvir and Smotrich on the other hand claimed provision of fuel was a sign of weakness. Netanyahu was sinking in the polls, his rating hitting an all-time low. Yoni Ben Menachem, Israeli journalist and ex-IDF intelligence, expressed the view that if Netanyahu defeated Hamas and released all the hostage he might survive politically; somewhat like arguing that if it rained only at night we could all stay dry in the daytime.

On 21st November, Farah Omar, a journalist in her twenties working for Al Mayadeen TV was killed, along with her cameraman Rabih Al Maamari, in a targeted attack in Tayr Harfa, southern Lebanon. How is this morally different from Putin's assassinations of Anna Politkovskaya or twenty or so other journalists since 2000? Putin is excoriated by the "West" as an enemy of free speech, Israel assassinates journalists and a few mild voices of disapproval are raised for a few minutes and the matter is forgotten. Without honest journalism, we are all in the dark. There is much dishonest reporting and commentary, but when power can silence its critics, any semblance of freedom is obliterated.

On the same day, the Scottish parliament debated the question of a ceasefire. The Welsh, Irish and Catalonian parliaments had already voted in favour. Humza Yousaf said too many had been killed and action had to be taken. The captives should be released. International law should be adhered to by everyone involved. The motion was passed, ninety in favour and twenty-nine against.

While the civilised Scots were calling for peace and the rule of law, the IDF killed twenty in the Al Nuseirat refugee camp, in case the world wasn't yet convinced of their belief in violence and lawlessness. There was a twenty-four-hour upsurge in violence, concentrated in the north. Beit Lahia was hit. Three houses in Jabalia were destroyed and an UNRWA school hit. In Gaza City there were intense battles against tanks. The Israeli Security Cabinet met to discuss an exchange deal. In a briefing from Beirut, Hamas claimed the IDF had made no practical advances, except for killing civilians.

According to Khalil Al Hayya the Al Qassam fighters taking on the IDF were "warriors of Allah" who didn't fear death. Gaza's hospitals were surrounded. The occupation was intent on making all hospitals unserviceable. They were no better than Nazis. Israel's stories about Al Shifa were propaganda, a silly charade no one could believe. The occupation was denying the Palestinians the basic means of life. Sadly, they had cover from Biden. The people were holding firm. There was no question of them leaving the Strip in spite of the genocide. The Palestinians would not be terrorised by Nazis. They would have their own State with Jerusalem as its capital. Rafah needed to be open continually. Only one hundred trucks a day were entering Gaza while five or six hundred were needed. Only ten percent of Gaza's food needs were being met. The Israelis were inflicting collective punishment. The siege needed to be lifted. The UN resolution was ten days old. Yesterday, Hamas responded. What was Israel's position? It wanted to carry on its insane war. For the Palestinians, it was either death or victory. As for the hostages, it was time for a truce, aid and a prisoner swap. The occupation was playing games.

Marwan Bishara argued that Hamas was upbeat and would keep up the struggle. Hayya had left Gaza in 2014.

Nineteen members of his family had been killed by the IDF. Hamas was in a difficult position. It couldn't reveal the whereabouts of the hostages. If there was to be a pause, Hamas would insist on no drones. The women and children in Gaza made things more difficult for Hamas and Israel would find a prisoner swap hard to swallow. For them, Hamas represented "pure evil". Palestinian kids caught throwing stones would get twenty years in prison. Hamas was now in the position that it believed it could gain momentum.

The Hamas comment from 21st November held true for months: Israel was achieving nothing of what it set out to do, but was killing civilians in droves. Comparing the Israelis to Nazis was sure to summon cries of hatred of Jews, the simple distinction between Jews and the State of Israel having been eroded by sustained propaganda. Interestingly, this would backfire in the middle of 2024 when orthodox Jews were forced to serve in the IDF, in response to which they explained their opposition to the Israeli State and its policies. That Israel had cover from Biden was true and a scandal. For the American right, of course, Biden was dangerously liberal, a measure of how far from reality thinking moves when constantly fed propaganda: Biden had always been a defender of Israeli power and had never raised any serious objections to its treatment of the Palestinians. To call that liberal is to rob words of meaning.

COCKROACH

Qatar announced on 21st November it was the closest it had been to a peace deal. It would oversee all the details, for example two hundred trucks per day into Gaza and humanitarian corridors. Qatar had been an active player in diplomacy for twenty years and was a focal point. It had brokered the deal between the US and the Taliban in 2021. The US proposal was for three Palestinians to be released for every Israeli. There would be a five day pause in the fighting. Biden declared he was "hoping to bring the captives home very soon." Netanyahu, Gallant and Gantz said once the hostage exchange was done, the fighting would go on. Smotrich and Ben Gvir, ever open-minded and rational, were firmly against any deal: no Palestinian prisoners should be released, despite many of them being children of unproven guilt.

The following day, nine were murdered in an attack on Al Nuseirat. The Kamal Adwan hospital was hit and the Al Maghazi and Jabaliya camps were under attack.

The truce was struck. Fifty hostages were to be returned and there would be a four-day pause. About a hundred and fifty Palestinian prisoners were to be released but concerns were raised that there was no barrier against them being rearrested. The question of the length of the pause was also raised. Why four days? It was suggested if ten more captives were let go, it could be five, but the question in the air was, "why not indefinite?". The Israeli response was unceremonious dismissal.

Three for one looked pretty conservative, given the customary Zionist view that the entire Palestinian population might be sacrificed.

Netanyahu was playing for time and trying to appease the growing dissent among the Israeli population. Neither he nor his war cabinet were serious about bringing the war to an end. For the PM, peace meant the end of his power and possibly his freedom. Randolph Bourne was right. Something Netanyahu understood perfectly.

Reem Alsalem, UN Special Rapporteur on violence against girls and women, who has caused controversy by insisting sex and gender must be kept distinct, and in this instance seems to be on the wrong side of the argument, failing to recognise that people born with female or male reproductive organs do not necessarily experience themselves as belong to the category those organs suggest, spoke of the "epic proportion" of violence against women and children in Gaza. They constituted seventy per cent of the dead. The "realities" were "apocalyptic". Thousands of the dead were buried under rubble. Women were giving birth in grossly unsanitary conditions. To allow it to go on was a scandal.

Emina Cerimovic of Human Rights Watch said Israel was not taking minimal measures to protect the fifty thousand disabled in Gaza. Why would they? It was their aim to wipe out or disable as many as possible.

Six were murdered in a raid on Tulkarem refuge camp in the West Bank. In Jabaliya where a residential building was directly targeted, twenty-five were killed in an hour, which must have had the IDF doing quick sums about how rapidly the remaining two million could be eliminated. Rafah suffered a direct hit. The attack on the south was unrelenting. Crowds rallied in Ramallah. A hundred unidentified bodies were discovered in a mass grave in Kahn Younis, a small part of the total tally of fourteen thousand one hundred and twenty-eight dead.

Mass graves are a metaphor for supremacism. While the dead of the supremacists are honoured, remembered, while royal and State flummery commemorates their disappearance, the low-level humans, those who are not really human, those who are dispensable and must be swept aside so they may not hinder the march of progress – the religion of capitalism – can be chucked in a pit like the carcasses of diseased cows, covered with dirt, their exit from life unrecorded just as their time on earth was unremarked, except for being deplored.

There was to be a six-hour pause in the fighting from 10.00 a.m. on the 23rd November. Qatar was hopeful that the proposed four-day pause could be extended. The aid and fuel to be admitted during the pause was to be handled by the Red Cross. Israel announced that during the pause there would be no return to the north for those who had fled south. Netanyahu held a press conference at the Ministry of Defence in Tel Aviv. It was reported that he, Ben Gvir and Smotrich had no choice but to agree, but they argued that the release of Palestinian prisoners would mean the murder of more Israelis.

Biden was "relieved and pleased", waiting to see the release of the first hostages and in touch with the negotiators. He hoped more aid would be forthcoming (a hope he could have turned into a reality with a single phone call). Polling showed the Biden figures were better outside the US than domestically.

John Bolton, that interminable fount of received bigotry, who supported the Vietnam War but pulled a little ruse so as not to actually fight, joining the Maryland Air National Guard, making him much less likely to be called up as the government was relying on the draft; who wrote, sweetly, in his Yale 25th Reunion Book: "I confess I had no desire to die in a Southeast Asian rice paddy. I considered the war in Vietnam already lost";who believes the US should invade Iran, Syria, Libya, Venezuela, Cuba, Yemen and North

Korea and bring down their governments – maybe he'll soon add Ireland or France to the list -; who defended Trump against the accusation of having plotted to overthrow the elected government by saying: "As somebody who has helped plan coups d'état…it takes a lot of work and that's not what Trump did"; was opposed to a pause and prisoner exchange. His line was hostages must never be swapped for hostages or cash. It would also give Hamas a chance to regroup. Palestinian prisoners were criminals. He was stunned the enemy had been given the right to determine the length of the ceasefire. If Netanyahu didn't destroy Hamas it would be bad for Israel and the US. Biden was strong on rhetoric but weak on action. His first advice to Israel was not to make the mistakes the US had made in Fallujah and Mosul; but at the same time he supported the assault on Gaza. He was saying go fast and go slow at the same time.

Bolton would be merely risible if he hadn't held so much power. He is an outstanding example of the twisted morality which accompanies the desire for power. Yet to accuse him of twisted morality is generous: he has no morality. He has described himself as an "Americanist". His belief that any violence, dishonesty, skullduggery engaged in to further America's ends is valid, flows from his demented acceptance of the myth of the US as an Angelic Nation. The idea that the US should apply to others the standards it expects to be applied to itself would shock him. Hence his amorality. A moral judgement has to be consistently applicable, even if there is no single principle in play, or it is simply hypocrisy. For Bolton, murder may be wrong, but not if it's done to advance American interests. That's the morality of a cockroach.

Of course, he genuinely believed all Palestinian prisoners were criminals because he believed all Palestinians are criminals. Their crime is to exist.

The UN said of the impending ceasefire it was a step in the right direction but there was much more to do. Hezbollah agreed to abide by the ceasefire if Israel did. The UN called also for a two-week Olympic truce. The release of the hostages would not begin until Friday 24th. Israel declared it would continue fighting in the interim. Three hundred trucks were to be admitted. Netanyahu said the release of the hostages was a "sacred mission" along with the "total dismantling" of Hamas. Gallant reaffirmed the defeat of Hamas as the objective. Gantz said the assault was the toughest thing he'd done in forty years of service.

Biden was in talks with the Emir of Qatar, Netanyahu and President of Egypt. He was not setting a high bar for Israel. There was no expectation of a longer ceasefire but Israel must protect civilians.

The assault on Gaza was not directly motivated by religion, any more than religion played the key part in seventy-six years of Israeli brutality, yet Netanyahu was keen to present his violence as essentially Jewish, plainly an insult to Jews. Melding Israeli State viciousness with Judaism was the only way to prevent it being seen for what it was: settler-colonial, supremacist atrocity. If it was a religious mission to release the captives, why did Netanyahu launch the assault? He could have had all the hostages released had he stayed his hand and made an offer to Hamas. Far from being a sacred mission, their release was a calculation. From the start, Netanyahu had played fast and loose with their lives, as many Israelis knew.

As for Biden's feeble bleating about protecting civilians, it was grimly farcical given the death toll of fourteen thousand five hundred and thirty-two. Biden cared far less about Palestinian lives than for the interests of US big business (standard US mentality). Palestinians have dark skins and are mostly Muslims after all, how can their lives have equal worth with those of white Christians?

Speaking on 23rd November, John Casson, ex-adviser to David Cameron and UK ambassador to Egypt, claimed Israel's policy was creating more Palestinian resentment and radicalism. Three things were necessary: serious aid, a policy for after the war and the replacement of Hamas and the Palestinian Authority by a new generation of Palestinian leaders. Cameron went to Israel to meet Arab leaders.

Pro-Palestinian protesters, displaying a banner calling for the expulsion of the Israeli ambassador, held up a meeting of Derry and Strabane council. Frank Gardner of the BBC said there was no place for guns in hospitals, giving credence, without evidence, to the Israeli claim that Al Shifa was a Hamas command centre. Ben Gvir, meanwhile, revealed the sweet generosity of his character by insisting Palestinians must display no joy when released from prison.

How does it happen that a plainly nasty man like Ben Gvir can hold high political office? Probably not one percent of the population of any country shows such egregious unpleasantness. It's a conundrum only to the naïve. Power is attractive to the inadequate, the pathetic, the immature, the regressed. No mature, autonomous person has any significant desire for power over others.

Balata refugee camp was invaded by one thousand IDF. What security threat did it pose? Ben Gvir tweeted that Israel would prevent any celebrations in East Jerusalem following the release of prisoners. A video circulated of him touring an Israeli prison full of Palestinians insisting the Israeli national anthem be played.

Al Thani, Qatar's foreign minister, announced the truce would start at 7.00 a.m. on 24th November. The first batch of hostages, thirteen women and children, would be released at 4.00 p.m.. Hostages from the same family would be kept together. Qatar and Egypt would continue to work for a longer pause and the release of more than fifty as they would supervise the truce. The US said the humanitarian priority was women and children. Aid was also crucial and should be admitted through Rafah as soon as possible.

It was no coincidence, argued Marwan Bishara, that Biden spoke of a two-State agreement immediately before Israel's assault: Israel won't accept anything which pleases the Palestinians, or even the US. His cabinet was occupied by fascists. A two-State agreement was a pipe dream. While Biden took his Thanksgiving break, things were going nowhere. Israel turned down every US suggestion and had no response to the question of its long-term plans.

Hakan Fidan, Turkish foreign minister, said once the war was over, Hamas would be a political player like any other. Qatar had played a great role. Turkey was saying to Gaza, "you are not alone, we will do all in our power to help." Many countries were helping. The whole world had woken up.

Maybe so, but Biden was asleep and all US allies snoozing. True though it may have been that Qatar had acted as a responsible intermediary, it was a depressing spectacle to see a dictatorship behaving more sensibly than the world's so-called great democracies. Qatar has a population of more than two million but only some three hundred thousand are Qataris, the rest are foreign workers, denied trade union rights and, according to some assessments, engaged in forced labour. Consumption of alcohol and sexual peccadilloes can be met with flogging. The House of Thani has been in effective control since 1825. The State's interest in bringing a resolution was in large measure due to its Islamic character, yet the fact the self-congratulating "West", loudly trumpeting its belief in democracy and human rights was complicit in wholesale slaughter carried out by a State in daily breach of international law, while a country engaging in medieval practices looked more committed to peace and adherence to international law, was shameful. Of course, it was easily explicable by reference to the ingrained hypocrisy of so-called democracies, whose elites were involved in a strenuous effort to undermine what they claimed to believe in.

Seventy-two IDF had been killed so far. Thirty-nine Palestinian prisoners were to be released on 24th. Israel released the names of those to be set free and notified the families. The hand-over would be conducted by the Red Cross at Rafah and the Israelis would be taken to hospitals in Tel Aviv.

Gallant announced there would be two more months of fighting while Netanyahu's popularity plummeted to its lowest level. The hostages were the most sensitive issue. People felt Netanyahu and his cabinet were not doing enough. Government communication was poor. People wanted to know what was going to happen to the hostages not scheduled for release.

Of course Netanyahu wasn't doing enough. His skin was at stake. He had elaborated three aims, two of which were impossible, to ensure the war would endure. The best outcome for him would have been a US attack on Iran and a regional conflagration. A ten-year war would have done nicely, making him eighty-four, at which point he might have spirited himself away to some friendly regime (if any could still be found) to avoid a jail term. He had no concern for the hostages or their families, beyond how he could use them to secure his nefarious ends. His colleague Gallant would turn out wildly optimistic in predicting two months more carnage.

Twenty-seven were killed in an attack on an UNRWA school in Jabalia. In Rafah City, two homes were hit. Israel, it was claimed, was killing an entire generation by targeting homes. A twelve-year-old boy was fatally shot in the chest. Maybe he had a pebble in his pocket and was therefore a threat to Israel's nuclear capacity.

On 24th November, David Cameron called for thirty million dollars to help the UN bring more aid to Gaza. Here was the urbane ex-UK Prime Minister apparently showing his country's commitment to humanitarian law. Yet Cameron never wavered in his support for Britain supplying arms to the Israelis. On the one hand, providing the weapons to murder civilians deprived of safe shelter, on the other calling for aid. This is very much the stuff of our so-called democracy. Cameron can look humanistic and in favour of legal means while simultaneously funding a racist regime engaged in daily war crimes. He was speaking as Foreign Secretary, though since 2016 he has represented no one. He was recalled to government essentially out of Sunak's desperation, but no significant objections were raised to a major office of State being occupied by an unelected figure. Interestingly, in the immediate wake of his general election victory in July 2024, Starmer would appoint eight unelected ministers, in spite of having four hundred and twelve MPs to choose from. In this, a mentality can be discerned which is characteristic of our democracy: its practitioners believe the people need to be kept out of decision-making. They can play a sanctioning, confirmatory role but no more. The party chiefs will decide on policy, the people will be permitted to choose between one set of handed-down policies and another; after that they should keep quiet and get on with what their betters decide for them. Had democracy prevailed, a ceasefire would have been arrived at quite early. Big majorities were in favour once the scale of Israeli violence became clear. Tens of thousands would die in Gaza because the supposed democracies saw their people as meddlesome. Power must be in the hands of those who know how to use it, the responsible people; that is, people with money.

At 5 p.m. on 24th November a four-day ceasefire began.

CEASEFIRE

James Elder of UNICEF reported things were quieter, there were people on the street but they needed water, tents, blankets. Much more was required, at least two hundred trucks a day. The devastation was testimony to Israel's brutal force. It was utterly confounding that the pause was limited, a stain on the conscience of humanity that war would restart. A political settlement was needed, only peace would keep the people safe. The skies were quiet. There were no drones, no bombs. Israeli helicopters flew to Egypt to collect the hostages. Some were IDF, there were a dozen Thai workers out of a total of twenty-three. The Red Cross was mediating.

Thirty-nine Palestinians were returned to their families. Tear gas was fired towards Ofer prison north of Ramallah. The Bethlehem home of one of the released Palestinian prisoners was raided in a warning not to celebrate.

Israel reasserted the very temporary nature of the pause. Hamas wasn't smashed, as all Israelis knew.

The White House declared that US passport holders were not in the first batch but were expected be among the initial fifty. The goal was for the process to be extended. There was, inevitably, disagreement between the Republicans and Democrats. The success of the ceasefire and the release of the hostages was important for Biden's domestic prospects.

Ghazi Hamad, senior Hamas member, who is reported to have called more than once for the elimination of Israel, said it was impossible to trust the Israelis. Israel was a brutal enemy. It was killing civilians not Hamas members. Israel would fail.

Hamad was right about Israel's brutality and its likelihood of failure if it continued on its current path, but his intervention was weakened by his previous ill-thought-out remarks. Everyone who opposes Israel's illegal occupation is in favour of its disappearance in its present iteration, but that needs to be spelled out. It's understandable a man like Hamad, whose father was killed by the IDF, is outraged, but his assertion that anything done in response to the Israel's injustice is justified undermines his moral position. Terrible is the fate of the oppressed: they have to fight their oppressors by the most moral means possible.

David Cameron reported he'd told the Israeli Prime Minister and President "over and over" they must obey international humanitarian law and the death toll was too high. There would be no security and stability for Israel until there was the same for the Palestinians. They must think of the future.

Did Cameron say the same to Biden? Netanyahu and Herzog were going to pay no attention to the monkey while the organ grinder was granting them *carte blanche*. What made Cameron believe Israel was interested in security and stability? The evidence of decades was that its leaders were much more interested in power even if the cost was continual violence and the necessity for a heavily militarised security State, good for profit, naturally. There was little evidence either that Israel's sponsor was deeply concerned for security and stability outside its own borders, and even internally it was happy to put up with perilous social division in the pursuit of wealth and power. The leaders of the US and Israel were perfectly aware of the beneficial effects of egalitarianism on stability and security, which is why they were so opposed to it. A world where people prefer peace to the pursuit of material wealth at any cost is a sick idea for the rich and powerful.

Marwan Bishara declared, "Israel can no longer use its fanciful theological claims to justify its violent racist prejudices. God does not sanction the slaughter of innocent children. And nor should Israel's American and western patrons."

In writing of Israel's theological claims, Bishara was separating Israel from Judaism. The latter, open to many interpretations as religions always are, was not under threat. It was Israel which was faltering under the burden of what Bishara rightly characterises as its racism. God, of course, can be invoked by anyone to justify anything.

Biden spoke of the trauma of the Israeli hostages but said nothing about the Palestinians. It was expected dozens more captives would be released over the next few days. There were leaks in the US press about preparations for a "victory lap". America was to raise questions about the death toll, but it was hesitant to pressure Netanyahu. There were no red lines for Israel.

Just what kind of questions were the Americans going to ask? Why were they asking questions rather than using their power to twist Netanyahu's arm? Given the history of American extreme violence, it's stunning they should be so timid in the face of a recalcitrant client; but having long ago recruited Israel to the category of Angelic Nations, they were lost in their delusions.

There was a significant demonstration in Washington. Muslim voters, the young, African-Americans were dropping Biden and dubbing him "Genocide Joe". He was worried the pause would admit more journalists to Gaza and the reporting would turn more opinion against Israel.

Nour Odeh, the Palestinian political analyst, speaking on 25th November deplored the lack of aid to northern Gaza. The Israelis were deliberately starving the Palestinians and destroying the health system. The north, the centre of economic, educational and political life, was close to uninhabitable. Everything happening was the result of deliberate decisions. There was an utter lack of international vision. The crisis was political.

The centre of that crisis was the US. Odeh was correct, the Palestinians were being massacred because of decisions taken in Washington. The UK media offered virtually no criticism of the US government. When your allies behave like barbarians, of course you stand shoulder to shoulder. There was plenty of comment in the media about the threat from China, though just how we were threatened, except by the Chinese doing what we had done for centuries in trying to develop their economy and conquer markets, wasn't made clear. The issue of Taiwan hovered in the background but no one discussed the One China Policy, agreed in the 1970s according to which Taiwan is part of China but neither it nor the US would engage in provocative acts. There was no evidence China was reneging on the agreement, the US, however, was tearing it up. No doubt this had much to do with Taiwan's production of semiconductors. Some ninety percent of the most advanced were produced by a single Taiwanese company. As usual, money trumps morality but naturally the US and its poodles have to offer pseudo-moral excuses because everybody despises rank greed and unfairness.

Nebal Farsakh asked where the injured and sick were supposed to go. There was nowhere in the north. Netnayahu's criticisms were invalid, there was no ease of access for the aid agencies, even keeping the aid workers from death or injury was hard. Establishing tent cities was a joke.

Akiva Eldar, the Israeli author and activist, complained of a lack of compassion in Israeli hearts. Even liberal-left Israelis were afraid to speak. Haaretz was the only Israeli newspaper to offer any serious reporting which was rewarded by State withdrawal of advertising. Israelis saw the disaster in Gaza as collateral damage. They compared Gaza to Dresden: there should be no mercy. Mercy was in short supply in Israel. The excuse was that Hamas hid behind civilians and therefore the IDF couldn't take risks. Israeli zealots were taking advantage. If the US didn't get things right, a regional war was likely.

It must have been lonely for Eldar, being willing to express such opinions. We should ask why compassion was so lacking among Israelis, why could they compare Gaza to Dresden. The comment about Haaretz provides the clue: the Israelis were a brainwashed people. Most had little inkling of what was really going on in Gaza. The Israeli State was intent on keeping them ignorant and prejudiced. War is peace. Freedom is tyranny. The Israeli propaganda machine had learnt a lot from Orwell.

There was minor trouble over the release of the hostages amidst alleged breaches of the ceasefire but by 7 p.m. on the 25th things were back on track. There were claims an Israeli used live ammunition and a drone. Thirteen more hostages were released including seven foreign nationals. Hamas confirmed that Qatar and Egypt would ensure Israel would observe the agreement but there was no assurance of an extension. Thirty-nine Palestinians were to be released, mostly teenage boys. Their families were warned , again, not to celebrate.

Israel had suffered a setback for its military and political establishment, argued Marwan Bishara. Its promise not to deal with Hamas was false. Six weeks had brought no release of captives by force. Only diplomacy had prevailed. Israel was in a corner through its own follies. Hamas created a kind of parity, asking for a fair process. The Palestinians were paying a heavy price which Hamas was required to justify. Israel's acts were criminal but Hamas felt it must bring something to the table. The big question had to be addressed: the way we got to this point had to provide a microcosm of what would come next. The political capital for the implementation of peace had been squandered. Some fourteen billion dollars had been spent on war. Imagine if that had been devoted to avoiding killing and if all the western officials had used their leverage with Israel. What had become obvious was that Israel couldn't attain peace without justice. The potential for diplomacy was small but clear. Why didn't Biden make the call to Netanyahu insisting on a ceasefire? His claim not to be a war monger was pretence.

That Israel was destroying itself as a putative democracy and responsible international actor was plain to everyone but the Israelis, just like the self-destruction of the addict. The cover provided by the fawning US and in particular the soggy-minded Biden who fell, hook line and sinker, for the Zionist misuse of the Nazi genocide, was a joke to the global south. Most people globally were convinced Israel was a rogue State engaged in systematic slaughter excused as pursuit of terrorists. The views of billions in the less developed nations were, naturally, nothing like as influential as those of one narcissistic old man hoping to hang onto power. In the context of a people being wiped out or expelled from its land, the long view matters little, but no sane person could doubt that in due course Israel's actions would take their place alongside those of history's greatest tyrants and psychopaths.

Bishara's point about Hamas having to justify the suffering of the Palestinians was pertinent. International law and morality would have been on Hamas's side had it confined itself to an attack on the IDF. The killing of civilians muddied the waters. Those fighting colonial oppression have enormously difficult choices. In all likelihood, had Hamas killed only Israeli soldiers and police, Israel's response would have been just as exorbitant and the excuses proffered by the US and its poodles just as threadbare, but the public couldn't have been so easily bamboozled into accepting their necessity.

Biden was the driving force behind the killing. It was pointed out many times he was one call away from ending it. The soft-pedalled diplomacy was an expression of belief in the rightness of everything done by the Israeli State. Just like the US, it was an Angelic Nation. It too had its Manifest Destiny. As, did the Palestinians: death.

Daniel Hagari, the unthinking purveyor of Israeli self-justification, declared the goal as far as the captives was concerned hadn't changed. Israel complied with the law. It would respect the deal. He declined to say if there were any red lines. The released captives were being interviewed and screened.

In other words, Israel had failed to learn that the way to get the hostage released was a permanent ceasefire and diplomacy.

"A complete dead-end" was Ghada Karmi's judgement of Israeli's trajectory. Destroying Hamas was a chimera. Palestinians were fighting Israel and the western world. It was deeply unfair. The western consensus was for the necessity of maintaining Israel which was supremacist, dominating and guilty of extreme cruelty against an innocent people. Karmi is reported to have called for Israel to cease to exist more than once, but, as previously mentioned, in its current iteration, Israel can't exist if there is to be an autonomous Palestine. US and European politicians customarily wriggle out of the difficulty of confronting Israel by speaking of a "safe and secure" Israel, or similar formulation, seldom qualifying what they mean by Israel. This sleight-of-hand lets Israel off the hook and pushes the possibility of Palestinian independence into an impossibly distant future. The refusal to specify that a safe and secure Israel must be different from today's, that it must withdraw the West Bank settlements, get out of the Golan Heights and East Jerusalem, implies Israel must be able to carry on as it is, and the Palestinians disappear.

Who was talking about the bombing of hospitals? asked Mustafa Barghouti. The mindset which permitted this was that of the Nazi genocide. Palestinians would never accept another Nakba.

Barghouti's remark about the similarity to the Nazis, would have led to his designation as a virulent Jew-hater by the UK media and the main political parties. Needless to say, he was given no exposure.

There were calls for an extension of the ceasefire and more aid. Eight Palestinians died during raids in the West Bank. The ceasefire was fragile. The damage to the Strip was colossal, especially in the south. Aid wasn't getting to people. Most water was contaminated, starvation and diseases were spreading. Gaza needed five hundred trucks a day. Police surrounded homes in East Jerusalem to prevent celebrations, proving once again that Israel was the only democracy in the Middle East.

One hundred and fifty Palestinians were to be released, eight had been killed during the pause. The physical health of the Israelis released was good but the body of nine-year-old girl said to have been killed by Hamas, was among those handed over. There were large gatherings to welcome the captives home and calls for more to be set free.

Hamas said it would agree to an extension if three Palestinians were handed over for each Israeli. Thirteen Israelis were exchanged for thirty-nine Palestinians near Gaza City. Hamas was making the point it was in control. Palestinians were fearful of escalation after day four.

Basem Naim pointed out that after fifty days of bombing, Israel hadn't destroyed Hamas, which still had full control in some areas. There was an urgent need for a complete ceasefire. Hostages were held in different places by different groups, making an extension necessary so they could be gathered and handed over. Israel had said it would extend the pause by one day for every ten released, but what was needed was a ceasefire. Hamas was ready to let the hostages go without a quid pro quo.

Naim insisted in more than one interview that Hamas killed no civilians on 7th October, a stance which seriously weakened his argument. Once again, we face the extraordinary responsibility borne by those fighting colonialism. Israel killed civilians with alacrity in its "mowing the lawn" but replicating the lawless psychopathy of oppressors is no way to liberation or justice.

Netanyahu appeared in Gaza in full military gear talking to IDF soldiers, the first visit there by an Israeli Prime Minister since 2005. Biden, meanwhile, whimpered he was hoping for a ceasefire while Hagari announced the IDF would return to fighting with full force.

US generals, however, expressed puzzlement over what the elimination of Hamas meant. Biden said there needed to be a surge in aid to two hundred trucks a day. Here was the most powerful man in the world, leader of an inordinately rich and extravagantly armed country, apparently baying at the moon, hoping that by some *deus ex machina* relief might arrive for the Palestinians, somewhat like a man looking at the rain pouring through his ceiling, saying what he needs is a bucket but doing nothing to get one. Biden, all through the horrific business, was a curious mixture of potential potency and actual impotence. Biden added a caveat to his insistence on the need for more aid: it would be provided only if more hostages were released, otherwise he would be a hundred percent behind Netanyahu. That's the leader of the "free" world pledging possible unreserved support for a supremacist neo-fascist.

An eighty-four-year-old woman was handed over and was in dire need of medical attention. Why take such an old woman hostage? Seizing IDF soldiers or police officers would make sense. That a woman of this age ends up a hostage looks like randomness and recklessness.

Israel cut off all communications in northern Gaza.

Three Palestinian students, Hisham Awartani, Kinna Abdalhamid and Tahseen Ali, graduates of the Ramallah Friends (Quaker) School were shot in Burlington, Vermont,. Two had dual citizenship one was a permanent legal resident. They were students at Brown University, Trinity College and Haverford College. Awartani was hit in the back and it was reported doctors feared paralysis. Two days later a vigil was held at Brown University where the students called for disinvestment from Israel. The gunman was Jason Eaton, a 48-year-old who had recently been fired from his job, had struggled with mental health problems and posted confused political messages. A former girlfriend also said he continued to send sexual messages after she said she wanted nothing to do with him. There was some resistance to the notion that Eaton may have acted because of his mental problems; such excuses, it was argued, aren't offered if coloured people engage in violence. True though this may be, untangling Eaton's motivation sufficiently to be able to designate him an Arab-hater is unlikely. He may well have been influenced by media coverage of the Gaza conflict and of Arabs in general, but he was clearly unbalanced and in need of treatment.

The day after, 27th November, UNICEF called the assault on Gaza a war on children which the world was happy to watch happen.

The EU and NATO called for an extension to the pause, Stoltenberg arguing it was needed to bring in aid and get the hostages out. Borrell claimed the pause was sustainable. Jordan asked for a permanent ceasefire. Some captives were with Islamic Jihad. Some were IDF soldiers. Hamas, it was argued, would demand a high price as when Gilad Shalit was swopped.

RUSI spokesman, Michael Clarke thought an extension likely. Hamas would agree and Netanyahu too if the ten hostages for each extra day formula was applied. Israel had lost control. The IDF was chomping at the bit to resume fighting. Israel's bombing campaign was an international outrage. Israel would raid Khan Younis and other places, but they were a long way from destroying Hamas which had some twenty thousand fighters. The politics would not go away, which was effectively what Israel was hoping for. Two States was the only answer. If the IDF tried to occupy Gaza it would be the worst of all positions.

MODERATE AND PRAGMATIC

Deputy Mayor of Jerusalem, Fleur Hassan-Nahoum, who was later to claim there were no churches in Gaza, said the pause could continue if the innocents were returned. Hamas was playing games. Israel had to threaten, its public opinion was in favour of dismantling Hamas and there was no way to do that but violence. Hamas was not a national actor but an ideological group like ISIS or Boko Haram. It was a proxy of Iran.

Ms Hassan-Nahoum's views were proof that high educational attainment and senior legal positions are no defence against irrationality.

The Palestinian Authority called for an extension of the pause as Qatar, Egypt, the EU and the UN warned of starvation in the Strip.

An extension of two days was announced on 27th November.

Ghazi Hamad, a senior Hamas official said there was support from the US, Qatar and Egypt for a ceasefire. There had been some violation of the agreement by Israel but so far the pause had been a success. Things could be moved on. A list of the details of the captives was being prepared.

Marwan Bishara was of the view that more captives should be set free. Maybe the pause could be extended to eight days, but however long, the US and Israel would soon be back to war. He was not optimistic. There were still a hundred and seventy captives, the majority members of the IDF and therefore not part of the deal. Between forty and sixty weren't soldiers. A bigger deal was needed, to include all the Palestinian prisoners. The notion of Israel releasing three times as many prisoners but scooping up more Palestinians day by day was bad faith on Israel's part. To release on the one hand and arrest on the other was a cheat.

Israel was continuing with collective punishment. Its war crimes were inflicting pain and suffering.

Regev announced that Gaza would be demilitarised and Hamas and its ideology defeated. Israel was balancing the risk. Its approach was "moderate and pragmatic". The Israeli operation would prevail. It was Hamas which had brought bloodshed to Gaza.

Perhaps Regev considered Genghis Kahn moderate and pragmatic.

The BBC reported that from December 2020, Hamas had posted propaganda videos on Telegram depicting rehearsals for an invasion including footage of the Izzedine al-Qassam Brigades, Palestinian Islamic Jihad, the Omar Al-Qasim Forces, the Al-Amar Brigades, Al-Nasir Salah, the Al-Deem Brigades, the Ayman Jonda Brigades, the National Resistance Brigades, the Jihad Jibreel Brigades, the Abu Ali Mustafa Brigades, the Mujahideen Brigades, the Abdul Qadir Al-Haseeni Brigades. They included the precise tactics Hamas would use on 7th October. They built mock villages replicating features of kibbutzim, like yellow gates. Five of the factions shown joined in the 7th October attack. The locations of these rehearsals were identifiable. Andreas Kreig, defence expert from King's College, London said there was clear evidence of training for attack, including paragliding, the use of motorbikes and underwater training.

There was no shortage of data for the Israelis but a terrible failure of thinking and interpreting. This was a strategic disaster, unless a more sinister explanation might be applied. Yet, though this reporting from the BBC was and remains easily available, it is virtually never discussed. No significant UK politician has brought attention to it. It occupied no headlines in any tabloid. Was Israel the victim of a surprise attack on 7th October? Was it ambushed by desperadoes who had given no prior indication of their intentions? It had ample evidence that an assault was imminent. Why did it choose to ignore or misinterpret ? This is hardly nugatory. Adequate response might have foiled the incursion and maybe also Netanyahu would have lost his position and found himself in some legal difficulty.

POWER AND PARANOIA

What had been achieved would have to be built on, said Majed Al Ansari the UK-educated, Qatari foreign affairs spokesman, but things were difficult and delicate; a pretty way of saying the Israelis were uncompromising and the US flaccid in the face of a hecatomb.

The White House welcomed the extension of the pause, Jake Sullivan stressing the need to get the hostages and US citizens out of danger. Palestinian citizens, naturally, have to put up with constant danger. Biden was said to be in contact with the negotiators and was in favour of a resumption of the fighting once the pause was over because of the genocidal threat from Hamas.

To US presidents, the world is full of threats, all of them existential. If people vote for economic democracy in Chile, well, that threatens America. If the people of Iran enjoyed democratic government in 1953, how could people in Texas sleep easy in their beds? If the people of Grenada had been left to sort out their own affairs in 1983 what might have become of New York ? What would have become of the people of Arizona if Haiti hadn't been occupied under martial law? As with the Dominicans? The examples go on, topsy-turvy, the most threatening State in the world constantly threatened by much weaker and poorer countries. That Hamas had the means to destroy Israel was ludicrous, yet such wayward claims were permitted to justify the carnage.

Antonio Guterres welcomed the ceasefire, it was a glimpse of hope and humanity. Would more humanitarian aid be provided? More crossings needed to be opened. The current number of trucks was limited, two hundred a day at least were needed. Communications were starting to be reestablished, the ceasefire might bring an end to the confrontation.

On 28th November the World Health Organization said more would die from disease than bombing if medical services were not restored. The new killers were diarrhoea, 'flu and respiratory infections.

The CIA and Mossad were in Doha for negotiations but little was forthcoming. Biden was said to want to build on the pause. He was under pressure domestically and internationally. Who would govern Gaza? The US was asking for precision in the violence, while simultaneously accepting inevitable mass casualties. Qatar wanted an extension to the ceasefire as a basis for a long-term solution.

Seventy IDF had been killed and a thousand wounded. While an orange balloon demonstration took place in Tel Aviv eleven Israelis and thirty-three Palestinians were released. The were mass arrests and two deaths in the West Bank.

WHO spokesman, Tarik Jasarevic, reported people were homeless, cold, without water or food. Things would get much worse if water and health care were not provided. They were particularly desperate north of Gaza. There were acute diarrhoea, serious malnutrition, lice, skin diseases. Four thousand people were sharing one shower, two hundred a single toilet. Unhindered access was crucial. Without fuel, hospitals couldn't function. Al Shifa was catastrophic. There needed to be a sustained ceasefire or there was not much hope.

Is an organisation like WHO a moral agent? It would be naïve to attribute to any organisation the moral agency which people enjoy, but some bodies are established with a remit to do, if not good, then at least no harm. If we set WHO's aim no higher than that, then it would be rational to judge that its positions are worth taking seriously. Maybe many people did so, but they were overwhelmed by propaganda: "Israel had a right to defend itself", "Hamas had to be destroyed", "Israel was a beacon of light". The Palestinians were being massacred and Israel was destroying itself, but US big business was, as ever, watching its profits soar.

Finland was supplying military aircraft to Israel, worth hundreds of millions, a readier explanation of its recent accession to NATO than any putative threat from Russia.

Irish MEP Grace O'Sullivan noticed a slight shift in the EU's position, Joseph Borrell recognising Palestine for example; but there was no clear line. Messages were mixed. Trade with Israel was in obvious breach of the law. There was double-speak and no clear direction. The German Greens, she pointed out were pro-Israel, hardly surprising given the weakness in the EU. Smaller countries were at a disadvantage, Germany had too much power. The Irish Ambassador to Israel was summoned to the foreign office because Leo Varadkar had posted that released hostage Emily Hind had been "found". The Israelis focussed on the first sentence of his statement: "An innocent child who was lost has now been found and returned", despite his later use in a mere three hundred and sixty words of "hostage" and "snatched". Simon Coveney pointed out that "lost" was a biblical usage, which brought the response of greater offence because it came from the New Testament. There was no call for a ceasefire which wasn't good enough.

Ever alert to any possible accusation of Jew-hating, the Israelis pounced on Varadkar's post as siding with Hamas, depicted, predictably, as worse than ISIS. The tenor of the message was delight at the child's release. It made no reference to Hamas and didn't include any suggestion that Varadkar was a supporter. Power and paranoia live and thrive together and the dishonesty necessary to maintain power has to be projected to sustain the delusion of virtue.

Martin Konecny, MEP, argued divisions in the EU were customary. Ursula von der Leyen's siding with Israel had increased them. Borrell was more balanced but there were divisions everywhere. The left coalition in France had broken down over Gaza, support for the far-right who were apologists for Israel and the settlements was growing. Konecny's view was echoed by Suzanne Lynch who said there was unity in the Commission over Ukraine, but not Gaza. A failing von der Leyen had been to Tel Aviv without consulting. The EU was on the back foot. Von der Leyen was a prisoner of her right-wing background. Germany was very pro-Israel, partly because of guilt over the Nazi genocide. There was no reaching out to the Arabs.

The hypocrisy over Ukraine was stunning. Old imperialist nations which still held sway over distant territories and intervened in alarming ways (France's support of Morocco for example over the Western Sahara) puffed out their chests and spewed an ocean of moralistic guff while sternly upholding Israel's right to defend itself against resistance to illegal occupation and intermittent, casual slaughter of Palestinians imprisoned in Gaza. Von der Leyen, smiling self-complacently as ever, praised the Israelis for making the desert bloom and declared "your freedom is our freedom", by which she meant "your colonialism is our colonialism."

An adapted French warship arrived in Egypt to treat Palestinians injured in Gaza.

The French ambassador to the UN, Nicholas de Rivière welcomed the pause and called for the release of all hostages. A full ceasefire was a priority. Israel had a right to defend itself but it must protect civilians and the provision of aid was vital. There was a need to convince the fifteen members of the Security Council and the parties on the ground. France had raised a billion dollars for Gaza and was taking things one day at a time. Qatar, Egypt and the US had to be thanked for their efforts. The Secretary General was right: there needed to be more than one crossing point, two or three if possible. China would be in the chair of the Security Council for the November meeting, could they bring more pressure to resolve the crisis. It was necessary to prepare the ground for two States as soon as possible.

Is there anything here but wind? Like every glib recycler of received supremacist wisdom, de Rivière dutifully asserted Israel's right to self-defence but had nothing to say about the Palestinians right to the same. Where were the Palestinian army, navy or air force? What was meant by the Israeli right to self-defence was in truth its right to shoot fish in a barrel. The IDF fired bullets through the heads of kids throwing stones, and that was self-defence. It "mowed the lawn" with extreme violence in response to home-made rockets which seldom reached their targets, and that was self-defence. Over and again these airy spokespeople failed to say the essential: Israel occupied Palestinian land unlawfully and inflicted appalling violence and oppression to continue to do so. By refusing to lay this groundwork, the implication was that the Palestinians were irrational terrorists, ever threatening the peace-loving Israeli State. What needed to be said first about Israel/Palestine was that Israel was a colonial power, a nuclear-armed tyrant and everything flowed from that.

Blinken was to visit the Middle East imminently. Three US military transport C17s were to be sent to northern Egypt carrying twenty-four and a half tons of aid. The US urged its international partners to step up.

Another visit from the ditheringly ineffectual Blinken was sure to make things worse. Twenty-four and a half tons of aid for two and half million people? That was stepping up?

There was no need for the US to urge anyone to do anything, it simply needed to tell Netanyahu to stop fighting. Biden had the power. The killing went on because US big business wanted it, and, as ever, the President was the servant of the corporates. The people wanted a ceasefire, but who, in a democracy, listens to them?

Ten Israelis and two Thais were released on the evening of the 28th November.

One of those set free was seventy-five-year-old Ada Sagi. The following day, her son Noam, a London-based psychotherapist was interviewed on BBC Radio 4 by the syrupy Nick Robinson. Her ordeal was "something we can't imagine" she was "an amazingly strong woman" who had survived "the most inhumane conditions". Some of the hostages had " no houses, no homes to go back to." Mrs Sagi was humanised. She had a name, fine characteristics, a family. Was this offered for any of the Palestinian dead or injured? They were numbers, by this point some fourteen thousand. Mrs Sagi was an Arabic speaker who worked for Israel-Arab understanding. Her son explained some of his family were refusing to talk to him because didn't unreservedly support Israel's actions. No sane person could fail to be sympathetic to an old woman taken hostage, nor either to hundreds of thousands of Palestinians forced from their homes, bombed, shot, denied food, water and medical care. There may have been rare examples of humanisation of the Palestinians but they were seldom as fulsome as Robinson's presentation. Behind most reporting was the unacknowledged assumption that the Palestinians deserved it. After all, that's what the propaganda system had been saying for decades.

UNRWA's Thomas White, with two and half years' experience in Gaza City condemned Israel's rhetoric: an entire suburb had been destroyed while they spoke of targeting. The city was unliveable, some parts hadn't been destroyed but there was no power or services. All the same, people preferred to stay rather than be displaced and then bombed. There had been a small increase in aid during the pause, but it was petty. People were anxious about what was to come. They feared a ground offensive in the south. Civil infrastructure was overwhelmed.

In response to the shooting of two children in the West Bank, Marwan Bishara said the soldiers were instrumental, merely following orders. The assault was fascistic. There was a pause in Gaza, meanwhile children were being shot in the West Bank. It was psychopathic. Insane.

Bishara is right that the instrumentality of the soldier makes possible conduct they wouldn't engage in otherwise, a very good argument against instrumentality. Plainly, all the IDF soldiers weren't psychopaths, yet in context their actions took on a demented hue. They were agents of the Israeli State. Can the State be a moral agent? To permit yourself to become its agent is to cede your capacity for moral decision. Where else can a moral decision be made but in an individual conscience? Which is not to say people can't act together for moral ends. it's a matter of one plus one plus one; but to be carried along by an outside agency, however plausible its claims, is to lose your moral autonomy. It makes sense to speak of a psychopathic culture when the characteristics of psychopaths are rewarded. All the same, the language of individual psychopathology never fits war.

Journalist Osama Bin Javaid said Hamas was willing to extend the pause. Israel indicated it might extend it to Sunday 3rd December. There was a lot at stake, more aid crucially. So far supplies for only one day had been admitted. Qatar was caught in the middle and was under pressure to get the parties to be serious. A CIA official had posted a picture of a Palestinian man on her profile, indicating the delicacy of the whole process. People were playing their cards close to their chests. Blinken was arriving in Tel Aviv before the end of the deadline at 7.00 a.m. on Friday.

The CIA posting of a man waving a Palestinian flag took place on 21st October. It was claimed the officer involved, whose name was withheld, had made similar postings some time earlier. This was accompanied by spreading dissent over Biden's handling by US diplomats and government employees. These were not radicals, anarchists or libertarian socialists, but sober-sided American careerists who were appalled by the viciousness and Biden's ineffectual response. Even among Trump supporters, millions were in favour of a ceasefire. Biden appeared to be lost in the mists of 1947, as if the terrible history of Israel's supremacism and brutality had never happened.

The Israeli police used force against the protesting families of the hostages outside the Knesset. Blinken claimed the US was trying to extend the pause and that aid was surging, not a word employed by the aid agencies. The objective, Blinken said, was to prevent a repeat of 7th October. It didn't appear to cross his mind that the lifting of the siege might be useful.

In South Africa there were big pro-Palestinian protests.

JERICHO WALL

Antonio Gutteres lamented the death toll and emphasised two-thirds of the dead and injured were children and women. More children had been killed than in any year during his tenure. Resolution 2712 should be observed. It was clear there were serious violations of international law before the war. The population was being pushed to the south. Nowhere was safe. Forty-five percent of homes had been destroyed. UNRWA shared the coordinates of its facilities, yet two hundred and eighteen had been killed in its schools. A hundred and eleven UN staff had been killed. Civilians must be defended and international law upheld.

2712 was by no means the only resolution respected more in the breach than the observance. The UN was an obstacle to US power, to "full spectrum dominance" or whatever high-falutin' title embellished thuggery. Gutteres and many more expressed consistently, common human sympathy, but in teeth of power and its limitless machinations they sounded like Sunday school teachers in a brothel.

In the UK a climate of intimidation was spreading. NHS staff were banned from displaying Palestinian flags at work. People were losing their jobs for criticising Israel yet the number of convictions for anti-Jewish hate crime was small. The discrepancy between Israel and Ukraine was glaring. In the latter case, people could display the country's colours in any context and receive congratulation for their humanity and love of peace; in the former, the Palestinian flag was deemed a call for the elimination of all Jews, even the few dozen in Iceland. In schools, pupils could talk freely about Ukraine and the heroic struggle for freedom and democracy while discussion of Gaza was widely outlawed. The logic that Ukraine was the victim while Palestine was, through the proxy of Hamas an aggressor, was perverse, as the most cursory glance at history betrayed. The general mood, however, was sympathetic towards the Palestinians. Remarkably, the common folk of Britain didn't relish seeing defenceless women and children being bombed to shreds. UK authors were effectively banned from writing about Palestine and the major political parties set up serious hurdles for anyone opposing the Israeli State. In a self-congratulating angelic culture of infinite respect for democracy and human rights, the official line was unquestioning support for a war cabinet of neo-fascists intent on targeting civilians whose humanity was acknowledged only in mealy-mouthed soundbites intended to mollify an increasingly doubtful public.

In New York, also, students were prevented from discussing Palestine. Canadian lawyer, Nora Fathalipour, reported being overwhelmed by inquiries after offering advice to those facing discrimination. Austria, Denmark, Sweden, Switzerland and the European Commission moved to restrict funding to pro-Palestinian NGOs on the specious grounds of links to terrorist organisations. Naturally, absolute freedom was granted to anyone wishing to support Netanyahu's evil war cabinet.

Clearly, Israel was losing the intellectual and moral argument. The hysterical cries about antisemitism at every mild rebuke to the Israel State had been evidence for decades that it was Israel not Judaism which was under threat. Netanyahu and his neo-fascist allies were driving their State closer to self-destruction and with every centimetre moved, the vice tightened on protesters in the so-called democracies.

Hamas released two Russian-Israelis, one an elderly woman.

Netanyahu declared the sole way to prevent another 7th October was to resume fighting. Gaza would have to be occupied for an indefinite period. There were no circumstances in which Israel would not go back to war. The entire war cabinet was agreed.

Well, there might have been one circumstance: if Biden had refused further arms, money or diplomatic support, but Netanyahu knew he was dealing with a deluded old man.

The Qatari Minister for Foreign Affairs announced thirty Palestinians, sixteen children and fourteen women had been released in a swap for ten Israeli captives, including one Dutch, three Germans and an American. Qatar was confident of an extension and was trying to rally global support. Qatar would play a crucial role. The US would pressure Israel. Hamas was yet to start talks on the IDF captives. Released Palestinians were threatened with rearrest if they spoke to the media. There were no journalists in East Jerusalem.

Jenin was raided by hundreds of soldiers. Gallant warned the war would resume "with intensity"..

The IDF would start seizing Gaza City overground, predicted Andreas Kreig. They would smoke Hamas out of the tunnels. Subsequently they would go for the south. Even the White House was a bit queasy. Israel reaffirmed the doctrine that the total destruction of Hamas was the goal and all else would be failure. Blinken, Brussels and NATO were saying "we're doing what we can". The Secretary of State was making his third visit to the region. Israeli media reported he might attend the war cabinet. Roger Carstens, US Special Envoy for Hostages was sent to help. The notion Israel was applying care for civilians was a joke.

29th November marked the International Day of Solidarity with Palestine. South Africa identified with the Palestinians. They were victims of apartheid. The South African parliament voted for the expulsion of the Israeli Ambassador and the cutting of diplomatic ties. There were protests around the country. The Israeli ambassador to the UN, however, claimed anyone supporting a ceasefire was in favour of the "Hamas reign of terror." All that was necessary to end the fighting was for the top Hamas leaders to surrender. Curious the possibility wasn't admitted of Israel taking its foot of Palestine's neck.

A seventh day of pause was agreed on 30th November. At the Ramot junction in Jerusalem three were shot dead and sixteen injured. Hamas claimed responsibility. Seventeen Thais were released, four were subject to medical tests.

Fifteen thousand had been killed and thirty-six thousand injured, according to Gaza Health Ministry figures.

Ahmed Yousef, senior adviser to Haniya, said the focus was a ceasefire. All prisoners on both sides should be freed and the terms of any ceasefire should be universally observed. Discussions in Qatar or Egypt might lead to a settlement. Palestinian autonomy was a way out. Both sides should get something of what they wanted. Hamas should let the women and elderly go. As for 7th October, no one expected it. The plan was to invade and kidnap IDF soldiers. No one but the fighters knew when the attack was to take place, the final decision was made only a few hours in advance. Taking civilians was wrong. Some Palestinian civilians who joined the attack made mistakes. The Al Qassam brigades were more disciplined. Israel's intention to destroy Hamas was misplaced. It was an ideology. Was a peaceful solution possible? Hamas was a resistance movement. It recognised Israel. The PLO negotiates. The resistance bore no hatred towards Jews but was the enemy of Zionism which had seized Palestinian land and displaced its people. The resistance had to continue.

Yousef may have been right that the plan was known only to a few until a matter of hours before the attack, but the preparations had been widely publicised for months. He may be right also that the plan had never been to kidnap civilians, and perhaps the somewhat difficult to explain absence of the IDF contributed to what he judges as wrong. Nothing, however, could justify Israel's response. Starving civilians, killing women and children in their thousands, laying the Strip to waste, was not a way of countering Hamas. The moral difficulty resides in Yousef's assessment that taking civilians was beyond justification, together with his equally correct assertion of the right of Palestinian resistance.

Two Levys offered radically differing perspectives. Elyon Levy, the mechanised purveyor of received Zionist wisdom, Oxford educated, as slick as he is superficial, said the IDF would resume its assault, destroy Hamas and ensure Gaza could never threaten Israel. If the hostages couldn't be freed by negotiations, then they would be set free by violence.

On the other hand, Daniel Levy, son of Lord Levy, friend and booster of the war criminal Tony Blair, chairman of the US/Middle East Project, ex IDF, claimed the US was disingenuous in thinking the IDF might behave differently once it resumed fighting. An all-for-all swap was under discussion but the Israelis insisted that even if that was forthcoming, they would still renew their attack with intensity. The IDF hostages represented high-value leverage for Hamas. Blinken would be in the area the next day, maybe there would be a breathing space. Soon the US would run out of road, it needed to act decisively. Biden was posturing. Israel was playing a clever game, occupying the space between the public and private.

Daniel Levy was hardly a fierce critic of Israel, indeed had previously been a government spokesman, but was in this and other interventions able to distinguish between Zionist propaganda and what was happening. Elyon Levy, on the other hand, was simply a propaganda mill, a man whose capacity to think had been frozen, as it always is, by adherence to ideology.

A Palestinian was arrested in Tubas, a daily occurrence in the West Bank where there were seven major raids overnight in which forty were arrested. Raids were becoming more intense. Three thousand three hundred from the West Bank had been detained so far.

Two Israeli women were released by 4 p.m., by 9 p.m. Hamas had handed over six more captives.

Blinken was talking to Abbas about post-war Gaza and a possible role for the Palestinian Authority. Blinken, apparently, emphasised the need to protect civilians, which must have given Netanyahu another good laugh.

Osama Hamdan argued that fifty days of destruction had brought Israel no closer to its aims. Israel, he said, could not be trusted. Hamas didn't know where all the hostages were. Israel's continued violence might kill some of them.

Hamdan has defended suicide bombings and called for the return of Israelis to where they came from. Bombings which kill civilians are morally indefensible. The call for Israelis to leave Israel defies international law. Israel is a functioning State in the international order, like any other, North Korea for example. However regrettable the founding of the State of Israel, its legitimacy is a matter of law. Is there a moral case for the expulsion of the Israelis? Most of the current population bears no responsibility for the Nakba. They enjoy rights of citizenship. There is no solution in seeking to do to them what was done to the Palestinians in 1948. Hamdan's hurt is understandable, but the future worth campaigning for is one of equal citizenship. All the same, Hamdan was right on all counts. Netanyahu didn't care about the lives of the hostages, as more and more Israelis realised, he cared for his power. There was going to be no end to the massacre while he clung on.

Ben Friedman, Policy Director of Defense (sic) Priorities, thought an extension of a day or two was possible. Then Israel would start again in the south. There was no clear aim. If Hamas was destroyed, what would come in its wake. The US wasn't exerting great pressure. Blinken was no threat to the Israelis. Bill Burns might have been pushing but wouldn't force Israel. The humanitarian cost of the war was unacceptable. Washington should rethink its fourteen billion dollars of support. The US wasn't an honest broker. It was never an unbiased arbiter. Biden was facing pressure from within but it was relatively weak. Trump would be more pro-Israel.

John Kirby said no nation should have to suffer what happened to Israel on 7th October. As for what had happened to Palestine for seventy-six years, not a word.

Lula da Silva criticised Israel. The world, he argued, lacked governance. What was happening was insane. What was it for ? The world had no heart. If the UN had any strength, there would be two States. Where was the UN Security Council? Where was humanity?

Da Silva is usually depicted as far-left in the UK media but while his programmes did lift millions out of poverty he also presided over huge banking profits. In foreign policy he has been more expedient than principled, perhaps, to some extent at least, inevitable. What his comments did represent, however, was the stance of the global south. US and European hypocrisy regarding Gaza was transparent to those on the receiving end.

In that regard, China put forward a five-point peace plan: a comprehensive ceasefire; effective protection of civilians; ensuring humanitarian assistance; enhanced diplomatic mediation; and seeking a political settlement. It was perfectly rational but straight out of Alice in Wonderland; a little like asking Regan and Goneril to be kind to their father. China, of course, had invested hugely in energy infrastructure in the Middle East and latterly was assisting the Gulf States with the transition from fossil fuels to renewables. It was hardly an impartial actor.

Pedro Sanchez remarked that he doubted Israel was abiding by international law, a comment which resulted in Netanyahu upbraiding the Spanish ambassador. Sanchez is a social democrat with a little edge of radicalism. That he stepped beyond the customary mealy-mouthed apologism of most European politicians is to his credit, but that such a mild rebuke about obvious law-breaking could elicit a dressing down was further evidence of the neurotic touchiness of the Israeli regime.

On 1st December, James Elder of UNICEF expressed his bafflement at the acquiescence of the powerful in the deaths of children. These people, he observed, needed to look the kids in the eye. Hospitals were at two hundred percent capacity, a catastrophe.

Common human sympathy is revolted by the slaughter of children, which is what Elder was saying. His bafflement, however, was somewhat out-of-place: the world economy is not organised to look after the needs of children, or of the poor or even the majority; its purpose is to feed the bottomless maw of the rich. They can't tell the truth, of course; hence the empty flummery about democracy and human rights and the freedom of the individual and free enterprise as they rig the global system. The rhetoric works only in so far as people don't bother to look behind it, and the propaganda system works hard to ensure they don't. Cynicism is well-placed, however, when extreme violence is commonly employed to further the interests of a wealthy tiny minority. No doubt Elder takes democracy, human rights and the rest seriously, but the people who rule the world don't. On the contrary, at the first sign of the common folk behaving truly democratically, they reach for the baton, the riot shield, water canon, the paraphernalia of torture, the fighter jets, the missiles and of course, the op-ed.

The IDF's Lieutenant Colonel Peter Lerner claimed Hamas had refused to release women and children. Israel was doing everything to protect civilians. All Hamas had to do was surrender and hand over the hostages and the fighting would be over. At the same time, however, Netanyahu was right: Hamas must be destroyed. Hamas was to blame for everything.

All Hamas had to do was surrender, and then what? Autonomy for the Palestinians? Surrender and go back to being imprisoned. There were no polls in Gaza to reveal the level of support for Hamas, but there can be little doubt that Palestinians were not willing to give up at the cost of losing any chance of independence. People do arrive at the point at which death is preferable to a life under tyranny, and much more quickly than many care to admit. The flaw in Lerner's thinking was that in Zionist thinking per se: the Palestinians are not quite human, not at the same level as the Zionists, not chosen by god, not an angelic nation. The simple fact of common humanity defies all ideologies of supremacism and the refusal to accept it is always the prelude to chaos, murder and madness.

At 7.00 a.m. local time on 1st December, fighting resumed. One hundred Palestinians were killed. Israel stopped the aid trucks. It also sent electronic messages about attacks but the Strip was without connectivity. Khan Younis was hit. The south was under attack. Qatar said negotiations were continuing.

If a street fight is under way outside the pub and people are getting their heads smashed, what use is it for people at the bar to be talking about how to stop it?

Moroccan sociologist, Mohamed Cherkaoui, said the victims were being made guilty. Now was the time for a longer ceasefire. Netanyahu had reverted to his previous mindset and was pursuing an irrational war against civilians in which his true aims were concealed. For him the goal was the eradication of the Palestinian population. He wouldn't stop. He wanted to change the human face of Gaza.

The modern world rests substantially on the guilt of the victim, as Franz Kafka knew. It wasn't always so. As Milan Kundera points out, the fault used to seek the punishment: Lady Macbeth drives her husband to murder and is tortured by conscience; but in the modern world, the punishment seeks the fault. To be accused is to be guilty and forced to examine yourself minutely in pursuit of your error. When did the change come about? Essentially when the common people began to take part in history. While power was in the hands of a few, it was convenient to apply a morality which punished wrong-doing (although much of it among the rich went untouched) but once democracy threatened, a means had to be found to inculpate the masses for daring to assert their humanity. When accusation was guilt the secret services, the death squads, the gulag and imprisonment without trial were empowered. This is not to say that during the long-period of rule by tiny minorities horrendous things weren't done in the name of power, but the fundamental shift to a code in which accusation became guilt was a vital weapon in the fight against democracy.

The *New York Times* revealed, on 2nd December the Jericho Wall document, evidence the Israelis had details of the 7th October attack more than a year in advance. Reporters Ronen Bergman and Adam Goldman explained the blueprint in the forty-page document was followed by Hamas with "shocking precision" In July 2023 a veteran analyst with Unit 8200 (the Israeli version of GCHQ) warned of an intense, day-long exercise. In response to claims by the IDF that Hamas lacked the capability, the analyst, a colonel in the Gaza division, said: "I utterly reject that the scenario is imaginary. It is a plan designed to start a war." In addition, a Defence Ministry memorandum of 2016 observed: "Hamas intends to move the next confrontation into Israeli territory." The document recognises the attack would begin with a barrage of rockets, drones to take out cameras and automated machine guns, followed by gunmen pouring in en masse in paragliders, on motorbikes, on foot. The plan was to break through at sixty points. The military base at Re'im was to be overrun, an aim realised on 7th October.

Did Netanyahu know of it? There is no evidence. All the same, the nonchalance of the Israeli top brass in the light of this alarming document is at best arrogant at worst complicit. Even they concede that had it been taken seriously it might have permitted serious resistance or perhaps prevention of the incursion. For a State which prides itself on its security and militarism and for a Prime Minister who staked his reputation on keeping his people safe, to have treated this warning with such insouciance is criminal. It would be unwise to connive at the advantages which may have accrued to Netanyahu and others from this neglect, but to have had in their hands a precise plan for what transpired on 7th October, though they didn't know the date, and not to have responded seriously places a heavy burden of responsibility on the Israelis for the events of 7th October.

AND THE SUN ORBITS THE EARTH

Senior Hamas official Khalil Al-Hayya accused Israel of dishonesty in its refusal to distinguish between civilians and soldiers. Mediation was in place but it wasn't able to stop the aggression. The White House was accusing Hamas of failing to produce a list of captives and declared its full support for Israel and the effort to prevent a repeat of 7th October. Blinken was reported to have told Israel not to do in the south what it had done in the north. International support could not be guaranteed for such action. The US laid all the blame on Hamas. No credence was given to the Palestinian story.

Hezbollah fired on positions in northern Israel. Raids continued in the West Bank. More than seven thousand Palestinians were in Israeli prisons, forty percent in administrative detention.

Gallant explained that Hamas understood only force. It was aiming for Tel Aviv. Israel told Egypt, Jordan and the UAE it wanted a buffer zone within Gaza. The Arab States were not likely to be in favour. John Kirby declared the US opposed: Gaza must be Palestinian.

Of course, Gallant was speaking for a State which proceeded always in the most possible peaceable fashion. It's interesting that the victims of violence of any kind are said to understand nothing else. From the wife-beater to the Head of State, the violent forever claim there were no other means at their disposal.

Elyon Levy claimed Hamas has chosen to break the ceasefire for which it would take "the mother of all thumpings". There was no convincing evidence of a Hamas breach, but Mr Levy was not a man for evidence. His conciliatory tone was typical. Like Gallant he knew Hamas understood nothing but killing. By extension this applied to the thousands of Palestinians being slaughtered, The notion they might understand peace, autonomy, prosperity and equality was, naturally, fanciful.

A US Gallup poll showed support for Israel at fifty per cent while a Reuters survey revealed only thirty-one percent agreed with the continued supply of weapons. How does it come about that almost seventy per cent of the population of the country said to be the world's greatest democracy support a policy, but their representatives do the opposite? The wisely cynical recognise the distinction between the flummery and the reality. The people in Congress aren't there to do what the common folk want, but to ensure their will can never be implemented. They are inheritors of the long tradition expressed by John Jay, one of the early architects of American ideology, that the country must be ruled by those who own it. There may have been some shilly-shallying by the Republicans over weapons for Ukraine, but arms for Israel were never in doubt. The American people had to be ignored, for their own good, as usual.

Marwan Bishara argued the US was one hundred per cent complicit in the massacre; its hypocrisy was at a high level, offering deadly weapons on the one hand and talking of limiting the damage on the other. What was the explanation? It was impotent to use its leverage over the use of its own weapons. The US had more concern for Israel than the Israeli government which was too fascistic to worry about its people. As for a buffer zone, the Strip was thirteen kilometres at its widest point. Thus, if the buffer was two kilometres, twenty per cent of Gaza was being stolen. It made no sense.

Netanyahu claimed Hamas was calling for the destruction of Israel. It was evil. The devil. Israel would continue to the end. Israel had strong morals. Attacks would be renewed. There would be war till all the aims were achieved. Israel was complying with international law. It would bring back stability. Hamas was making terrorists of children. He was in touch with the US media and with Congress but at the end of the day, Israel made the decisions. There would be security and safety in the north and south of Gaza. The people should trust him, he knew what he was doing. The Palestinians were not religious people. As for resignation, he wouldn't discuss it. Opinion polls were not his business. He was working towards one goal. He had the support of the US. There were some differences, but he overcame them. There wasn't full agreement on humanitarian aid, but Israel made the decisions. There was time ahead to convince the US everything he had done was right. The hostages were being tortured, subjected to violence and starvation. He wouldn't discuss 7th October. It would be investigated in due course. In regard to the Red Cross, Israel was dealing with terrorists. The Red Cross didn't understand that. He was trying to pressure Qatar and Egypt. Israel gave priority to the safety of women and children. Having the Palestinian Authority in Gaza would change nothing. It would take years to guarantee Israel's safety. The Palestinians teach their children to hate Israel. Israel was identifying safe places. The people of Gaza knew they could go there. Israel doesn't touch civilians. It goes after only Hamas. He had made sure there would be no humanitarian catastrophe in Gaza.

And the sun orbits the earth.

Netanyahu withdrew Mossad from the negotiations in Qatar, claiming they were getting nowhere. Hamas announced no more hostages would be released till the end of the war.

Tamar Qarmout, professor in the Doha institute for graduate studies, said most of the remaining hostages were IDF.

Netanyahu would treat them as collateral damage. Israel, not the US was in control. It was very worrying. Could there be a renewed Palestinian Authority? Israel was after the leadership in the West Bank. Palestinians had no say. The prevailing mindset was colonial. Netanyahu was viewed badly by the Israeli population. The opposition wanted him removed, especially the generals. He was likely to last out the war. The US wouldn't seek his removal. The EU was more pragmatic and its policy had long been carried by France, for whom Lebanon was an important matter. There were protests in Tel Aviv calling for more releases. The end of the temporary ceasefire was a major blow for the common folk.

Kahn Younis and southern Gaza were hit.

Macron in Doha said Israel must define its goals precisely. There would be no security for Israel at the price of Palestinian lives. The destruction of Hamas would require a ten-year war.

If Macron was right, was the "West" willing to see the carnage continue for a decade? It seems the French President was struck by a moment of sanity. Hamas couldn't be defeated militarily without a prolonged, hugely destructive war which would almost certainly also destroy Israel whose economy was nose-diving and society fracturing.

Disagreeing with Macron's view that Netanyahu's aim was the destruction of Hamas, Mads Gilbert argued it was rather to wipe out the Palestinians. They were starving and freezing to death or being killed by disease. Southern Gaza was now in zones. Hospital transfers were no longer possible. Medics were improvising. The WHO estimated a hundred and fifty thousand civilians with infectious diseases. Soon there would be massive deaths. As for Al Shifa, he had been in Gaza in January and June and seen no sign of a military presence. There were a hundred and thirty medical facilities in the Strip, why did Israel accuse only one of harbouring the IDF? It was a fig-leaf. Where were the world's leaders? They were impotent. A sadistic punishment of the Palestinian people was taking place, two and a quarter million people being treated in a medieval fashion. The dignity and solidarity of the Palestinians in the face of what was being done to them was remarkable. They must not give up. He was speechless at the sadism of the IDF supported by the US and the EU.

Gilbert was right to point out undemonstratively that Netanyahu was annihilating the Palestinians. His problem, of course, was that to keep his fig-leaf in place, he had to do it bit by bit. Carpet bombing to kill thousands or tens of thousands at a time wouldn't have been compatible with the story of the IDF going after Hamas in targeted raids. The corollary was the aggression was going to have go on for a long time. Maybe Netanyahu was hoping viruses and bacteria would do the work for him. Perhaps cholera would sweep through and decimate the population. No doubt, also, he could calculate the restrictions on aid would lead to the deaths of many of the vulnerable; but it's likely his calculus was in line with Macron's view. A long war, the slow grinding down and slaughter of the population, and perhaps a tipping point at which some escape route would be provided for those remaining. The speechlessness at the sadism needs to be extended back many centuries. The world hasn't yet cast off the false notion that slaughter is morally justified in pursuit of lucre. The delusion is a simple one, captured in simple language, Manifest Destiny the Monroe doctrine, the White Man's burden, but the consequences are devastating. An equally simple step needs to be taken, from the airy rhetoric of human rights, to the reality that no one has the right to be aggressive to anyone else to suit their advantage. All human lives really are of the same worth.

Israel issued an evacuation order. Leaflets containing a QR code were dropped over the north, of great use to the Palestinians as there was virtually no connectivity. The UN pointed out eighty per cent of the population was already displaced. Israel claimed the tiny, barren Al Mawasi was a safe zone.

Kamala Harris said the US would not permit the forced movement of people in Gaza and enunciated four further principles she would stand by: a unified Gaza and West Bank governed by the Palestinian Authority; no reduction in the territory; no occupation by Israel and no terrorist influence.

Marvellous. If only the US's actions had risen a centimetre towards these high aspirations. The forced movement of people was taking place every day as they were chased round the Strip like a bluebottle round a kitchen. Netanyahu had set his face against any linkage of the West Bank and Gaza years earlier, as he had asserted Gaza would have to be under some form of Israeli control. If no terrorists were to have influence, didn't that exclude Israel?

Jabalia refugee camp was attacked and a hundred killed. People pulled bodies from the rubble by hand. Rafah was bombed driving people to try to return to the north.

Academic and author, Dov Waxman argued Netanyahu was getting a better press abroad. Since 7th October, he had been the subject of much criticism. He had delayed meeting the families. He believed that Israel was the same as Netanyahu which was coterminous with Churchill ie he was the great war leader who would be a national hero. He saw himself as the leader of the Jewish people, an attitude hardly marked by modesty. Since 7th October he had been on the defensive. His only thought was his own survival. Gallant's recent press conference in which his differences with Netanyahu had become clear suggested the divisions in the cabinet could become a liability. Netanyahu was always militaristic. He would countenance no move other than the annihilation of Hamas. Yet he was under pressure from the US to restrain the IDF. The tensions were significant. Likud was getting ready for the demise of Netanyahu.

To associate Netanyahu with modesty was like linking Stalin with honesty. His megalomania was stunning.

Saleh al-Aroui, who would be assassinated by Israel on 2nd January 2024, announced there would be no more prisoner releases till the war was over. Women and children were not Hamas's targets. The Israeli claim that woman and children were still held was a lie. There would be no negotiations about the captives till the fighting stopped.

Lloyd Austin called on Israel not to drive the civilian population into the arms of the enemy. The only way Israel could win was by protecting civilians.

Austin's tiny bit of wisdom came a little late. Israel had been driving the Palestinians into the hands of Hamas for two months. If the only way Israel could win was by protecting civilians, its strategy was ensuring defeat. Why was the Secretary of Defence of the most powerful military bleating in this pathetic manner? The US's military might was feeble, because it was morally disabled. The US's moral position, that Israel by definition is always in the right, just like itself, ensured that Austin sounded as foolish as Canute.

On 3rd December, the Israeli navy sank ships said to be associated with Hamas. In the West Bank, ten masked raiders attacked a restaurant. Just an ordinary day for Palestinians.

James Elder of UNICEF reported seeing children with third degree brain injuries. The bombing of hospitals was relentless. The amount of aid was hopeless. Diseases were spreading. He predicted as many children would die of illness as from the violence. Why not stop the bombing and let the supplies in? The social fabric of the Strip was smashed. It was like a game of chess. The people were sent to so-called safe zones which were nothing but pockets of dry sand. They were zones of death. Israel was callous, cold and calculating. The levels of panic among the Palestinians were very high. An entire generation was traumatised. Any decent person would be heartbroken. What Israel was doing was both immoral and illegal. To remain silent was complicity.

John Bolton, choosing his language as carefully as ever, intent on spreading human sympathy far and wide, said Palestinians do not have a problem, they are the problem. With the typical purblind mentality of the our-ideology-is-the-truth right-wing, he was blithely unaware of his pure racism. Two States was the wrong idea. Palestinians should be resettled. The problem was the Arab States didn't want to take them. The Palestinian refugees were being weaponised. The Palestinian Authority wasn't an alternative. Gaza was one big refugee camp, which wasn't the best solution for the Palestinians. The Republicans offered Israel unconditional support while the Democrats were split. There was plenty of anti-Semitism in the US and it was now on show.

Bolton might have come straight out of nineteenth century Europe, especially England. The victims of colonialism were the problem. How did they dare exist, and in places we wanted for ourselves? It's interesting how metaphysical the politics of colonialism is: the world was made for the whites to rule and exploit. The rest were put on earth to be slaves, industrial ants or corpses. The flimsy house of cards which is this mentality can't withstand even the slightest breath of reason, yet it persists while reason veils her face.

Sarah Leah Whitson, a lawyer from Democracy for the Arab World Now, responded that resettlement didn't serve the interests of the Palestinians but Israel's desire to ethnically cleanse. The Oslo Accords were stale and impotent. It was an insult to the Palestinians to depict them as an Iranian proxy. Iran may take sides like many other States do, often unfortunately. The Palestinians in Gaza had been under siege since 2006, they were stifled and strangled. If it wasn't Iran offering support, it would be someone else. The Palestinians had a fundamental grievance. Biden was an utter failure. His aim was to align Israel with the Arab States and to by-pass the Palestinians. His scheme had exploded. There could be no stability if there was oppression. It was a natural human instinct to resist tyranny. She hoped the Arabs would re-think their nasty little scheme.

Whitson is no radical. She worked for Goldman Sachs. It requires nothing more than common human sympathy and moderate intelligence to arrive at her kind of view. Understanding the oppression of the Palestinians is not hard science. Every child in the playground understands fairness because it's part of our biological inheritance. It requires extraordinary effort to suppress this and to denature people to the extent they elaborate a phoney moralism to defend fundamental injustice. Whitson's simple formula, that there can be no stability where there is oppression, is obviously right. Everyone can see it, even those who profit from the oppression; but they must engage in constant self-deception. How do we prove this? We can't. In the end, it's a matter of faith. There is supportive evidence, but no proof. We have to trust to human sympathy, it is all that can save us.

Gaza's Health Ministry spokesman Ashraf Al Qudra claimed medical staff had been seized and tortured by Israel. The injured were being left the bleed to death. The remaining medical facilities in the north had been bombed. Getting people out was virtually impossible. Since 1st November only four hundred and three had been removed. Displaced people were in hospitals and UNRWA facilities without basic provision. There were many communicable diseases. He appealed to the conscience of the whole world. There was a need for an effective global mechanism. Fifty-six ambulances had been destroyed. Paramedics were being arrested.

Al Qudra's call for world conscience is interesting. The world is ruled by States and they are not moral actors. They make no moral decisions, rather they defend interests. At least it can be said of the US that it is sometimes honest about this. In its most cynical politicians, the doctrine that the US does what it must to defend what it sees as its interests gains expression; but how is that in any way moral? An individual who declared, "I do what I have to do to pursue my interests" would be correctly viewed as sociopathic. We recognise without difficulty that morality is about the interests of others. To see no interests but your own is pathological. Every murderer, rapist, robber and paedophile can say they did what they had to do to pursue their interests, given their interests are demented. A world conscience can be nothing more than the combined moral decisions of all the world's individuals. There is no morality in the rule of States.

HANNIBAL

The scale of the casualties, Marwan Bishara observed, showed the war was intensifying. Seven hundred had been killed in the past few days. Was the US exerting pressure? The more Blinken talked to Israel, the worse things became. Hamas was being incorrectly likened to ISIS. The US says nothing and doesn't show up or if it speaks or appears, things do downhill. The assault was against civilians. Hamas was collateral damage. Israel was making use of US hypocrisy. The stores of US weapons in the region were open to Israel. How many would have to die? Did Albright think half a million dead Iraqis was enough? The aim was to decimate the Palestinians. What would the real "day after" look like? The infrastructure of the Strip would be destroyed. University professors were being killed, scientists were enemy combatants, in other words, Palestinians, not Hamas, were the enemy. Biden was employing the wrong diplomat. Blinken should resign, either he was no good or he was being played like a fiddle. Perhaps Lloyd Austin could do better. It was going to be a tactical win but a strategic loss for Israel if the huge civilian casualties continued. Arab countries were doing nothing. Israel understood what that meant. Arabs have leverage but Egypt couldn't bring one truck into Gaza without Israeli permission. The Arabs were very weak. However, a bunch of Hamas fighters had stopped the mighty Israeli army. Israel was winning the war against children but not against Hamas.

Blinken comes from a line of diplomats, which may explain his destination. It isn't always wise to follow in the footsteps of your forbears, however convenient it may be. He supported the 2003 invasion of Iraq, after which he proposed the country should be split into three independent regions: Shiastan in the south, Sunnistan in the north and Iraqi Kurdistan. Good old colonial, carving-up the spoils stuff. Of Obama's decision to kill Bin Laden he said, "I've never seen a more courageous decision made by a leader." One of Bin Laden's children and a woman in the compound were killed in the raid. Perhaps it takes courage to kill people against whom there is no evidence of wrong-doing. The raid was a violation of Pakistan's sovereignty, but who cares, they're only blacks after all. Imagine if Palestinians decided, given the US's long and unflinching support for Israel's oppression, to carry out a daring assassination of an American general in the Pentagon. Would that be an act of great courage? That Bin Laden should have been brought to justice is beyond question, but to kill him on foreign territory when he was unarmed and might have been arrested is typical US arrogance. Blinken also supported Saudi Arabia's attack on Yemen, maybe that was courageous too; and in April 2024 he refused to act on recommendations of the Israel Leahy Vetting Forum regarding abuse of Palestinians in the West Bank by Israel. No wonder every time he intervened, things got worse in Gaza.

Israeli legal scholar and international women's right advocate Ruth Halperin-Kaddari, speaking on 4th December, protested that Palestinian women were being raped and mutilated. Footage of bodies showed evidence of rape, mutilation and execution. First responders were producing numerous accounts of violence. It was too prevalent and systematic not to have been planned. On 8th October she had written to the Red Cross and the Special Rapporteur for Violence against women. Crimes against humanity were being committed confirmed by experts from around the world. Until a week earlier no one at the UN was speaking of "sexual violence". Antonio Gutteres has recognised the problem and called for an investigation. There was a conventional framing of Palestinians as victims which got in the way of the truth being revealed. The cruelty being inflicted on Palestinian women exceeded what was done by ISIS. Israel's actions were consistently presented as defensive. The suffering of the Palestinians was blamed on Hamas.

In spite of continuing claims by Israel and its apologists, no evidence had been produced of rape by Hamas fighters on 7th October. No eye-witnesses had come forward, nor any survivors. On the other hand, there was plentiful evidence of rape of Palestinian women, but very little media interest. Women non-combatants fit badly into the official picture. They quickly become prey to wound-up, frustrated soldiers, but the heroes of the IDF can't be associated with bestial behaviour, nor the attack itself linked to a precipitous decline in moral judgement, so they have to be air-brushed away. War, being by definition a form of violation, rape always flourishes. The official view, unstated but ever-present, is that the cause is good even if it entails the most debased means.

Qalandiya in the West Bank was raided, shops destroyed, the Star of David sprayed on buildings. One person was killed and seventy-seven injured. One hundred and fifty IDF took part asking local people, "where are the guns?", "where are the narcotics?". People were beaten and put in handcuffs.

Six Palestinians had died in Israeli jails since 7th October, There were, reportedly, beatings, strip searches, threats of rape. Since the start of the attack, the rules had gone out of the window.

The Dutch State was referred to the ICC by aid organisations for its export of fighter jets and F35 spare parts to Israel.

Deaths in the Strip were averaging two hundred and seventy a day, more than British deaths during the Second World War.

Elijah Magnier argued that the US was at some distance from Israel's war crimes and crimes against humanity. Why was Israel killing civilians? Because it was permitted to. The Presidential campaign was uppermost in American minds. We were far from a ceasefire and Israel was equally far from achieving its aims. The Palestinian resistance was doing well though Hamas didn't have the capacity to strike Tel Aviv. Netanyahu, he predicted, would go to jail. Israel was weak in the face of a guerilla campaign.

Former Egyptian Foreign Minister Hussein Haridi called for solidarity with the Palestinians. Soon the Israeli war cabinet would have to listen to the US. We were one step from the US calling for a ceasefire. Senior officials were pushing for it. It was a near certainty that Israel was planning to push Palestinians into the Sinai and out of the West Bank into Jordan. Pamphlets had been dropped warning of a second Nakba. Egypt wouldn't accept Palestinians being driven onto its territory. It was in talks with the US and insisting on no forced displacement and was issuing warning upon warning, as well as engaging in exercises on the Egyptian side of the Rafah crossing.

The Israeli cabinet included those paragons of enlightenment, Smotrich and Ben Gvir. They were a very long way from accepting a ceasefire, whatever the US said, and were willing to tip Netanyahu's government into the sea to get their own way.

Palestinian lead for Oxfam, Bushra Khalidi, said safety no longer existed for the Palestinians. There had been six previous military escalations. People had been displaced over and over. People were losing hope. Nearly two million people were packed into an area the size of Heathrow. The

World Health Organisation was predicting an epidemic. Sixty per cent of Gaza was rubble. The arrival of aid was far too slow.

On 5th December, leaflets were dropped telling Palestinians to leave Khan Younis for Rafah. Khan Younis was targeted. The Al Aqsa hospital appealed for blood donations.

Robert Jenrick, Tory MP, who was, for a time, chair of the All Party Parliamentary Group for the prevention of Genocide and Crimes Against Humanity, said on Radio 4 that "we support Israel". Just who the "we" was he didn't make clear, but it wasn't the British people who, in poll after poll, were heavily in favour of a ceasefire. Privately educated, Jenrick was elected in a by-election in Newark on 5th June 2014. The Electoral Commission ruled in 2017 the Tories had breached spending rules during the contest, and in two others. The party was fined £70,000. Of course, marinated in the shamelessness characteristic of modern politicians, the self-regarding Jenrick saw no reason to apologise. In April 2020 the *Sunday Times* reported the ex-lawyer had claimed £100,000 for his third home from the taxpayer. Jenrick, it seems, continues to suck £2,000 a month from the public purse for a house in his constituency, though he owns three. Naturally, he dislikes public spending and benefit scroungers. In June 2019 he was the UK representative at the Israeli-Palestine peace initiative led by that beacon of enlightenment, Jared Kushner. To call this a peace initiative is a little like calling kicking someone in the teeth orthodontics. In a speech to the Conservative Friends of Israel in January 2020, he said he looked forward to the day the British embassy would be in Jerusalem. In November 2020 the Public Accounts Committee judged that funding provided by Jenrick's department for projects in Newark was "opaque and not impartial." Jenrick approved a £1 billion luxury housing scheme in the Isle of Dogs funded by Richard Desmond, a Tory donor. Tower Hamlets sought a judicial review. Jenrick conceded the scheme was "unlawful by reason of apparent bias." Jenrick was also the kind-hearted soul who had pictures of Mickey Mouse and Baloo painted out in a reception centre for children in Kent. If Jenrick came from a social housing estate he'd have been banged up as a serial offender long ago. Hamas, he explained, had to be destroyed. That Israel was, according to informed international opinion, engaging in daily war crimes and crimes against humanity, didn't seem to conflict with his previous position as chair of the APPG group. Why would it? For the likes of Jenrick, war crimes can take place only against allies. Ripping the bodies of women and children to bits is fair game when you're defending the rights of the rich.

The IDF pushed into the south and increased the bombing in the north. Jabaliya, Israel claimed, was a Hamas hot-spot. The IDF had to "close the back door". The UN said its facilities were threatened by Israel. The World Health Organisation was moving its supplies of drugs to prevent them from attack. Tanks were on the outskirts of Khan Younis. The Kuwaiti hospital in Rafah was hit. Residential areas were bombed. Israeli snipers were killing people fleeing Kamal Adwan hospital. The aim of the IDF was to divide the Strip into north, central and south. Kamal Adwan was under siege, dead bodies everywhere. A health worker from Kamal Adwan called Netanyahu "the Hitler of Israel" and said of the IDF "you are the neo-Nazis". At 12.30 GMT there was a raid on Jenin.

David Cameron, pointed out the US State Department was imposing visa bans on those involved in settler violence, as if this would in any serious way mitigate the violence inflicted on the Palestinians. Such action had been promised by Biden years earlier, but nothing had been done. Biden's main worry was his re-election. Resignations from his administration were doing him harm.

The Gulf Co-operation Council of six Arab States called on the Security Council to end the barbaric war. Netanyahu was endangering the region. He must not be allowed to get away with his war crimes.

Calling on the Security Council to end the massacre was like calling on Al Capone to put an end to bootlegging. Any one of the five permanent members could scupper any resolution and as one of them was a criminal State which had flouted international law for decades, a State founded on genocide, developed by slavery, consolidated by the Jim Crow laws and resting on the mass incarceration of coloured people, why would it blench at the slaughter of a few thousand non-whites?

Marwan Bishara said the GCC had intervened too tardily. The focus should be a ceasefire not a pause. The US didn't want a ceasefire but its stance was backfiring because Israel's plan was to depopulate the Strip. However, the Israeli argument that all Palestinian civilians were guilty was boomeranging: if there were no civilians in Gaza there were none either in Israel. On 6th October, Hamas was not popular in Gaza, now for every dead fighter there was at least one new recruit.

Bishara was correct: the US didn't want a ceasefire. As usual, its calculation was about its supposed "interests". Yet at the same time, it purported to be a moral actor, something, as pointed out above, States never are. They exist to defend and promote perceived interests. Institutions don't make moral decision. There is much wild talk about computers becoming as "intelligent" as humans, even though the world's most powerful computers know nothing and can't think. Yet the debate seldom strays into the arena of moral decisions, the most important we make. If it were possible to produce a computer which could make moral choices, what would be the point? We do it all the time because we evolved for it. It would be as useless as a computer which could cough or unrinate. The problem we face isn't lack of computing power, but how to dismantle the States which get in the way of our moral choices prevailing.

Osama Hamdan, Hamas spokesman, evoked the Nazi occupation, condemned all those who supported Israel and celebrated those who refuse to leave their land. Gaza would be a cemetery for the aggressor. He saluted the youths who rebelled in the West Bank. What was taking place was a terrible massacre of the unarmed. Hospitals and schools were targeted. The Palestinian people were displaying heroism. The US was the sponsor of the violence, it supplied the weapons. It was no sponsor of democracy. The will of the Palestinian people would not be broken. Gaza was an open war zone. The target was every living thing. In 1956 in Suez we saw how France, the UK and the US behave. The same was true today. The enemy had failed to remove us. Netanyahu's aims were unattainable and he would be proven a war criminal. The Palestinians had resisted for seventy-five years. There would be no victory against them. Netanyahu was sinking in the swamp of Gaza. Rabbis who supported him were justifying rape and genocide.

Hamdan is no moral genius, nor is it the case that Hamas can't be criticised, but those on the receiving end of injustice merely have to say what has happened to them to have the moral upper hand. A child abused by a priest rises to higher moral height than her abuser simply by telling the truth. The descendants of coloured people lynched in the American south need do nothing more than dispassionately recount the events, to be the moral superiors of the perpetrators. Apart from his predictions, everything Hamdan said was straightforward fact. Above all, he was right about the US: it permitted the continuation of a massacre it could have ended any day, except it foolishly believed its interests were served by not doing so.

In response to Hamdan, Bishara emphasised his tone of defiance. He was taking the confrontation to the US and had dismissed the accusations of rape and so on against Hamas. The Arab countries should rally to try to break the siege. A report from the Washington Post claimed most of Hamas's forces were in place. About five thousand of the original thirty were dead, which underlined Hamdan's point: the IDF was committing war crimes but failing to achieve its aims.

BBC news claimed rape and mutilation took place on 7th October but the only evidence was anecdotal and provided by Israel. There was no third party confirmation.

On 4th December, Robert Jackson of New York University and Joshua Mitts of Columbia published a paper, Trading on Terror, which claimed there had been a spike in short selling before the 7th October incursion. "Days before the attack," they wrote, "traders appeared to anticipate events to come…And just before the attack, short selling of Israeli securities on the Tel Aviv Stock Exchange increased dramatically…Our findings suggest that traders informed about the coming attacks profited from these tragic events." The authors have acknowledged they made a mistake about the scale of the profits by assuming some shares were traded in shekels when in fact the currency was agorots. Doubt has been cast on their findings by, for example, Carson Block, a short seller, who claims Mitts begins from his conclusion and backfills by cherry-picking data which he casts in mathematical mumbo-jumbo people can't see through. Block has criticised previous work on the same issue by Mitts. Of course, as a short seller, Block is hardly impartial. The paper was criticised also by Yaniv Pigot, a Tel Aviv Stock Exchange executive. Once again, not someone able to view the matter from the third person perspective. There is apparently no controversy over the fact that almost four and half million shares in the Israeli bank, Leumi, were sold between 14th September and 5th October. The Israeli Securities Agency doesn't dispute this. Nor does there appear to be any doubt that there was a spike in short selling from 2nd October. It isn't possible, without expert knowledge, to draw a firm conclusion, but there is at least a suggestion that Jackson and Mitts were onto something.

Far less doubtful is the testimony of Colonel Nof Erez who called 7th October "a mass Hannibal" "The Hannibal Directive," he declared, "was apparently applied at a certain stage." On December 18th the IDF admitted Israeli combatants were killed by friendly fire but argued it "was not morally sound to investigate." In January 2024, *Yedioth Ahronoth* claimed the Directive had been used from noon on 7th October. On 28th March 2024, Captain Bar Zonshein said in an interview he had fired tank shells at vehicles not knowing if they contained Israeli combatants. "I decided," he said, "that this is the right decision." In June 2024 a UN Commission report said the ISF used the Hannibal Directive in several instances on 7th October. In July 2024 *Haaretz* reported the Directive was employed several times, the first being 7.18 a.m.

None of this is esoteric. It's easily available online. Nor does understanding it require special intellectual capacities. Yet the media line is that some twelve hundred Israelis were killed by Hamas on 7th October. By now, every media outlet in the world should have informed people of the truth. The Israelis, almost certainly, killed some of their own people. How many, no one knows. Nor will we, as long as Israel claims finding out is not "morally sound". That the propaganda position remains that all the victims were killed by Hamas, when evidence of the opposite is at hand, is testimony to the stunning efficiency of the propaganda system. It could be argued that people should find the truth for themselves, but no ordinary citizen has the time to research every issue. We rely on journalists to do that. They, of course, work for media which are principally in the hands of the rich. Hence the widespread misconceptions.

THE SOBBING OF THE VIOLINS

French ambassador to the UN from 2003 to 2006, Gérard Araud said Israeli settlers were frank about deliberately preventing territorial compromise. Ben Gvir was a fascist. There was a need to move the Israeli public. Israel was annexing the West Bank. To get both sides to agree a peace deal was impossible. There was no Palestinian leadership and Israel was in the hands of the far-right. Israeli public opinion was looking for security. Israelis were deeply insecure, convinced the Palestinians wanted to wipe them out. It was necessary to convince the Israelis that two States would make them secure. Pressure on Israel from the international community never worked because Israel is obsessed by security. The US needed to twist Israel's arm, it had to be more creative and make an offer to Israel which could break the stalemate. Macron's first reaction after 7th October, unconditional support for Israel, went too far. There was a big difference between France and the US. The US was fully supportive of Israel as, he claimed, the 1991 Madrid Conference showed. Relations between France and Israel were always a bit more uncomfortable. Biden had hit two barriers: the Israelis take no notice of him, and the Democrats are divided. The youth especially were turning against him. The settlers were always vocal. The Israelis were engaging in "retail ethnic cleansing" ie bit by bit. "Diplomacy," Araud observed, somewhat gnomically, "is not the sobbing of the violins of autumn."

For an ex-diplomat, this isn't bad, given that diplomats are puppets ventriloquised by the States they serve. Ben Gvir, of course, is a fascist, but he thrives on the designation. A significant proportion of the Israel population is at ease with violence directed at the Palestinians; hardly surprisingly given their depiction in Israeli media as less than human and intent on slaughtering Jews. Perhaps it would be more useful to point out the lack of connection between ben Gvir's politics and Judaism. The more he's called a fascist, the more he likes it; but he may be less enamoured of being depicted as anti-Judaic. That there is no Palestinian leadership is an extraordinary comment which plays into Zionist ideology. Israel makes a habit of wiping out Palestinian leaders, precisely because they are, to some degree or other, effective. At the very least, they provide a focus. Even the old and compromised Abbas does that. There is always someone to negotiate with on the Palestinian side, if the Israelis are willing to meet them halfway. By the time of the Gaza debacle, it had long been Netanyahu's strategy to ensure the Palestinians looked leaderless to confirm his assertion he had no one to talk to.

Araud's use of "Israel" is problematic, as this usage in the mouths of western spokespeople always is. Did he mean the Israel of the West Bank settlements, the siege of Gaza, the illegal occupation of the Golan Heights? If so, everyone who upholds international law should reject that definition. The only Israel consistent with international law is one within, at most, the 1967 borders, but crucially one which pulls out the settlements, lifts the siege, gets out of the Golan Heights, permits the establishment of a link between the West Bank and Gaza and an autonomous Palestinian society. When Israel demands its security and when western politicians speak of a safe and secure Israel, what they imply is Israel in its current iteration.

Araud is right: the US should twist Israel's arm. Why doesn't it? When the US looks at Israel, it looks in the mirror. To condemn the ethnic cleansing of 1948 and everything that has followed, would be self-criticism. It would require the insight the US State lacks. How can States be expected to have insight? The US State exists to defend the interests it has established through genocide, slavery, conquest and exploitation. Why would it face down a client State which does the same?

On 6th December it was reported Netanyahu had told his ministers over the past few days he was the only person who could prevent a two-States agreement. On the one hand, the US and its poodles spouted their customary platitudes about two States, on the other Netanyahu set his face against it, as he had done for years, and not a bleat of criticism came from the supposedly principled west.

Israel claimed it had intercepted a surface-to-air missile in the Red Sea near Eilat and that the Houthis were a proxy for Iran. It also approved a far-right march on the Al-Aqsa mosque set for 7th December.

Ben Gvir was furious when Gallant issued an arrest warrant for a settler involved in violence. The West Bank, he asserted, was his constituency. Three were killed in Al Fara refugee camp in the West Bank, two teenagers. Seven were injured. Balata refugee camp was raided.

Blinken announced the visa ban might apply to families, which must have terrified the settlers.

An "utter deepening horror" was how Antonio Gutteres had described Gaza, according to Marwan Bishara. The US was engaged in deflection and deception as it pretended to do something. There was more and more comedy in the tragedy: the settlers the US claimed to be punishing had its support. For decades there had been networks in America raising money for settlements from US taxpayers. Jared Kushner ran such a charity. Nothing was changing. If there was a visa ban on Netanyahu or Gantz or Gallant, that would be different. As it was, there wasn't even a slap on the wrist. It was an insult to intelligence. The fact this nonsense was being discussed was indicative: the true issue was sidelined. There was a pretence of action. The US was in fact blindly supportive of Israel. If there was a land invasion of Rafah, the result might be hundreds of thousands of deaths. Was a ceasefire on the cards? No, because Netanyahu was opposed and would continue the war selectively whatever was agreed. The US and Israel were sitting back and watching Palestinians die. At the moment, the Palestinians were refusing to move, but once the destruction became absolute, people with young children or facing desperation might try to leave. Maybe Egypt would be pushed to take in Palestinians in return for US aid. The US was complicit in ethnic cleansing. Israel was using starvation as a weapon. It was engaged in sadistic collective punishment. Gaza's infrastructure was obliterated. Talk of safe areas was humbug, genocide was under way. Netanyahu was playing a game between his cabinet and war cabinet.

The factitious US and EU moral outrage at settler violence in the West Bank was farcical. It was an opportunity to claim some form of moral objection to aggression, while yawning and dozing as Israel, the original aggressor in Palestine, went about eliminating the population of Gaza. No one can repudiate moral discrimination entirely, apart, perhaps from a small minority of psychopaths, because it is so inscribed in our nature. Thus, those who push their narrow interest, disregarding moral boundaries, are forced to drag in a phoney moralism; hence the inauthenticity of State morality.

Mohammed Ghalayani, an atmospheric scientist from Manchester, who escaped Gaza during December, described Khan Younis as terrifying. He had spent three hours collecting water. Some were going for ten days without any. There was extreme poverty and a desperate need for aid. Bombing was intense. To the question why Palestinians didn't simply leave, he answered, "Would you?". Leaving was no guarantee. There was no safety. It was textbook genocide.

Among the common folk of the world, there was sufficient imagination to understand a ceasefire was necessary. Statesmen and women, however, are not conspicuous for their imagination. Once again, interest blinds insight. When nothing but your interest matters, there is no space for empathy. Most ordinary people had enough native sympathy to want relief for the Palestinians, as well as release of the hostages. The politicos could see only *Realpolitik*, a preposterous misnomer, as what it means is retreat into fantasy.

Antonio Gutteres directed the Security Council to meet invoking Article 99 which permits the General Secretary to bring to the attention of the Council anything he or she thinks may be a threat to the maintenance of peace and security. He claimed the humanitarian situation in Gaza was close to collapse. Used only four times previously, the measure permits the General Secretary to convene the Council for discussion, but the veto power of the five permanent members remained the obstacle to a ceasefire.

In response, Marwan Bishara said the UN was trying to face down the US, which was the only obstacle to peace. There was little hope. The US was slow-walking everything, frustrating every positive move. Gutteres's duty was to the UN Charter. His voice was more important than any member State. The majority of countries wanted a ceasefire. Gutteres understood what was taking place was genocide. His move was a call to arms, an attempt to ramp up diplomatic pressure. Public opinion in the US and the EU was shifting. The US had often stood alone in support of Israel, this time things were more grave. The US's credibility was on the line. It was becoming a laughing stock. The clock was ticking. International public opinion was pro-Palestinian. Israel was getting nowhere in securing its military aims. The patience of the States in the region was running out. Would the US listen?

Trying to get the US to listen was like trying to make an alcoholic see their drinking is a problem. By "the US", of course, is meant the US State. This shorthand is very misleading. The media is replete with claims that the UK thinks one thing, France another, China another. States, like computers, don't think. Only individuals think. So-called "group-think" is merely a set of individuals conforming. Groups don't think. Tens of millions of Americans thought there should be a ceasefire, but they were not included in the standard definition of "the US". What Bishara's question really meant was, would Biden listen? He had the power. One phone call and he could have ended the fighting. Thus, the foolish delusions of one old man became "the US" and thousands of people were sent to their painful deaths so his distorted view of reality could go unchallenged.

The Palestine Solidarity Campaign was overwhelmed by the size of protests in South Africa. The NDN Collective of indigenous peoples said that ancestrally they had faced what the Palestinians in Gaza were facing. Indigenous people should call for a ceasefire. Usuf Chitke, professor emeritus at Stellenbosch University said apartheid had been a humiliation. Resistance had been spectacular. The struggle of the South Africans was incomplete without the freedom of the Palestinians. The South Africans were linked to the Palestinians through resistance.

On 7th December, Rabbi Mirvis, often invited onto Radio 4's *Thought for the Day* slot, claimed the BBC had reported sexual abuse of Israelis by Hamas fighters on 7th October, despite there being no third-party evidence. It appears no Palestinian spokesperson has been invited to the same feature.

Fatah's offices in Nablus were attacked. The Palestinian Authority was criticised by Palestinians, seven were injured in Jenin refugee camp during a nine-hour attack. Tanks, drones and snipers were used in West Bank raids. Balata refugee camp was raided. Jabaliya refugee camp was bombed.

Human Rights Watch accused Israel of targeting journalists on the Lebanon border. Aya Majzoub of Amnesty International said there was clear evidence Israel struck a group of journalists on 13th October, which needed to be investigated as a war crime. Israel had a long history of killing journalists. In 2000, a Lebanese journalist working for the BBC was assassinated. More than twenty years later, no one had been held accountable. Why? Where were the eyes and ears of the world?

Israel argued Antonio Gutteres was threatening world peace. The UN's human rights chief, on the other hand, pointed out Israel had not responded to requests for evidence about allegations of rape on 7th October.

James Elder of UNICEF said anyone watching the events must be heartbroken. Israel was prosecuting a war on children. It was deeply wrong, indiscriminate and merciless. People were plunged into darkness for long periods, were dying of thirst. Aid wasn't getting through. There was only one functioning entry point. His role was to bear witness.

Elder was right that anyone who had not lost their basic fellow feeling would be heartbroken, unfortunately such sentiment is a disadvantage for those seeking power. Needless to say, that means wealth too: no one in power is ever poor. The interests of States can't be defended by those without property. Human interests can, of course. There is no need for wealth in order to be wise or kind. The State, however, is always and everywhere first of all a defender of property. A society without great differences of wealth could dispense with the State. Far from being heartbroken by the deaths of tens of thousands, Netanyahu, a thoroughly dehumanised man, would have been delighted. Likewise, the hundreds of members of Congress who heartily applauded him a few months later, as the political leaders who went on providing weapons. George Orwell once remarked that decency is found only among those without power. When people are defending a property interest, they lose, to some extent or other, their capacity for common human sympathy, hence the mercilessness Elder rightly highlighted.

Men arrested in Beit Lahia in the north of the Strip were shown naked except for their underwear, forced to sit, heads bowed on the ground, before being taken to Israel.

No doubt this ritual humiliation too greatly pleased Netanyahu and his backers. The sadism of power is never satisfied.

Tulkarem was raided. Twenty-one Palestinians were arrested in raids on the West Bank, sixteen-year-old Omar Abu Bakr was killed by a shot to the chest. It's good to be able to put a name to a victim. Most of those murdered by the IDF will remain nameless except to their close relatives.

Two hundred ultra-nationalists were granted permission to march through the Al Aqsa compound to the Wailing Wall in protest against the administration of the area by the Waqf, a Muslim organisation.

Anthropologist, Sami Hermez, said he assumed what Israel was saying was true: its aim was to destroy the Palestinians in the Strip. Hamas was a secondary matter. How many Hamas fighters had been killed? Who knew? Israel could hit Hamas but not destroy their aim. A temporary ceasefire might take eyes off Gaza which would give the Israelis an opportunity to push the Palestinians out. A ceasefire and the end of the siege needed to be simultaneous.

Hermez was percipient: in August 2024 the US and Israel would optimistically promote a possible ceasefire, but Netanyahu would let the cat out of the bag by telling the families of hostages the Israeli military must stay in the Strip. Hermez made an elementary point: the assault was said to be against Hamas yet no reliable tally of fighters killed was offered. Israel could go on decimating the Palestinian population until it was wiped out, while claiming it was going after only Hamas. No great intellectual capacity was required to see this. It was plain to everyone. As plain as the fact that the US was happy to let the carnage continue on the thoroughly specious grounds Israel was a progressive democracy. In that regard, Israel's primary claim to Palestine presented a problem: the land was, so the argument went, given to Abraham by god some three thousand years ago or so, and this donation was, implicitly, irrevocable. Democracy is at odds with eternal, irrevocable rights. The people, supposedly, can choose and can change their minds. If Israel was a democracy, there was no reason the people shouldn't, at some point, decide to hand the land over to the Palestinians, or strike an agreement with them to share it. The notion of a fixed inheritance divinely granted is incompatible with the essence of democracy, which is why Zionists often argue against the inheritance of the Enlightenment.

At six o'clock on 6th December poet Rafaat Alareer, along with his brother, sister and four nephews was killed in a targeted attack in northern Gaza after a long period of death threats, evidence not only of Isreal's monumental cruelty, but also its ingrained stupidity. Poets can be influential, but seldom in the short term. A regime that kills poets is in utter desperation. Alareer's final poem was quickly translated into dozens of languages. Were he still alive, many people who've read it and remember his name wouldn't know of him. The flat he was in was pinpointed. The Israelis were clearly paranoid. Even people writing sonnets were a threat.

Netanyahu told Israelis lighting candles for Hannukah not all the hostages would be released, what he didn't mention is he that he was the reason.

Martin Griffiths said there was no humanitarian operation in southern Gaza, the pace of the attack in the south now equalled that of the north. No place was safe and aid was in tatters. The arrival of trucks had become nothing more than humanitarian opportunism. It was erratic and not sustainable.

A career diplomat, Griffiths took a principled and humanitarian position throughout, but he made his way by serving the British State, hardly a body with clean hands. Diplomats can be effective and can assist those most in need, but usually to do so they have to push against the limits of what their position permits, as Craig Murray discovered when he dared to set his face against tyranny. Every servant of the State is hidebound. As Hemingway puts it in *For Whom The Bell Tolls*, "Continence is the foe of heresy." Diplomats are required to be continent. In March 2024 Griffiths announced he was leaving the UN for "health reasons". Maybe protocol prevented him saying it was because of the horror in Gaza.

ARTICLE NINETY-NINE

Gutteres said he was ready to speak to the Security Council on 7th December. He wanted a humanitarian pause. There needed to be negotiations towards a resolution, but the US was opposed. Robert Wood, Deputy US Ambassador to the UN said the question of a pause should be left in the background. Gutteres said Gaza might never recover.

Wood's position was inordinately cruel. Why leave in the background the matter of a pause which could save thousands of lives and permit the arrival of desperately needed aid, except to serve the needs of American business and its allies? Images of the smartly-dressed Wood entering the plush surroundings of the UN building contrasted starkly with the nastiness of his message.

Chair of the Council on American Islamic relations, Nihad Awad, highlighted a report which claimed two thousand one hundred and seventy-one cases of Islamophobia in two months, an increase of a hundred and seventy-two per cent on 2022. Free speech was stifled in schools and colleges. Pro-Palestinian voices were silenced. People were being sacked or discriminated against at work. CEOs were sending e-mails to employees warning them not to support Palestine. A young woman on a train had been threatened with beheading. There was an effort to silence US Muslims. The White House and Congress were engaging in dehumanisation of the Palestinians and supporting Israeli violence.

Islamophobia was on the rise in Europe too, though you wouldn't have suspected so if you'd attended to the British Board of Deputies, the CST or the UK government. The figures provided by the CST were recycled by the UK media without question, as if it were an utterly unbiased, objective body. It's known to have spied on British citizens and to have passed information to the government. One of its founders, Gerald Ronson, served six months for his role in the Guiness fraud. It was heavily involved in the campaign to dub Jeremy Corbyn a racist and the Labour Party under his leadership institutionally antisemitic. Complaints have been made to the Charity Commissioners about its alleged political activities, a breach of its charitable status. Its designation of incidents as antisemitic is often dubious, yet such is the pusillanimous compliance of the UK media and political Establishment, everything it claims is taken as beyond question. When serious riots took place in August 2024, Muslims, asylum seekers and refugees were targeted. No one was threatening Jews. Neither the UK media nor leading politicians have whipped up ill-feeling toward Jews. Serious evidence suggests antisemitism is a peripheral problem in the UK, while Islamophobia is more prevalent. Yet the official line tallies with the perspective of the CST, for obvious reasons.

On 8th December, Blinken observed there was a gap between Israel's promises and what was happening on the ground. This unprecedented reservation towards Israel might have encouraged some to think the US was about to show some steel. Events at the UN would reveal it as flaccid as ever in defence of the democracy, human rights and the rule of law it claimed to uphold.

Sheikh Mansour of the UAE told the assembly the Israelis were trying to destroy the Palestinians. The call of the majority of countries should be heeded. In the name of humanity, it was time for courage and decisiveness.

Gilad Ardan, Israel's ambassador to the UN, complained that article ninety-nine had not been invoked over the attack on Ukraine, nor over Yemen or Syria but only for Israel's "defensive war". Hamas had to be eliminated. The path to peace was Israel's war. (Why didn't he simply say War is

Peace?) Hamas was a Nazi organisation which had engaged in a massacre on 7th October, including beheadings. If Israel wiped out Hamas, there would be no more horrors. Hamas had said it would repeat the attack. Hamas was responsible. Hamas ruled Gaza with an iron fist. A ceasefire would ensure this would continue. It would leave Hamas in control of Gaza. A ceasefire would mean Hamas was forgiven. Diplomacy would not release the hostages. There would be terror forever. Hamas murdered civilians and would drive the Israelis out of their homeland. They hide behind civilians, in hospitals and schools. They operate a reign of terror. The death tolls they claimed were fabricated. Israel was falsely blamed for casualties in hospitals. Hamas kept rockets in children's bedrooms. They exploited civilians as human shields. Israel was a law-abiding democracy. Hamas was writing the script of death. Hamas was the root cause of all the trouble. Why was Hamas not held responsible? Tell the truth. Hamas had violated the terms of the first pause. Israel had allowed fuel and other supplies in, had evacuated families, set up field hospitals. Israel had kept its side of the bargain. Hamas broke the hostage release terms. It fired rockets at Israeli towns and villages. Why didn't the UN demand that Hamas stop its violence? Why wasn't a ceasefire demanded from Hamas. Israel was making every possible effort to improve the situation. Recently, thirty-five thousand trucks and seventy thousand tons of aid had been admitted. Israel had agreed to increase the supply of fuel. Hundreds of aid trucks were in a log jam caused by the international aid agencies. Israel welcomed all aid. There was footage of Hamas shooting people queuing for aid. Aid was concealed in Hamas tunnels. Israelis were celebrating Hannukah. They have faced millennia of potential annihilation. It was a miracle the Israelis had survived, the triumph of light over darkness.

There is nothing to say about this as an objective assessment. It stands as evidence of the capacity for self-deception. Erdan's problem was he couldn't tell the truth, which would have been something like: "We see ourselves as a benevolent nation. Whatever we do is justified. Whoever we kill is a terrorist. International law is a conspiracy against Israel and the Jews. All Palestinians are legitimate targets. We will kill them all or drive them out. The land is ours. God gave it us. Anyone who disagrees is an antisemite. If we have to starve them to death, we will. We are superior. The Palestinians are less than human. The UN is antisemitic. We recognise no law but our own. If we have to destroy the region or beyond to get our own way, so be it."

He couldn't have said this not only because the world would have seen it as morally vicious, but he would have too. Tyrants almost always have to find some moral justification for their barbarity. Even Genghis Khan believed the supreme deity Tengri had destined him for world domination, a neat way of not admitting to himself it was his own diabolical motivation which was to blame. Of course, that motivation gained its energy through institutions, which is where the threads of extreme violence always lead back to. Without the institutions of the Mogul Empire, Khan would have been impotent, like Hitler or Stalin without their respective States. It isn't the psychology of leaders we should focus on, but the nature of the institutions which permit them the get away with murder.

Erdan knew he was lying. With the eyes of the world on him, in one of the most crucial international bodies, he was prepared to fib on a grand scale, yet in the west he received very little censure. The current world order is kept in place by consistent professional lying, and this is assumed to be normal.

Robert Wood spoke to the Security Council about US diplomacy. Hamas was to blame for the end of the ceasefire. The UN was guilty of moral failing in not condemning 7th October, including the rapes. Hamas still held the hostages and was in control of Gaza. The US was in favour of a durable peace but not a ceasefire. Hamas didn't want two States. War was tragic and the loss of life heartbreaking, but Hamas embeds in the civilian population. Israel must respect the law and protect civilians. A deconflicting mechanism was necessary. Israel must avoid further mass displacement and provide humanitarian support. There must be no reduction in the territory of Gaza. Humanitarian workers must be protected. Attacks on UN facilities were not acceptable. Infrastructure must not be destroyed. Violence on the Blue Line (the Israel-Lebanon border) must end. Resolution 1701 (2006) must be respected. The Iranians and the Houthis were one and the same. Iran had a choice. Settlers in the West Bank engaging in violence must be held accountable. Visa restrictions would be imposed. Our people had suffered the worst attack for decades.

Wood sounded like nothing so much as a parent upbraiding a recalcitrant teenager but refusing to use any sanctions to get her to clean her bedroom, come home at a reasonable hour and stop raiding the wine rack. His words fell impotently into the void because he represented the sole power which could bring about all he said was desirable, but which was unwilling to do anything but speak. It was pure theatre. High-level filibustering while thousands died. The spectacle can be greeted only with the greatest cynicism. Smartly-dressed, calm and eloquent, Wood was in effect saying high-falutin' platitudes were all the US could offer and if the result was mass death, who cared?

Marwan Bishara pointed out that the US was responsible for the Middle East arms race: Israel was not just massively armed by America it was shielded diplomatically and propped up financially. Biden engaged in hyperbole but the US was helpless. Invoking the myth of rapes on 7th October was a distraction technique because the US hadn't the will to change Israeli policy. It was stunning that the world's superpower behaved like a puppy and a parrot. Designating the Israelis as "our people" made him sound like the Israeli ambassador. Reagan in 1982 had called Begin and warned him about "another holocaust" in Beirut and had expressed "outrage" at the bombing which scuppered the Habib talks. Biden couldn't see the genocide. Why not support Israel and a ceasefire.? The US had abstained on resolution 517, to end the bombing of Beirut, on 4th August 1982, ensuring it passed by fourteen votes for and none against.

Biden didn't raise his voice to Netanyahu as Reagan was reported to have done to Begin because he was fully behind Israel's actions, however much he feebly lamented the loss of civilians. Bishara's essential point was pertinent: what was wrong with support for Israel and a ceasefire? In fact, the only way to rescue Israel from increasing isolation and opprobrium which, in the long term was bound to threaten its position, was to insist on a ceasefire. Biden was assisting Israeli suicide, risking a regional war and scuppering his chances of a second term because of his unwillingness to stand up to Netanyahu.

In the Security Council, the US vetoed the resolution for a humanitarian ceasefire put forward by the UAE.. The vote was predictable: thirteen for, one abstention (UK) and the US against, its forty-fifth abstention over Israel-Palestine. Jeremy Bowen remarked that the US couldn't go on using its veto against a ceasefire for ever. Ninety-seven nations had called for a General Assembly resolution. The Chair of the ICC had gone to Israel to meet the families of hostages but had made no mention of Gaza. There were three hundred and sixty-two F16s in Israel, the second largest number after the US.

On 9th December Professor of Economics Eyal Winter, argued Israeli agriculture was important but imports more so. The country's agriculture was in trouble. Some farmers had been evacuated, many foreign workers had gone home. Israelis were volunteering but not in sufficient numbers. Many labourers were from Thailand and Malawi. Israel was a leader in agricultural technology and had great potential to help out Gaza.

There wasn't a great deal of coverage of the economic effect of the war on Israel and virtually nothing about how the war was impacting on the poorest in Israel. As usual, when eyes are raised to focus on glory, those being trampled underfoot become invisible.

Oman called the US veto "a shameful violation of humanitarian norms." Pakistan said it was "deeply disappointed". Médecins Sans Frontières declared it "against the values the US professes to support". Norway described it as "tragic".

It's interesting to ask what values the US does profess to support. From a superficial and naïve perspective, it can be taken to be a defender of democracy, human rights and the rule of law, but such a view requires almost total ignorance of its actions over the last half century, at least. In its actions, the US supports exactly what it was doing with regard to Gaza: the use of extreme violence to get its own way based on the unquestionable assumption of its benevolence.

There were big demonstrations in London and Paris, BDS was gaining attention on X and TikTok. Ben Jamal of the Palestine Solidarity Campaign argued the UK anti-disinvestment law was evidence of Israel's influence. In Turkey, Nestlé products were banned from restaurants.

McDonalds' sales had fallen by seventy per cent in Europe. In the US Starbucks was in trouble after suing a union.

Netanyahu celebrated the defeat of the resolution and declared he would go on till his aims were achieved. Other countries, he said, could not support Hamas and call for a ceasefire. The IDF claimed Hamas was disintegrating in the north. It would take several months to wrap up the first phase of the war. Jabaliya would be captured in days.

Just what was meant by the "first phase" is hard to know, maybe the annihilation of the people of Gaza.

The World Food Programme said the food chain had collapsed. UNRWA claimed only fifty trucks a day were getting through. Lazzarini said his brief of relief and education was becoming impossible. Money was ceasing to be able to buy anything in Gaza. Dramatic change was needed or UNRWA was done for.

No doubt the complete collapse of UNRWA would have been sweet news to Netanyahu for whom every international agency represented an antisemitic conspiracy.

One hundred and thirty-two UN staff had been killed. Israeli planes struck the supposedly safe area of Deir Al Balah early in the morning. Speaking of these things, however, could get you in hot water, as was being demonstrated far away in Pennsylvania.

HASBARA

From 22nd to 24th September 2023 Pennsylvania University hosted the Palestine Writes Literature Festival. By and large, literature festivals don't attract the attention of CEOs or leading politicians, literature being thought a harmless eccentricity and not something anyone who wants to get on in the world would bother with much. Of course, the powerful like to present themselves as cultured, as they like to present themselves as moral: because a sense of morality is native to us, so is imagination. Speakers at the festival included Dana Abbas, Nasreen Abd Elal, Nevine Abraham, Randa Abdel-Fattah, Maya Abu Al-Hayat, Zeiad Abbas Shamrouch, Mosab Abu-Toha, Bassam Abun-Nadi, Mayss Abu Ghoush, Susan Abulhawa, Salman Abu Silta, Laura Albast, Laila Al-Arian: academics, poets, novelists, journalists, lawyers. The Anti-Defamation League engaged in its usual defamation, claiming the speakers had supported antisemitic stances. By now, only the most naïve or uninformed can have failed to grasp that when the ADL or the CST or the British Board of Deputies, or Labour Friends of Israel etc speak of antisemitism, they mean no more than criticism of the State of Israel. Marc Rowan, CEO of Apollo Global Management, a major donor to the university threatened to pull out and called on others to do likewise. Rowan's estimated wealth is $6 billion. He donated, along with his spouse, $1 million to Trump's campaign in 2020. He has also supported Republican politician Virginia Foxx who opposes abortion in any circumstances, invests heavily in tobacco companies and is against the legalisation of cannabis. Rowan claimed he was critical of the University's President, Liz Magill, because she failed to condemn the festival. Ronald Lauder, another billionaire, heir to the cosmetics empire, also threatened to pull his financial support. Lauder gave $200,000 to Trump's 2020 campaign and has donated some $1.5 billion to Trump causes. He is a supporter of Netanyahu. Ross Stevens, CEO of Stone Ridge Holdings, yet another billionaire also warned of withdrawal.

A handful of tendentious billionaires presume the right to tell the rest of us what we can hear. What serious evidence was presented that any of the speakers were Jew-haters, which was the protesters claim. To cite "antisemitism" when that term has become so elastic it could be applied to a parrot taught to say "Netanyahu is a fool", is meaningless. Susan Abulhawa is published by Bloomsbury, who might be somewhat surprised to be told they've promoted a Jew-hater. The power of money, combined with support for purblind Zionism derived from messianic supremacism, elbowed aside reason, free speech and democracy when Liz Magill, on 15th October, succumbed to the bullying and said she should have criticised the speakers' views, without specifying which speakers and which views. Were all the views of all the speakers Jew-hating?

On 5th December Magill testified before a Congressional Committee. She was attacked by Republican Elise Stefanik who supported Trump's claim of having won the 2020 election and blamed Nancy Pelosi for the 6th January assault on the Capitol on grounds of negligence. She opposes abortion. Stefanik implied the speakers had called for the genocide of the Jews and that the chant "Intifada" amounted to such a call. Questioned as to whether she believed support for the genocide of the Jews was antisemitic, Magill responded it depended on context. Not the wisest of answers. There had been antisemitic incidents at the University, offensive messages to staff, graffiti, but there was no evidence this was related to the Literature Festival. 7th October gave those after the skins of academics accused of supporting Jew-hating their excuse. What validity can be ascribed to questioning by a woman who backed Trump's ludicrous claims of victory and was accused of fraud when she claimed votes had been cast by various categories of the ineligible? How could this be anything but a witch hunt? All the same, Magill resigned on 9th December, driven out by slander, viciousness and manipulation. Not that she was anything more than a conventional careerist, had she been, she would never have been appointed. The campaign against her was a fierce assault on free speech and intellectual liberty.

The latter is of the utmost importance. Universities must be arenas where ideas which will offend the majority can be advanced. If they are flawed, it's for intellectuals to demonstrate it. If an intellectual wishes to advance a theory that James Joyce wasn't Irish, she must be permitted. Evidence and argument will defeat her.

Free speech is a slightly different matter. It isn't what Elon Musk thinks: the right of everyone to say what they like, because it has to apply equally to all. If I use my right of free speech to call for you to be murdered, I am denying to you a right I claim for myself. Free speech is not like property: if I own my books, you can't. Property excludes. Free speech implies equality which also implies I have to restrain my speech so it doesn't interfere with yours. To call for the elimination of the Jews, or the decimation of Gaza, would not be examples of free speech whose essential characteristic is respect for the right of others to express themselves as freely as oneself. Not something readily enjoyed by corpses.

At 2 a.m. on 10th December, Tulkarem was raided, bulldozers and tanks rolling through the streets.

In Geneva, thirty-six members of the World Health Organisation, including the US, voted for "unfettered" access to provide immediate humanitarian aid. Meanwhile,

Netanyahu called on Hamas to surrender. Footage was released claiming to show Hamas fighters doing exactly that, but badly edited, it clearly showed a switch of guns in IDF hands from one side to the other. It was a poorly staged PR, indicative of Israeli arrogance.

Mads Gilbert claimed fifty-two doctors and eighty-seven nurses were among two hundred and eighty medical staff killed. Antibiotics, water, drugs and surgical equipment were lacking. There was no security for Palestinians. Israel tanks had shot at a hospital in the north. Where was the International Committee of the Red Cross? Health workers were displaying enormous dedication.

The Palestinian Medical Agency said half the population was starving and three hundred and fifty thousand had infections.

Lazzarini accused the Israelis of trying to remove the population, a view endorsed by the Jordanian Foreign Minister.

Eylon Levy, on the other hand, claimed the IDF was doing nothing but going after the "monsters who did 7th October".

Mustafa Barghouti accused Netanyahu of pursuing ethnic cleansing. Its aim was to make Gaza uninhabitable. People were starving. There would be epidemics. The world community wasn't doing what it should. A ceasefire, an exchange of prisoners and an end to the occupation were needed.

Barghouti was always a reasonable voice, but what "world community" did he mean ? The economic, political and military power of the US had been overwhelming since 1945. If there was a "world community", how did it make decisions and let its views be known? The UN was nothing like such a community because of the absurd vetoes in the Security Council. The US could always get its way. Had there been a genuine "world community" the war would never have begun because 7th October would never have happened. Israel occupied the West Bank and imprisoned Palestinians in Gaza because the US permitted it. Barghouti, of course, was invoking the "world community" which should exist, a real partnership of equals in which every country can make its voice heard; but the world was a very long way from that while Manifest Destiny and the Monroe Doctrine bubbled in the American mind. The problem with referring to a "world community" was the reassurance it provided to the rich and powerful countries that they represented such a thing. Better to point out the absence of a "world community", to assert that the Palestinians in Gaza were being slaughtered because, as usual, the world was being run, before all else, in the interests of US big business.

Juliette Touma of UNRWA said she had seen misery, desperation and huge needs. The Palestinians had lost everything. More than a million were in UNRWA shelters and were not safe. The position of the UN was there were no safe zones. It wasn't possible for one party simply to declare a safe zone. One quarter of the territory of Gaza was now occupied by the entire population. A ceasefire was the only way out.

Touma, like all the others who pointed to the obvious, was right: a ceasefire was the only way out for the Palestinians. For Netanyahu, however, it would have been a disaster. Every time people like her expressed the common reaction that the massacre and the suffering were appalling, Netanyahu, Ben Gvir, Smotrich, Elyon Levy and their cronies must have been delighted. For them, the Palestinians were no better than rats, an unwelcome infestation which had to be expunged in the interest of health. That people can think in this way about others is regrettable, but all too easy when their minds are filled with demented notions of supremacism and god-given rights to territory.

Professor Mukesh Kapila said the events in Gaza were unprecedented. In Syria, Iraq, Bangladesh, he had seen nothing like it. The safe zones needed safe access. The Security Council wasn't calling for safe zones but for a ceasefire. There was an easy answer: open the border and let the Palestinians shelter in the Sinai. What was taking place was a religious war.

Kapila's suggestion of an escape route into the Sinai was playing into the hands of Israeli supremacism. Imagine if Mexico invaded Texas, slaughtered the population, laid the place to waste; would anyone suggest the Texans should take refuge in Oklahoma? To advise an exodus by the Palestinians was to imply their guilt and the rightness of the Israeli cause. Nothing about the Israeli cause was right. 7th October was a response by an imprisoned people. The unexamined notion that Israel had the right to defend itself is without validity. They had humiliated and oppressed the Palestinians by the use of appalling violence. Rightness was with the Palestinians, however the actions of Hamas might be criticised.

The notion of a religious war was convenient for the right, a way of masking the colonial nature of Zionist seizure of Palestinian land, the creation of an exclusively Jewish State, and the brutalisation of the indigenous population. For the right, the invocation of a religious war provides an excuse for unfettered support for Israel and creates the ground for depicting the Palestinians as backward medievalists. The religion, of course, was coming from the Muslims. The Israelis were progressive, democratic, modern. Thus, it was the duty of the "West" to side with the advanced society and to defeat the purblind fundamentalists. Not that the tens of millions rallying to Trump could belong in such a category.

It's interesting there is evidence of arrogant ill-treatment of the Palestinians by Jewish settlers as early as 1891. Asher Zvi Ginsberg, the Jewish writer, usually known as Ahad Ha'am, who visited Palestine in that year wrote of settlers who: "behave towards the Arabs with hostility and cruelty, trespass unjustly on their boundaries, beat them shamefully without reason and even brag about it." The Jewish population of Palestine was very small at the time. In Ginsberg's view, freed from their slavish position in their countries of origin, the settlers behaved like kings. No doubt there's some truth in this essentially psychological explanation, but what did those people bring with them which convinced them they had the right to mistreat the Palestinians? Ginsberg was an advocate of Cultural Zionism, distinct from the Political Zionism of Herzl. While he accepted the idea of a Jewish State, he didn't envision it as a State of the Jews and he warned of conflict if the settlers abused the rights of the existing population. There were, of course, pre-Herzl Zionists who took a more colonial line but Political Zionism proper was born with Herzl's *The Jewish State*. Perhaps Flapan gives us a clue to the mentality when he writes in *Birth of Israel*: "There is no intrinsic connection between Judaism and democracy. There always was an orthodox, fundamentalist current in Judaism, characterised by racial prejudice toward non-Jews in general and Arabs in particular." Speculatively, it might be that some of those early settlers who considered it their right to throw their weight about, abuse Palestinians and brag about it, were motivated by this "fundamentalist current". If so, is it reasonable to argue there was religious element to the settler attitude and behaviour? Would it then be reasonable also to suppose the extension of this religiously motivated megalomania through the years of the British Mandate, to 1948, 1967, 1973 and into the twenty-first century, bringing us to the current assault on Gaza? Is there an irreducible strain of fundamentalist Judaism which still fuels the aggression towards the Palestinians and the denial of their rights? If so, it might be sound to conclude that pushing religion aside and insisting on the colonial explanation denies an important thread. Is what is taking place in Gaza as this is written partly a religious war, but not one produced by putatively backward Islam, but rather, to a degree, by a nasty and virulent, if minority strain of Judaism?

H.A. Hellyer of RUSI pointed out the obvious: Israel had been the occupying power since 1967. International law was failing the Palestinians. In the calculus of death, one Hamas fighter was equivalent to hundreds of civilians. The IDF was behaving as if the sensible way to respond to a gunman in a school was to destroy the school. He took exception to Kapila's view: Egypt was right not to permit Palestinians to be ethnically cleansed into the Sinai. There were seven land crossings, six were controlled by Israel. It could open them to let aid arrive. However, if Palestinians were to leave, they would never return.

Abu Obaida, spokesperson of the Qassam Brigades, said the hostages would not be returned through military means. Netanyahu claimed it was the beginning of the end for Hamas which should surrender.

Obaida's comment was a veiled threat, but he was right that the way to get the hostages released was diplomacy. The double bind for the oppressed is always the same: if they resist, they are vicious, amoral, anti-democratic, murderous, never to be trusted. If they don't, they are weaklings who have no self-respect and therefore deserve their position. The difficulty is to resist while avoiding the accusations. Sometimes impossible, but fighters for freedom have to operate at the highest moral level. Those who recommend violence without consideration of its negative reception fall into the trap oppressors lay for them.

Footage appeared of IDF soldiers ransacking a shop in an act of pure vandalism. No one in the media seemed to ask how this could be interpreted as action against Hamas.

Blinken simultaneously called for the minimisation of civilian casualties and by-passed Congress to sell arms to Israel, including fourteen thousand tank shells. Presumably, US politicians and diplomats are so accustomed to speaking out of both sides of their mouth, to saying one thing and doing another, they do so without thinking. No doubt the usual emotional turmoil such mental conflicts engender is buried beneath specious self-justification: the US is ever-benevolent, if it engages in double-speak Orwell would wonder at, that's merely a reflection of its moral perfection.

A CBS poll showed approval for Blinken's approach falling from forty-four percent to thirty-nine. Disapproval had risen to sixty-one. Among Democrats those who thought the US was providing Israel with the right level of support fell from sixty-two to fifty-four. Polls are interesting, and they are often fairly accurate, but they are meaningless when policy is decided by the rich. Had Biden acted in accordance with US opinion, the war would have ended months earlier.

Germany's Foreign Minister called for more protection for civilians, as if he was calling for rats to use the bathroom. Al Magahzi refugee camp was hit and twenty-two killed.

On 11th December Grant Shapps, or Michael Green or Corinne Stockheath or Sebastian Fox sent a British warship to the Red Sea. In the West Bank there was a general strike and calls for the action to be repeated elsewhere.

The withdrawal of labour by West bank Palestinians raises the question of support for the Palestinians from international organised labour. In the UK, intimidated by the Labour Party which, with monumental pusillanimity warned its members to stay away from pro-Palestinian demonstrations to avoid contact with the wrong sort of people, the unions, with a few honourable exceptions, were dismally absent. What global issue could have engaged more potently the Labour movement's supposed commitment to universal values than Gaza? Yet the TUC was either silent or mealy-mouthed, a fine example of the retreat from defence of the oppressed.

Yossi Mekelberg of Chatham House accused Israel of a second Nakba. Israel effectively controlled Gaza. The Israeli government must change, as must the Palestinian leadership. The International Community must alter its stance.

What stance, a reasonable observer might have asked? The International Community was a chimera. The US was in control, its exorbitant military power the assurance of it getting its own way.

The phoney videos produced by Israel were being parodied online, an interesting and amusing phenomenon but of little use to the victims of Israeli violence. Palestinians were forced out of Beit Lahia where residential buildings were hit. Smoke bombs were thrown into refugee camps. The north and east of Gaza City were evacuated, the displaced people sent to the west, where they were bombarded. In Deir Al Balah, the safe zones were hit. One million people were herded into Rafah. The Omari mosque in Old Gaza City was razed, only its minaret remaining. Clearly, this was necessary to disable Hamas. Equally obviously, the "West" offered no serious condemnation. Recall when St Paul's was hit by the Nazis on 29th-30th December 1940. Didn't it become, instantly, a symbol of resistance?

Professor Dina Matar highlighted Israel's hasbara, roughly translated into English as "explanation" but being much closer to bamboozling, deceiving, dissembling, it is the essence of Israel's propaganda and an example of extreme chutzpah. It might be compared a previous example of explanation: "…the great masses of the people..more easily fall victim to a big lie than to a little one, since they themselves lie in little things, but would be ashamed of lies that were too big. Such a falsehood will never enter their heads, and they will not be able to believe in the possibility of such monstrous effrontery and infamous misrepresentation in others."

White lies are part of the bread and butter of life, but no one expects big lies to be commonplace. Does Is this how hasbara works? The Israeli State justifies its monstrous and infamous behaviour through its conviction that it is the eternal victim and therefore justified in whatever it does as a way to shrug off its victimhood. The latter derives from the conflation of Israel and Jew. As the Jews have been persecuted and were subject to arguably the worst crime in history, then if Jew and Israel are coterminous, Israel is the victim and beyond criticism.

The strategy of hasbara, Matar claimed, is to legitimize. It made use of an antisemitic frame: Israel is surrounded by a world of antisemites. Its aim was to change the perspectives of the West. Regev made use of it all the time. It works, she said, but was starting to crack. Among the young especially the lies and misinformation were starting to be seen through. The hasbara propaganda machine was well-funded. BICOM for example flooded the public space with pro-Israeli views. Stunning was the spectacle of the leaders of the so-called "free world" soaking up the propaganda like kids absorbing the latest pop hit.

ERDAN SPEAKS

On 12th December, Netanyahu declared his refusal of what was agreed in Oslo, in other words asserted that the Palestinian Authority must have no power. Biden, at the same time, said he was opposed to an Israeli military occupation of Gaza. He offered, however, no clue as to how Gaza was to be administered post-war if the PA was to be excluded. Members of the UN Security Council had visited the eastern side of the Rafah crossing prior to a vote. The day before, the US had said it was worried about the use of white phosphorous. Not worried enough, of course, to do anything serious about it. The WHO reported that health workers had been beaten by the IDF, a half-naked Red Cross employee was handcuffed and blindfolded, which also brought no action from the US. An UNRWA school in Beit Hanoun was destroyed, on the customary pretext. Forty were arrested in Silwad. Seven were killed in a raid on Jenin.

In emergency session the General Assembly of the UN voted for a resolution with twenty-one co-sponsors calling for a humanitarian ceasefire. One hundred and fifty-three were in favour, ten against and twenty-three abstained. Those voting against were the US, Israel, Austria, Czechia, Guatemala, Liberia, Micronesia, Naurau, Papua New Guinea, and Paraguay. Amendments from the US and Austria, objecting to the omission of reference to Hamas failed to gain the necessary two-thirds majority. The first received eighty-nine votes in favour, sixty-one against and twenty abstentions while the second had eighty-four supporters, sixty-two against and twenty-five abstentions. Thomas-Greenfield, speaking to the US amendment said, "Our goal must be to stop the death and the destruction for the long-term and that is simply not a future Hamas wants to see." Just what kind of future did she think Hamas wanted and on what basis did she claim to know what the organisation favoured for the future? It can't be said too often that after its success in the elections of 2006, a success the US deplored and immediately set about undermining, Hamas offered to recognise Israel and renounce violence in return for an autonomous Palestine. Naturally, the US is suspicious of anyone who renounces violence, given extreme forms are its way of maintaining its global control. Both the US and Israel require Palestinian violence. Neither can countenance a Palestinian willingness to live in peace with a Israel. Israel is founded on the notion that Jews (Zionists in fact) can't live with the rest of humanity. The history of nation-creation involves many variations, but nations whose fundamental rational is that rest of humanity can't be lived with are hardly typical.

Gilad Erdan's response to the resolution included: "Not only does this resolution fail to condemn Hamas for crimes against humanity, it does not mention Hamas at all. This will only prolong the death and destruction in the region, that is precisely what a ceasefire means…So why would anyone want to aid Hamas in continuing their rule of terror and actualizing their satanic agenda?"

Perhaps most of interest is the medieval language. "Satanic"? Typical of Zionist rejection of Enlightenment thinking and its regression to Manichean notions of good and evil, easy to identify and having nothing to do with context, this lack of reasoning makes any settlement with Hamas impossible. They have no legitimate grievance or claim. They are Satan.

Just what Erdan meant by their "rule of terror" is puzzling. What did they rule? Certainly not Gaza by any sensible definition. Nothing went in or out of Gaza without Israel's permission. Its people were not free to travel. It was subject to Israel's periodic "mowing the lawn". As for terror, mostly, Hamas was using home-made rockets against a nuclear-armed State. Its capacity for terror attacks was limited. It was a prison.

How would a ceasefire prolong death and destruction? Hamas was responsible for some of the deaths on 7th October, but so was Israel. The evidence for that is clear. As for destruction, the damage wrought by the incursion on that day was a bagatelle compared to the razing of Gaza.

To hear Erdan speak in one of the most elevated bodies on the planet was a dispiriting reminder of how little reason prevailed in international affairs. True, he was in a small minority and there was comfort in the hundred and fifty-three votes, yet power was heavily on his side in the US opposition and the abstentions by the UK, Italy, Germany, the Netherlands, Argentina and notably Ukraine. Here was a country which appealed to the world for support against a criminal invasion setting its face against a ceasefire to relieve the suffering of an occupied people who suffered ethnic cleansing and had been oppressed for seventy-six years. This was Zelensky siding with the US and Israel. Why, any rational person might ask, where we offering unconditional support to a leader presenting himself as a courageous fighter for autonomy who was clearly ambiguous about independence for Palestine?

UN peacekeepers warned that the Lebanese border war could worsen. Israel floated the idea of a buffer zone on the border, an ostensibly safe zone, possibly manned by French and US troops. In the Bab-el-Debab Strait a ship carrying oil from Norway to Israel was hit by Houthi fire.

On 13th December the Kamal Adwan hospital was stormed. Yaakov Amridror, ex Israeli National Security adviser whose mother was in the Irgun (ie a terrorist) and who drew up the list of candidates for the far-right Jewish Home party for the election of February 2009, accused Hamas, originally, of using human shields. Hamas, he claimed, wouldn't let people leave Gaza. It should be punished. Israel was creating safe zones while Hamas set up its centres in hospitals. To kill Hamas it was necessary to kill civilians. The population of Gaza had voted for Hamas. "We gave them all the opportunities," he asserted.

It's amazing how ungrateful people can be. Over a period of fifteen years, four major assaults killing thousands were launched and the victims insist on fighting back. If only they would understand that being dead is in their best interests. As for voting, half the population of Gaza was under eighteen. Imagine if a retired general from the UK, France, the US etc were to argue killing civilians is necessary to defeat the enemy. Amridor could get away with it because he's Israeli, Israel is conflated with Jewish, Jewish means victim because of the Nazi genocide, any criticism of whatever is Jewish is antisemitism, which was at the core of Nazi ideology and practice. Thus, to demur from absolute support for Israel was to align yourself with fascism. Of course, fascists were sitting in the war cabinet threatening to scupper Netanyahu's administration if he dared strike a peace deal.

Reports emerged of displaced people sheltering in a school in northern Gaza having been shot, execution style. Babies appeared to have been executed. The IDF was flooding the tunnels with seawater, risking contamination of drinking water. Non-stop rain was adding to the Palestinians' misery. Ten IDF had been killed over the past twenty-four hours, including a colonel.

Lazzarini bemoaned the "indifference of the international community", the "lack of empathy" and warned "we are losing our humanity". People might never be able to return to their homes. Despair might force them to leave Gaza.

Trucks bringing aid were being stopped and the food eaten on the spot. Lawlessness and social breakdown were growing. There was widespread hunger if not yet starvation. Outbreaks of diarrhoea, skin diseases, hepatitis were common. The matter of war crimes would have to be dealt with in the long-term but hospitals and civilians had to be respected. Where was the required proportionality? UN premises giving refuge to a million people were hit. The primary problem was Gaza was under siege. The Rafah crossing could no longer admit what used to arrive. Prior to 7th October, Karem Shalom was a major crossing. Israel was fully responsible for the siege. Erdan claimed the problem was log-jam but hundreds of trucks had got through. This wasn't true. The West Bank was on the verge of economic collapse but it was overshadowed by the catastrophe in Gaza. The number of dead was staggering. There was an organised campaign to liquidate UNRWA, then the refugees would be forgotten. During the Madrid period there had been hope. The Arabs spoke Hebrew the Israelis spoke Arabic, now there was complete mutual alienation.

Taher Herzallah of Minnesota University said Biden was breaking ranks a little more with Israel. M16 rifles for Israel were delayed because of worries about the West Bank. Everyone was breaking from Israel. It was an uphill battle the US couldn't win. The moral claims made by the US no longer cut any ice.

The Jenin refugee camp was subjected to a forty-eight-hour attack involving one thousand four hundred reservists. Jake Sullivan was in Saudi Arabia. There was a danger of a wider war which Saudi could prevent. Saudi was in favour of a two-States agreement but Netanyahu was opposed. Kirby was asking for more results from Israel without, however, using the US's leverage.

On 14th December the Head of Mossad refused to go to Qatar to discuss the release of hostages. The delivery of twenty-one thousand rifles from the US to the Israeli police was held up because of fears they might go to settlers. Rafah was struck. Netanyahu said he will go on to the end with or without support.

The Prime Minister's comment is akin to a thirty-year-old still living in a bedroom in his parents' house claiming independence while having all his bills paid. Israel was almost totally dependent on the US and diplomatic support from the EU, Australia and others. Its ability to prosecute its war in Gaza was thoroughly dependent on the US. Israel was the feral child among nations.

Sami Hermez pointed to polling showing forty-four percent of Palestinians in the West Bank supported Hamas, eighty-eight per cent in both Gaza and the West Bank wanted Abbas to go, and in the West Bank alone, ninety-two percent. There weren't many options. The PA would have to be granted a role. The onus was on Palestinian unity. All factions needed to be included.

The problem with Palestinian unity was every time it showed a glimpse of being achieved, the Israelis scuppered it. No one was more opposed to such unity than Netanyahu. Martin Griffiths made the remarkably subversive suggestion of asking the Palestinians and topped his temerity by saying Hamas must have a say. On the other hand, straight out of Lewis Carroll, David Cameron announced he was imposing a travel ban on settlers convicted of violence in the West Bank.

Netanyahu told Sullivan it would take a few more months to finish off Hamas. In the previous twenty-four hours two hundred Palestinians had been killed. It was reported that Kamala Harris was pushing the White House to focus on Palestinian suffering. Seventy staff and civilians were arrested at Kamal Adwan hospital. Israel claimed they were all Hamas fighters. At Khalil Suleiman hospital in the West Bank a seventeen-year-old was shot dead. Israel claimed it had arrested six hundred "suspects" in Jenin. Huge destruction was inflicted on Jabaliya by Israeli air strikes. Most victims were women and children.

If Harris was pushing the White House, she wasn't pushing very hard. The dismal Biden, a doddery, self-proclaimed Zionist apparently ignorant of what assuming that definition implied, continued to treat Israel as a saintly haven of reason, kindness and high moral reasoning. His inability to grant equal value to Israeli and Palestinian lives was blatant supremacism and his feeble lip-service to two-States utterly hollow. Complaisant towards a regime including self-confessed fascists, he continued to blather about democracy, human rights and international law.

As for Israel's definition of Hamas fighters, it would have included more than half the world's population.

Gallant contradicted his leader, asserting killing off Hamas would take more than a few months. Sullivan called for a timetable to end the fighting. There was dissent in the War Cabinet. Gantz thought Qatar should be involved.

Sullivan asking for a timetable was, as usual for US interventions, risible. The US could have imposed any timetable it liked. Time and again, the greatest military power the world had ever known, which threw its weight around like a playground bully on crack when it felt its interests were in question, behaved like a timid child summoned to the headteacher's office.

In Denmark arrests were made of people claimed to be planning attacks on Israeli and Jewish targets. Footage emerged of an IDF soldier at the pulpit in a mosque reciting a Jewish prayer. Ben Gvir, displaying once more his sensitive, thoughtful nature, said he should be congratulated.

Lazzarini said the lucky ones were in UNRWA shelters, the rest were destitute. The IDF seemed to be of the same view, hence its unending attacks on UNRWA facilities.

On 15th December, Al Jazeera journalists were targeted by the IDF. Youcef Bouandel of Qatar university said Netanyahu was aiming to eliminate the civilian population. The US was not tough enough. Netanyahu was fighting for his survival but Sullivan's visit won't do the trick in bringing him down. Pressure must come from within Israel. The US could stop the war but it had no will.

The targeting of Al Jazeera and the US failure to stop the war were not unconnected: Israel needed to ensure the world didn't know what was going on and Al Jazeera was a crucial outlet. Bouandel's view that the US wasn't tough enough is interesting. It couldn't have been tougher on the Palestinians. Biden's warm words about the scale of casualties and two States were belied by his constant claim Israel was pursuing terrorists. Schools were bombed, hospitals attacked, civilians decimated, and it was all justified. As usual, the US was comfortable with extreme violence and unspeakable suffering among those it designated enemies of its interests. Bouandel was right, Netanyahu was on thin ice, he could have been drowned had the US insisted, but in spite of his embrace of fascists, the US was on his side because the Palestinians were perfidious, backward Arabs. The will of the US was unbreakable with regard to its pursuit of continued global domination and its purblind willingness to murder anyone who got in the way.

A three-day assault on Jenin resulted in twelve dead and led to calls for an end to settler violence. IDF graffiti and a star of David appeared on the walls of damaged houses. Palestinian prisoners spoke of torture and abuse. Bernie Sanders called for an inquiry into aid for Israel. Support for

Israel was diminishing. Leo Varadkar said division over Gaza was undermining the EU.

How incongruous Sanders' intervention seems. Illustrative of how narrow were the terms of the debate. He didn't insist on the removal of aid, merely that it should be looked into, but that itself was heretical. The weight of opinion, most of it based on little but self-serving and lies, was enormously in favour of unquestioning support for Israel. All else, as the Zionists claimed, was giving succour to terrorism.

Jodie Ginsberg of the Committee for the Protection of Journalists said the toll among reporters was huge. Blinken had been told journalists were civilians and must not be targeted. Wael Al Dahdoh, the veteran journalist was wounded and his cameraman, Samer Abu Daqqa killed while reporting on the Haifa School attack. Al Dahdoh lost several members of his family, including his wife and son to IDF violence. He continued to work after being injured. Pointless to ask whether anyone will be brought to justice.

Hezbollah fired eleven rockets into Israel summoning an unrestrained Israeli response. Maersk and H. Lloyd suspended shipping in the Red Sea as insurance premiums soared.

Demonstrations were staged in Yemen, Tripoli and Amman. Celtic football fans were shut out of their stadium for supporting the Palestinians. The Green Brigade is a socially conscious, committed group of supporters. How odd they should be punished for behaving responsibly.

MAKARIOS, MANDELA, MCGUINESS

On 15th December, three Israeli hostages waving white flags were shot dead by the IDF. The trio, Samer Talalka, 24, Alon Shamriz, 26, and Yotam Haim, 28, were killed in Shuja'iyya. Haim was injured in the first volley, retreated for cover, but was then dispatched by an IDF soldier acting against orders. The official Israeli line was that they were taken for Hamas fighters. That they were unarmed and surrendering cut no ice, the Israeli view being that the perfidious Arabs will use any means. Wouldn't it have been possible to disable them? A bullet in the ankle could have rendered them harmless. Rules of engagement require positive identification, and the rule is not to fire on surrendering soldiers. It was to emerge later that a combat dog sent into the building where the hostages were held during a firefight five days before the incident had recorded the voices of the captives on its Gopro camera. The Israeli line was a farrago of excuses, bluster and mendacity. The obvious conclusion was that the IDF was trigger happy, shot first and thought after.

Marwan Bishara said the initial probe showed the soldiers had breached rules of engagement. The hostages were bare-chested, carried no explosives, Haim shouted in Hebrew. Every detail of the incident indicated common IDF practices in Gaza. The IDF was so cowardly, so afraid of the Palestinian resistance, it would shoot at its own shadow. Every military attempt to free the hostages had failed, only diplomacy could succeed. There was no incentive for Hamas if only a short ceasefire was agreed. Why would they release the hostages on those terms? There was a huge imbalance as more than four thousand had been arrested in the West Bank. What would convince Hamas was a once-and-for-all ceasefire and an all-for-all hostage swop.

Of course, the standard Western position that Hamas was a terrorist outfit and therefore could not be negotiated with, was the surest way to avoid a settlement. All virtue to us, is always a dishonest slogan. Archbishop Makarios was once a terrorist who had to be spirited out of Britain by the secret services and held in the Seychelles so he might not engage in the campaign against colonialism in Cyprus; but he ended up a statesman. As did the terrorist Nelson Mandela and the terrorist Martin McGuinness. They're all terrorists until they become statesman, just as western leaders are all statesman until they become terrorists. Change places and handy-dandy. The lexis of terrorism and statesmanship is nothing but a smokescreen for colonialism and tyranny. Toussaint L'Ouverture was a terrorist, Stalin was a statesman.

Footage produced by B'Tselem showed Israeli military police shooting two men on 8th December. The human rights organisation claimed this was an everyday occurrence but most instances were not recorded and chances of conviction were rare. There was a green light for the army and the police because of the right-wing nature of the government.

Osama Hamdan warned the hostages would not survive unless there was a ceasefire. Israel didn't care about its soldiers in Gaza. The UN was impotent because of the US veto. The world was run on Nazi lines. Israel was lurching from disaster to disaster. International broadcasters were changing the story bit by bit.

Daniel Hagari said Israel killed all fighters and aggressors. It had support from important allies, chiefly the US which provided the capacity to bring down drones. Three of the hostages had died but the IDF was doing what it could. Investigations were under way. Lessons were being learned. Israel would bring the hostages home, they were being released because of Israel's actions.

It would be interesting to know how Hagari defined an aggressor.

There was a major rally in Tel Aviv expressing outrage at the failure to secure the release of the hostages. At Kamal Adwan hospital, twenty were crushed by bulldozers, the pharmacy was shelled, the IDF were in the hospital, the manager was arrested, the staff interrogated.

Such paranoid actions are inevitable when people know what they are doing is wrong. Zionists cannot but be haunted by fear because the emotional tenor of their doctrine is disturbing. It takes extraordinary continued effort to convince yourself you belong to the chosen people and have the right to make life hell for those who don't. The balance of a mind trying to maintain such a falsehood is always fragile. We aren't so constituted that we can assume any definition of our humanity we like. We have a given nature, not easy to specify but which rebels at efforts to deny it. Impossible mental conflicts are set up when we try to be more than human. Jews aren't the chosen people, they are products of evolution and natural selection like everyone. They have no special qualities which distinguish them, nor do they have an eternally granted right to particular parts of the earth. They may believe these things, but believing a triangle has four sides doesn't alter the geometric facts. Belief is necessary only where we can't prove. No one has faith the square on the hypotenuse equals the sum of the square of the other two sides. Faith is unnecessary as proof is available. That Jews have the right to believe themselves chosen is beyond question, just as anyone has the right to believe there are fairies at the bottom of their garden; but to kill others because they don't believe in fairies is to mistake your belief for truth. This is the essence of Zionism. . It is a doctrine of faith. How would we respond if the Palestinians had been ethnically cleansed because they refuse to believe in fairies?

Gemma Connell, a UN humanitarian worker said Gaza was revealing the best and worst in humanity. Thousands were in desperate need. The NGOs would not give up. Al Shifa wasn't functioning but the health workers were heroic. There was neither water nor power. The situation in the south was desperate. People were running for their lives. There were no safe places in Gaza. The war had to end, aid had to flow, a deluge of assistance was needed, all crossings should be opened.

On 17th December six were killed by a strike on the Tulkarem refugee camp. The head of Mossad was in Europe trying to negotiate the release of the hostages. The UK and German Foreign Secretaries called for a ceasefire. The killing of Samer Abudaqa, the Al Jazeera cameramen in Khan Younis who was left to bleed to death for five hours, was referred to the ICC. Two women, Nahida Anton and her daughter, Samar Anton were killed in Gaza's Holy Family Catholic church the day before. Pope Francis said, "It is war. It is terrorism." Vincent Nichols, Archbishop of Westminster said, "They were shot in cold blood." Fleur Hassan-Nahoum, Deputy Mayor of Jerusalem said there were no churches in Gaza. Layla Moran, UK Lib Dem MP, tweeted that members of her family were trapped in the grounds of the church. Israel claimed the church was used to launch missiles. Whether the two women deliberately targeted by a sniper were involved in firing missiles the IDF didn't explain.

Marwan Bishara commented that from day one Netanyahu had predicted a long war. Biden's intelligence services judged Netanyahu had a personal intertest in extending the war. Israel had a criminal as its war leader. His logic was that military means would bring the release of the hostages, but his entire logic was a failure because his personal interest came first. The calculation was that Saudi would rejoin the Abraham Accords. That would be Netanyahu's reward. After 7th October, any freedom for the West Bank was unthinkable for Israel. 7th October meant Israel was not secure, but who talked about security for the Palestinians? There was no trusting Israel. It had subjected the West Bank to years of abuse.

The US intelligence services knew Netanyahu was prosecuting war to save his own skin. They didn't go so far as to look at the evidence that he knew the 7th October attack was in the offing. They wouldn't have had to search very hard. Hamas had made its intentions public for months. Here was the US, self-proclaimed lover of democracy and defender of human rights, supporting economically, militarily, diplomatically and politically a man as evil as any of history's great rogues and tyrants; a man willing to see tens and maybe hundreds of thousands die for the sake of his own warped ambition. This was the US State hitting the moral nadir and Biden, who could have ended the killing with a single phone call, was the instrument of this absolute ethical collapse.

Palestinians were scrambling for aid at the Rafah border. Twenty-five thousand people were packed into the Al Mawasi evacuation zone where there were no basic facilities, refuse was everywhere and heavy rain was expected. Shipping in the Red Sea was halted by some companies, the Hong Kong Co, for example. France called for a truce after a French citizen was killed on 13th December. "

Lindsey Graham, who on 1st November claimed Hamas was "trying to slaughter the Jews" and therefore there should be no limit to civilian deaths in the war, expressed the view that an autonomous Palestinian State was a prerequisite of normalisation between Israel and the Arab countries. That being so, why didn't the US tell Netanyahu to get the settlements out of the West Bank, lift the siege of Gaza, return the Golan Heights to Syria and get out of East Jerusalem What Graham was acknowledging, though he appeared not to realise, was that the assault on Gaza was taking place because of the occupation. Without it, what reason would there have been for 7th October

The French Foreign Minister said there were too many dead and there must be an immediate ceasefire. Peter Ricketts, argued a ceasefire must be sustainable. The fighting must stop now and the killing of civilians end. There needed to be a plan for the day after. It was clear Israel was not paying enough attention to protecting civilians. Israel had to make moderate Arab leadership possible. Israel couldn't defy international opinion indefinitely. The question of a ceasefire was a matter of timing, too soon and Hamas would fight on.

Ricketts was once an advisor to Lockheed Martin. He studied English Literature at Pembroke College, Oxford, which might lead you to expect he would be familiar with Owen's famous denunciation of the lie which sends young soldiers to their deaths or with Shakespeare's

Witness this army, of such mass and charge,

Led by a delicate and tender prince,

Whose spirit with divine ambition puffed,

Makes mouths at the invisible event,

Exposing what is mortal and unsure

To all that fortune, death and anger dare,

Even for an egg-shell.

But apparently the chance of pocketing a few quid for advising one of the biggest death machines on the planet was irresistible. The notion that the timing of a ceasefire might impel Hamas to fight on was bizarre. There was no reason for Hamas to fight if a deal was struck and a ceasefire was supposed to be the first step towards the long-promised two-States everyone claimed to want but nobody with any real power did anything to advance.

Lloyd Austin was in Bahrain, to what purpose was anyone's guess. Israel declared that the current phase of the war would end in December. Eight US hostages were still held. Young US Jews, in keeping with the trend since 2008, were protesting.

The fact that after two months US citizens were captives wasn't without significance. What prevented Biden, on 8th October, ordering the Israelis not to attack Gaza because US lives were at stake ?Why didn't he make the release of the US hostages the priority? Why didn't he push, immediately, for a deal with Hamas to release of all the hostages in a prisoner swap in return for no war and negotiations to remove the settlements from the West Bank? The reason this sounds like a fairy tale is because it is. Biden would never have dreamt of telling Netanyahu to remove the settlements. This was Israel, a name he couldn't utter without a tear in his eye. This was the State that could do no wrong, like the US. Such is the childish sentimentality which rules the world and sends hordes of innocents to their deaths, while an evil manipulator like Netanyahu, struts the globe like a modern Attila.

Rana Hajjeh of the World Health Organisation said Gaza was a scene of horror. There was a handful of doctors. Medical services were functioning minimally. Pain medication was virtually unattainable. There were reports the IDF was burying people alive.

Mohamed Elmasry opined it was too early to tell what would happen. The US had all the cards and always gave

Israel leeway. The Israeli view was that Gaza was a David against Goliath conflict. The world was antisemitic. Israel was deaf to what the world was saying. Israelis were angry about how the war was being waged, Hamas was not suffering defeat. The hostages hadn't been returned. Three IDF soldiers were killed and there was outrage, tens of thousands of Palestinians died and the Israeli public was content.

On 18th December Ben Wallace published a piece arguing that Netanyahu knew nothing of the 7th October attack. Writing in the *Daily Telegraph*, the ex-defence secretary was highly critical of Israel's tactics in Gaza, predicting they would lead to half a century of war. There was a "bull in a china shop approach" from some of Israel's military leaders. Israel's "killing rage" was undermining its moral authority. Perhaps, he reflected, Netanyahu's failure to foresee the 7th October incursion had left him with a sense of shame for which he was trying to compensate. Israeli spokesperson Eylon Levy dubbed Wallace's comments "unfortunate", but then he would probably say the same about the theory of evolution. Wallace's remarks were relatively balanced, relative, that is, to the wild intemperance of Israeli officials, and more sensible than the US's slavish adherence to every syllable of Netanyahu's incoherence. He granted Israel the right to defeat Hamas but deplored the mass civilian deaths. However, it's interesting that he should assume Netanyahu was blindsided by 7th October. Hamas could barely have done more to advertise its intentions. Isn't it at least possible that Netanyahu was perfectly aware of the impending attack?

Eli David, brother of one of the hostages, said he knew nothing of what was being done to release them and could only speculate. He hoped the government was acting and they would soon be released, but there seemed to be no plan.

The international community hadn't done enough. More pressure needed to be brought to bear on Egypt and Qatar. Hamas would not allow visits to the hostages.

Freeing the captives, one of Netanyahu's key aims, seemed utterly remote from his tactics. No one believed military action would set them free. Those released so far were let go because of a pause in fighting. The one step which was most likely to secure their freedom was what Netanyahu most opposed. To any wide-awake observer, it was obvious Netanyahu was as willing to sacrifice the hostages as the Palestinians. That the world was watching the machinations of a megalomaniac on speed seemed lost on most commentators, and unimaginable to the brainwashed Israeli public.

Eylon Levy declared he couldn't comment on the negotiations. For Israel, everything was possible. Unrelenting military force would secure the hostages' liberty. Hamas had broken the terms of the ceasefire on 1st December. The Red Cross was useless and was bringing no pressure for setting the captives free. As for killing of the Nahida and Samar Anton, Israel's investigation wasn't consistent with them having been killed by the IDF. Perhaps it was Hamas. Who knows, maybe Hamas assassinated Abraham Lincoln. There was no combat in the area. There was no alternative to total victory. Hamas had spent sixteen years embedding itself in schools , hospitals and mosques. Civilians should evacuate. UN agencies were driving them to areas of conflict. Israel listens to the US. We could swoop in and would but Hamas was hiding in schools and hospitals. We told civilians to get out of harm's way and were establishing specific evacuation zones. UN agencies offered no condemnation of Hamas rockets. Israel wanted to protect civilians but Hamas employed sick tactics, witness the beheadings of 7th October.

Jonathan Swift and Voltaire couldn't outbid Levy in absurdity. Levy knew, of course, he was lying but pushed his lies to such a limit, people would be hard pressed to believe he could be guilty of such monstrous effrontery and infamous misrepresentation. Levy was simply obeying his political masters, there was no thinking behind what he said. Whether he is capable of thinking at any level which matters can't be concluded from his utterances. Levy's statement was Israel declaring military force would free the hostages, an assertion for which there was no evidence. There was no plan for their release, simply a set of tactics, like trying to build a house by putting the roof on first. A to-do list of tactics gets nowhere in any enterprise, what matters is the organisation of tactics towards a desired end. In the best of schemes, of course, things go wrong, but without a strategy what you get is a blind man on a bike negotiating a rush-hour motorway. Israel knew full well the best way to save the hostages was a ceasefire, but Netanyahu feared that. Israel's claim that the deaths of the Antons might be the fault of Hamas was, once again, without evidence. Yet, it was taken for granted that whatever Israel asserts is beyond question. Any attempt to subject their lies to the test of evidence is responded to with neurotic outrage. . The line that there was no alternative but total victory begged the question of what such a victory might look like. It's distressing that such playground bravado falls from the mouths of the world's leaders. Whatever form "total victory" might take there were many alternatives; for example, asking the Palestinians what they might agree to, what might be their minimum demands for agreeing to give up armed struggle. What Israel was really saying, through its robotic mouthpiece, was it would have its own way at any cost. Nothing but the triumph of Zionism was acceptable, which is the attitude of the kid who takes her skipping rope home if she doesn't get to dictate the game. If

Israel was trying to protect civilians, it was proving woefully incompetent. As for beheadings, at the time of writing there is still no evidence.

Zionism has no basis in reality. Hence its adoption of the technique of outrageous lying. What a tragic irony the Israelis were dooming themselves to the same historical pariah status as the man who slaughtered millions of Jews out of pure delusion.

A PLO spokesperson argued there was no military solution. The "day after" must be decided by the Palestinian people. Two States were essential. What, however, about the day before? What was to be done about Israeli supremacism, the occupation, violence by settlers in the West Bank? Only a Palestinian State could suffice.

Ex-jailbird, Ehud Olmert, appealed for support from the international community whose concern about Israel's manner of operating was slowing the process. More time was needed for Israel to attain its fundamental aims. He reminded the world of the 7th October beheadings. Greater tolerance of Israel from the international community would come. Ben Wallace's "killing rage" would solve nothing. The aim of destroying Hamas was ambitious, but at least its command could be broken down. As for worries over civilian deaths, Hamas was embedded in the centre of towns. No Palestinian had been killed by trigger happy IDF soldiers.

Perhaps Olmert believed the world should rally to Israel and celebrate its daily breaches of international law; maybe he imagined people across the globe were delighted by images of Gaza devastation and death; possibly he was so far gone in delusion he thought every Israeli lie or excuse was the shimmering truth which should be piously embraced by every man woman and child. What was obvious from his kind of statement was that Israel fell for its own propaganda, that its apologists were incapable of accepting any view but theirs as valid, as if Zionism were mathematics rather than a faith. What we can prove is relatively restricted. Our cognitive abilities don't permit us to establish clear relations of cause and effect. Once we enter the political field, because people are defending advantages and entrenched interests, we quickly fall into assertion with no basis but belief. Yet, this is the twenty-first century, the minimum we should be able to assume is the recognition of a distinction between what we believe and what we can prove. Israeli apologists assume the opposite: there is no distinction, whatever they believe, however fanciful, is proven. Beheadings but no severed heads. Alice in Wonderland.

Tory, Alicia Kearns, Chair of the Foreign Affairs Committee called for a humanitarian truce which would lead to a sustainable ceasefire. Bombs would not destroy Hamas ideology, rather they were a recruiting sergeant. What was required was counter-terrorism rather than war. Israel had lost moral authority by breaching international law.

Kearns has worked in counter-terrorism in various trouble spots. Her faith in it may be somewhat naïve, but it was refreshing to hear a Tory dismissing Israel's assault on Gaza and pointing out its loss of moral authority. Unfortunately, the Labour Party was led by a man who seemed to think Israel was a synonym for innocence, purity and righteousness.

Marwan Bishara argued public opinion was turning against the war which was genocide in plain sight. Even CNN was covering the war. There was a make-believe the US was doing something. It was embarrassing. Netanyahu wasn't listening to the US. Netanyahu's timetable didn't correspond to America's; they needed a quick de-escalation, he needed to drag things out. The wisdom of the average person was showing up the idiocy of the political leaders. People were getting worried. Whenever the US appeared, things got worse.

Things were going to get much worse and entirely because of Biden's refusal to use his leverage. Netanyahu was running rings round him, exploiting his weakness and confusion for purposes entirely nefarious which would cost the lives of tens of thousands and drive the world towards destruction.

CONTENTS

7th October………p5

All Out Assault……….p17

Blunder……….p27

Irresolute Resolution……….p37

Friend of Hamas……….p48

Impeccable Virtue……….p58

From The River To The Sea……….p69

420 A Day……….p80

The Man Who Shot Liberty Valance……….p90

Mind Your Language……….P101

Bombing The Bakeries……….111

From Gaza to Dearborn……….p121

Fanciful and Farcical……….p130

Mugs……….p141

Dread Democracy……….p151

Arab Solidarity……….p159

Woe To The Vanquished……….p168

Genocide Joe……….p180

Ubu Roi……….p192

No Words……….p200

Amalek………..p209

Bravo!……….p220

Cockroach……….p230

Ceasefire……….p240

Moderate and Pragmatic……….p251

Power and Paranoia……….p255

Jericho Wall..........p261
And The Sun Orbits The Earth..........p273
Hannibal..........p283
The Sobbing of the Violins..........p294
Article Ninety-Nine..........p304
Hasbara..........p311
Erdan Speaks..........p323
Makarios, Mandela, McGuinness..........p332

END OF VOLUME ONE

SELECT INDEX

, John McTernan, 36
"indiscriminate bombing, 201
1922 Committee, 153
7th October, 5
A Kayum Ahmed, 202
Abbas, 215
Abbé Dinouart, 185
Abraham Accords, 25
Abu Obaida, 210, 320
Action Aid, 65
Ada Sagi, 260
Adam Shatz, 217
Adam Smith, 153
Adorno, 154
Afrasiab Anwar, 95
Afza Khan, 197
Ahed Tamimi, 125
Ahmed Abofoul, 147
Ahmed Alnaouq, 166
Ahmed Yousef, 266
Ahmet Goksun, 113
Akiva Eldar, 244
Al Aqsa, 212
Al Fakhoura, 212
Al Magahzi, 321
Al Quds, 24
Al Thani, 236
Alan Fisher, 113
Alice Rothschild, 171
Alicia Kearns, 344
Al-Jazeera, 35

Allende, 58
Alog Cohen, 22
Alon Shamriz, 333
al-Qassam brigades, 210
Al-Wafa, 33
Amalek, 212
Amnesty International, 226
Amos Goldberg, 217
ANC, 10
Andreas Kreig, 253
Andrew Fisher, 38
Andrew Mitchell, 186
Andy Burnham, 45
Andy McDonald, 75
Andy Slaughter., 197
Angela Davis, 57
Angela Rayner, 28
Angelic Nation, 13
Anthony Zurcher, 97
Antonio Guterres, 10
apartheid, 10
Arab Centre for Research and Policy, 82
Aryeh Golan, 8
Atlantic Council, 60
Aya Majzoub, 301
Ayman Safadi, 25
B'tselem, 63
Bahrain, 339
Balata, 236
Bangladesh, 318
Bantustans, 208

Bar Zonshein, 293
Barak, 14
Basem Naim, 249
Basma al Sharif, 214
BBC, 6
Be'eri Kibbutz, 8
Beit Lahia, 23
Ben Friedman, 269
Benzi Sanders, 30
Bernie Sanders, 331
Bill Burns, 117
bin Farhan Al-Saud, 25
Blinken, 15
Boko Haram, 252
Botticini, 12
Bradley Bowman, 15
Braverman, 22
Brett McGurk, 187
Bridget Phillipson, 133
Bushra Khalidi, 65, 191
Catherine Russell, 82, 224
ceasefire, 25
Centre for Constitutional Rights., 182
Chris Gunnes, 39
CIA, 117
Cindy McCain, 116
Cleverly, 24
Clive Betts, 36
Commission of Inquiry on Palestine, 63
Corbyn, 36, 61
Corinne Stockheath, 321
Cornell West, 178
Cyril Ramaphosa, 192
Dail, 196

Dan Gillerman, 34
Dana Erlich, 196
Daniel Hagari, 15, 54
Daniel Levy, 218
Danielle Rachiel, 9
Dany Kruger, 144
David Satterfield, 117
Defense for Children International-Palestine, 182
Diana Buttu, 177
Dima Khalidi, 59
Dina Matar, 322
Dov Waxman, 279
Dovev, 176
Dr Ahmed Mokhallalati, 146
Dr Amal Saad, 100
Dr H.A. Hellyer, 187
Dr Omar Abdel-Mannan, 189
Dr Tanya Haj-Hassan, 112
Eckstein, 12
Edward Bernays, 155
Efraim Halevy, 15
Egypt, 5
Ehud Olmert, 208
Elad Goren, 148
Eli David, 340
Eliajah Magnier, 33
Elias Farhat, 94
Emily Hind, 257
Emina Cerimovic, 232
Erdogan, 31
Erik Fosse, 201
Ethnic cleansing, 52
EU, 12

Eyal Winter, 311
Farah Omar, 228
Faris Al-Jawad, 129
fascists, 46
Fatah, 41
Fergal Keane, 66
Fikr Shalltoot, 173
Filippo Grandi, 84
Finnuala Ni Aolain, 24
Fleur Hassan-Nahoum, 252
Frances Leach, 35
Francesca Albanese, 92
Frank Gardner, 236
Gadi Eisenkot, 57
Galaxy Leader, 218
Gantz, 63
Garrison, 8
Gavin Stevens, 153
GAZA, 3
Gemma Connell, 336
General Assembly, 47
Geneva Convention, 18
Geoffrey Bindman, 190
Geoffrey Nice, 54
George W Bush, 11
Gérard Araud, 295
Ghada Karmi, 247
Ghazi Hamad, 241, 252
Gil Hoffman, 87
Gilad Erdan, 41
Gilad Shalit, 44
Golan Heights, 19
Golda Meir, 14
Grace O'Sullivan, 257
Grant Shapps, 321
Greensill,, 174

Haaretz, 244
Hagana, 10
Haiti, 7
Hamas, 5
Hamza Yousef, 102
Hananya Naftali, 13
Harlan Ullman, 60
Harold Shipman, 48
Hasan Barari, 192
hasbara, 322
Hezbollah, 33
Hillel Neuer, 63
Hisham Awartani, 250
Holocaust, 9
Houthis, 218
Human Rights Watch, 48, 63
Humanity First, 128
Hussein Haridi, 287
Ibrahim Freihat, 225
ICC, 40
IDF, 5
Ilan Pappé, 59
Imran Hussain, 133
Indonesian hospital, 225
International Committee of
    the Red Cross,, 140
Ione Belarra, 139
Iran, 53
Irgun, 10
Iron Dome, 5
ISIS, 11
Islamabad, 127
Islamic Jihad, 33
Israel, 5
Jabalia, 20
Jack Keane, 136

Jalazone, 23
James Elder, 241, 270
James Heappey, 173
James Joyce, 315
Jason Eaton, 250
Jawad Anani, 128
Jeremy Bowen, 6
Jeremy Hopkins, 55
Jess Phillips, 197
Jew-hating, 21
Jewish Power, 228
Jews, 9
Jihad, 23
Joe Biden, 10
John Bolton, 233
John Casson, 122, 236
John Entwistle, 207
John Kirby, 79
John McDonnell, 135
John McTernan, 36
José Rizal, 185
Josep Borrel, 203
Joseph Trumpeldor, 94
Joshua Mitts, 292
Judith and Natalie Raanan, 19
Juliette Touma, 212
Justin Cromp, 54
Justin Webb, 38
Kafr Bir'im, 176
Karim Kahn, 190
Kealeboga Maphunye, 129
Keir Starmer, 10
Ken McDonald, 22
Khalid Mahmood, 35
Khalil Al Hayya, 229

Khan Younis, 213
Kinna Abdalhamid, 250
Kiryat Shmona, 94
Kristen Saloomey, 226
L'art de se taire, 185
Labour Party, 21
Labour Zionism, 177
Lapid, 6
Lazzarini, 46
Lebanon, 19
Lehi, 10
Linda Thomas-Greenfield, 47
Lucy Willimason, 198
Lula da Silva, 39
Lyndon La Rouche, 153
Lyse Doucet, 116
Macbeth, 181
Mads Gilbert, 68
Magnier, 87
Mahjoob Zweiri, 115
Majed Al Ansari, 255
Makhachkala, 70
Maleeha Lhodi, 128
Manila., 185
Marcuse, 154
Marjorie Taylor Greene, 217
Mark Owen Jones, 166
Mark Regev, 55, 172
Mark Thomas, 163
Martin Griffiths, 20
Martin Konecny, 258
Marwan Bishara, 24
Marwan Jilani, 46
Marwan Kabalan, 82
Mazen Sinokrot, 22

Medea Benjamin, 86
Medical Aid for Palestine, 53
Mehdi Hasan, 210
Menachem Klein, 77
Michael C Ryan, 83
Michael Clarke, 251
Michael Green, 321
Michael Herzog, 224
Michael Howard, 188
Michael McCaul, 5
Michael Minnicino, 154
Middle East, 5
Mike Noyes, 149
Miriam Cates, 153
Mishal Hussein, 54, 173
Mitchell Plitnick, 157
Mohamed Elmasry, 339
Mohammad Shtayyeh, 206
Mohammed bin Salman, 161
Mohammed Galayini, 74
Mohammed Ghalayani, 298
Mohammed Nabulsi, 150
Mombasa, 157
Morris B Abram, 64
moshav, 176
Mossad, 15
mowing the lawn, 5
MSNBC, 210
Mubarak, 56
Mukesh Kapila, 318
Muslim, 16
Mustafa Barghouti, 52, 208
Nablus, 51
Nadim Nahif, 213
Nat Turner, 7

Natalie Raanan, 19
Navi Pillay, 63
Naz Shah, 197
Nazis, 41
Nebal Farsakh, 244
Nelson Mandela, 203
Netanyahu, 6
Nicholas de Rivière, 258
Nicholas Noe, 221
Nicholas Soames, 163
Nick Ferrari, 28
Nihad Awad, 305
Nikki Haley, 165
Noam Chomsky, 59
Noam Sagi, 260
Noam Tibon, 106
Nof Erez, 293
Nora Fathalipour,, 264
Norman Finklestein, 77
Norwegian Aid Committee, 201
Not In Our Name, 185
Nour Odeh, 243
Ofer, 241
Omar Baddar, 217
Omar Shakir, 48
Omer Bartov, 216
Orwell, 190
Osama Bin Javaid, 261
Osama Hamdan, 181
Oxfam, 31
Pacinthe Mattar, 165
Palestine, 10
Palestine Authority, 56
Palestine Legal, 59
Palestinian Red Crescent, 46

Pastor John Hagee, 217
Pat Ryder, 50
Patrick Ryder, 95
Paula Barker, 197
Pearl Harbour, 79
Pedro Sanchez, 40
President Herzog, 167
President Ruto, 157
Professor Abdelhamid Siyam, 39
propaganda system, 40
Putin, 43
Qassam Brigades announced they would release some hostages in the next few days. Elijah, 87
Qatar, 23, 140
Qualandiya, 33
Rabbi Alissa Wise, 213
Rabelais, 209
Rabih Al Maamari, 228
Rachel Hopkins, 197
Rachel Reeves, 197
Radio 4, 43
Rafaat Alareer, 303
Rafah, 20
Rami Khoury, 68
Rami Mortada, 102
Rana Hajjeh, 339
Rashida Tlaib, 138
Reem Alsalem, 232
Richard Falk, 39
Riham Jafari, 65
Riyad Mansour, 40
Robert Jackson, 292
Roger Carstens, 265

Rosena Allin-Khan, 43
Rupert Jones, 32
RUSI, 187
Ruth Halperin-Kaddari, 285
Sabri Saidam, 168
Sadiq Kahn, 144
Sadiq Khan, 45
Salah Al Din Street, 73
Saleh al-Aroui, 280
Samer Abu Daqqa, 332
Samer Abudaqa, 336
Samer Talalka, 333
Sami Hermez, 302
San Francisco State bridge, 205
Sarah Leah Whitson, 282
Sarah Owens, 197
Schultz, 59
Sebastian Fox, 321
Security Council, 33
Sergey Lavrov, 26
Settler violence, 34
Shaikh Group, 170
Shaista Aziz, 36
Sheikh Mansour, 306
Sherif Mansour, 84
Shin Bet, 81
Shireen Abu Akleh, 84
Simon Moutquin, 165
Sir Mark Rowley, 22
Sir Stephen O'Brien, 29
Sir Tom Winsor, 143
Siyan Abdehamid, 89
South Vietnam, 58
Sri Lanka, 128
Stephane Dujarric, 49

Stephanie Fox, 216
Steve Bell, 20
Steve Hartshorn, 153
Stokley Carmichael, 62
Stoltenberg, 251
Sultan Barakat, 155
Sunak, 59
Syria, 19
Taghereed El-Khodary, 225
Taher Herzallah, 328
Tahseen Ali, 250
Tal Katz, 8
Taliban, 231
Tamar Qarmout, 276
Tamer Quarmout, 125
Tanya Haj-Hassan, 115
Tarik Jasarevic, 256
Tel Aviv, 20
The Community Security Trust, 223
the Eisenhower, 11
The Elders, 203
The Hague, 40
The NDN Collective, 300
The Omari mosque, 322
The peace process, 176
The World Food Programme, 48
Thomas McManus, 202
Thomas White, 260
Tjada McKenna, 173
Tom Tugendhat, 97
Tunisia, 31
Turkey, 31
Tuval Escapa, 9

Twin Towers, 79
two-States, 12
UAE, 25
UN, 20
UN High Commissioner for Refugees, 84
UN Watch, 64
UNICEF, 24
UNRWA, 35
USS Ford, 11
Usuf Chitke, 300
Vincent Fean, 150
Vincent Nichols, 336
Voltaire, 13
Wael Al Dahdoh,, 332
Waqf,, 302
Washington, 19
West Bank, 5
Yaakov Amridror, 326
Yahya Sinwar, 156
Yasmin Porat, 8
Yasmin Querish, 35
Yasmin Qureshi, 38, 197
Yasser Arafat, 47
Yedioth Ahronoth, 293
Yigal Amir, 162
Yoav Gallant, 20
Yoni Ben Menachem, 228
Yossi Mekelberg, 322
Yotam Haim, 333
Youcef Bouandel, 331
Youman Elsayed, 83
Zionism, 10
Zionists, 10

www.ingramcontent.com/pod-product-compliance
Lightning Source LLC
Chambersburg PA
CBHW071236160426
43196CB00009B/1080